Nomos Universitätsschriften

Betriebswirtschaftslehre

Band 10

Martin Sternal

Mergers and Acquisitions by Digital Technology Giants

Three Perspectives on Value Creation

 Nomos

The Deutsche Nationalbibliothek lists this publication in the
Deutsche Nationalbibliografie; detailed bibliographic data
are available on the Internet at http://dnb.d-nb.de

a.t.: Darmstadt, Technische Universität Darmstadt, Dissertation, 2020

ISBN   978-3-8487-7672-6 (Print)
        978-3-7489-1047-3 (ePDF)

British Library Cataloguing-in-Publication Data
A catalogue record for this book is available from the British Library.

ISBN   978-3-8487-7672-6 (Print)
        978-3-7489-1047-3 (ePDF)

Library of Congress Cataloging-in-Publication Data
Sternal, Martin
Mergers and Acquisitions by Digital Technology Giants
Three Perspectives on Value Creation
Martin Sternal
183 pp.
Includes bibliographic references.

ISBN   978-3-8487-7672-6 (Print)
        978-3-7489-1047-3 (ePDF)

Onlineversion
Nomos eLibrary

D 17

1st Edition 2020
© Nomos Verlagsgesellschaft, Baden-Baden, Germany 2020. Overall responsibility
for Manufacturing (printing and production) lies with Nomos Verlagsgesellschaft mbH
& Co. KG.

Table of Contents

List of Figures

List of Tables

List of Abbreviations

BMP-test	Standardized cross-sectional test developed by Boehmer et al. (1991)
CAAR	Cumulative average abnormal return
CAR	Cumulative abnormal return
CEO	Chief executive officer
e.g.	For example
et al.	And others
FCF	Free cash flow
i.e.	In other words
IPO	Initial public offering
IS	Information systems
M&A	Mergers and acquisitions
N.A.	No author
OLS	Ordinary least squares
p.	Page
R&D	Research and development
RQ	Research question
SDC	Securities Data Company
SIC	Standard Industrial Classification
US	United States of America
vs.	Versus

1 Introduction and Motivation

1.1 Research Topics and Motivation

The economical and societal influence of large digital technology companies is steadily rising. These firms have experienced unprecedented growth in the last decade and expanded into a diverse range of industries (e.g., Mims, 2017; N.A., 2019; Zweig, 2018). Seven digital technology firms, which this thesis defines as digital technology giants, led the list of the largest publicly traded companies at the end of 2017 (see table 2.2.2). The business of these firms is continuously evolving, and they have entered a wide range of submarkets. The group includes the eCommerce-focused company Amazon, the two product- and service-focused companies Apple and Microsoft and the following four service-focused companies with their respective core businesses: Alibaba with marketplace platforms, Alphabet with online search and advertising platforms, Facebook with social networks and Tencent with social networks and online gaming. These firms are the owners of leading digital platforms and dominate the digital technology industry.[1]

The market environment of the digital technology industry is characterized by three main dynamics. First, strong economies of scale and scope that foster rapid growth and favor large firms (e.g., Furman et al., 2019; Mchawrab, 2016; Uhlenbruck et al., 2006). Second, high levels of direct and indirect network effects and complementarities that strengthen the value of related products and services (e.g., Amit and Zott, 2001; Crémer et al., 2019; Shapiro and Varian, 1999). Both dynamics decrease competition. Third, easy customer access, the potential of multi-homing and easily imitable products that lower market access barriers and increase competition. Additionally, the competition for customer attention, markets and capabilities is strong and establishes another competitive context for leading digital platforms (e.g., Chen and Hitt, 2002; Evans, 2013; van Gorp and Batura, 2015). The group of digital giants shows a distinct financial strength that

---

1 In this thesis, the terms digital platform and digital business are used interchangeably and refer to a set of digital technologies, products and services that can be the basis of an ecosystem with complementarities by third parties according to the definition of external platforms by Gawer and Cusumano (2014).

distinguishes them from other firms in the industry (Dolata, 2018). They conduct a large number of transactions that can initiate learning effects.[2] However, while high levels of liquidity and strong market valuation ensure financial flexibility, they can also drive managerial motives and make these giants particularly vulnerable to corporate governance issues (e.g., Haleblian and Finkelstein, 1999; Jensen, 1986; Moeller et al., 2004).

Digital platforms experience special dynamics and can be determined by different types of value. With digital technology breaking down industry and product boundaries, digital platforms are continuously advancing and evolving over time (Staykova and Damsgaard, 2017; Yoo et al., 2010). Value creation and capture are enabled through the recombination of digital resources, which can be driven by firms and users (Henfridsson et al., 2018; Yoo et al., 2010). Owners can initiate this internally through research and development (R&D), but also externally through cooperation or by means of mergers and acquisitions (M&A). Two different types of value can be distinguished – user value and owner value – with both types interlinked (e.g., Brousseau and Penard, 2007).[3] Acquisitions can generate a competitive advantage and provide value to users. They create value for owners in combination with positive profitability (Sirmon et al., 2007). A similar reasoning is followed by user-based valuation in marketing (e.g., McCarthy et al., 2017) and finance (e.g., Damodaran, 2018).

Research has identified several M&A drivers that can create value for owners, including market concentration, efficiency improvement, resource and knowledge redeployment and management replacement (e.g., Eckbo, 1983; Chatterjee, 1986; Agrawal and Walkling, 1994; Capron et al., 1998). However, empirically no overall agreement exists on the shareholder value effect for acquirers (e.g., Andrade et al., 2001; Bruner, 2002; King et al., 2004; Martynova and Renneboog, 2008). King et al. (2004) conclude that, in contrast with the effect across industries and firms, specific subgroups can create value in mergers and acquisitions.

The group of digital giants offers a promising field of study for potential value creation and can differ from previously leading groups. Nearly two decades earlier, the dotcom boom represented the first rise of the digital technology industry. It brought forth a group of leading digital technology-focused dotcom giants (Cisco, IBM, Intel, Microsoft, Nokia and Oracle), but the boom came to an abrupt end with the burst of the dotcom bubble in March 2000 (e.g., Griffin et al., 2011; Ofek and Richardson, 2003). Some

---

2 The terms transaction, deal, merger and acquisition are used interchangeably.
3 The terms owner value and shareholder value are used interchangeably.

observers note similarities between both digital technology booms and giant groups (e.g., Driebusch and Farrell, 2018), but there have also been significant developments in the years in-between which can have opposing effects on value creation (e.g., Chambers, 2015; Cusumano et al., 2019; Evans and Schmalensee, 2016). For the digital technology giants, the special characteristics of the digital technology industry and the firms' distinct position influence the value creation potential. In addition to the effect on shareholder value of the acquirer, the new information that is revealed with a transaction also affects the shareholder value of other firms in the industry (Binder, 1998). The rivals' share prices reflect the impact of the M&A activity and the rivals' reactions that are anticipated by capital markets; this can range from no reaction, imitation to other moves (Smith et al., 2001). A range of rival effects theories concur with the different possible reactions, including Market Concentration Hypothesis (e.g., Eckbo, 1983), Efficiency Hypothesis (e.g., Akdoğu, 2009), Acquisitions Probability Hypothesis (e.g., Song and Walkling, 2000) and Growth Probability Hypothesis (e.g., Gaur et al., 2013).

To sum up, this dissertation is devoted to the topic of digital technology giants' mergers and acquisitions for three key reasons. First, digital giants are the largest and most important companies in the 21st century. They hold a key role in the digital technology industry and can have influence on other companies, industries and the society as a whole. Second, digital platforms are continuously evolving and owners need to repeatedly alter their business. Mergers and acquisitions are a key approach to expand platform boundaries and can create value for users and owners. Third, mergers and acquisitions by digital giants merit attention because of the special market dynamics experienced by the digital technology industry and the distinct factors influencing the group of giants. The market environment and the company-specific characteristics can have key impact on the value creation. The next section discusses the research goals of this endeavor in more detail and derives the specific research questions.

1.2 Research Goals and Course of Analysis

This dissertation analyzes mergers and acquisitions by digital technology giants from three perspectives – it sheds light on the value creation for acquirers and for competitors, and compares the value creation effect with other firms' mergers and acquisitions.

The thesis addresses *three key research goals* here, and fills a range of research gaps. First, the dissertation enriches the knowledge on the group of digital technology giants and platform boundary expansion. It develops a definition for the group of digital technology giants that is strict and replicable. The analysis is based on an unique M&A dataset combining multiple sources to ensure that it correctly reflects the group's acquisition activity. In addition, the thesis integrates different perspectives on value creation and mergers and acquisitions at theoretical and empirical level. It links user value to owner value built on the concepts of user-based valuation, user value and resource based-view and M&A activity to platform boundary expansion built on digital innovation, platform evolution and firm-initiated recombination of resources. Hence, the thesis is able to examine the value effects of platform boundary expansion in terms of mergers and acquisitions on user and owner value.

Second, the dissertation sheds light on the influence of the digital technology industry on the value creation for digital technology giants and competitors. The market environment of the industry is therefore analyzed based on different areas, including finance, information systems (IS), strategy and economics. IS-related concepts (e.g., network effects, switching costs) are combined with strategy-related concepts (e.g., relatedness, diversification) and economics-related concepts (e.g., economies of scale and scope, competition), and are analyzed from a finance perspective on the basis of shareholder value. Furthermore, the dissertation links discussions on competitive dynamics in IS-literature with rival effects theories in finance literature. It shows the effect of competitive actions and reactions on shareholder value of acquirers and competitors. Additionally, the dissertation differentiates between rival groups, and analyzes the effect separately while discussing different potential rival stories.

Third, the thesis provides a better understanding of the distinct role of digital technology giants in the digital technology industry. It shows the interaction between the influence of the market environment and the distinct financial strength of the digital giants. It links the high economic endowment and leading position of the firms to alternative acquisition motives like managerial self-interest and managerial hubris. Moreover, it investigates the unique societal and economic influence of the digital giants by analyzing the rival returns and signaling effects of the transactions and by comparing the deals with the M&A activity of dotcom giants as another group of acquirers. The comparison with the dotcom giants' deal sample enables an analysis of the special characteristics of digital giants as acquirers, the transition of leading digital technology companies and the impact on M&A activity and value effects.

The dissertation accomplishes the research goals by answering the following *three main research questions (RQ)*:

RQ 1. Does platform boundary expansion with regard to mergers and acquisitions create value for digital technology giants?

RQ 2. How do other firms react to digital technology giants' competitive actions in terms of mergers and acquisitions?

RQ 3. What can digital technology giants learn from dotcom giants, and do capital markets exaggerate digital technology giants' value creation?

The remainder of this dissertation is structured in three studies that approach the research questions successively (chapter 2–4), and in a concluding part (chapter 5). Figure 1.2.1 illustrates the structure of the thesis.

Chapter 2 investigates the impact of digital giants' mergers and acquisitions on the value creation for acquirers to shed light on the effects of platform boundary expansion. 435 transactions by digital technology giants are thus analyzed and two opposing effects observed. On the one hand, transactions that are related to the core business can create owner and user value due to positive influences of the market environment in terms of network effects, complementarities and decreasing competition. On the other hand, value dilution is driven by a distinct financial strength and by unrelated transactions. High liquidity can trigger corporate governance issues, and unrelated deals seem to have limited value potential but high opportunity costs.

Figure 1.2.1: Structure of the Thesis

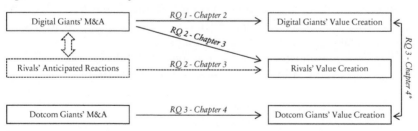

Figure 1.2.1 presents the structure of the thesis and shows the analyses of the different chapters. The dashed lines indicate that the reaction is not directly measured. * indicates that chapter 4 also includes the rival effects analyses of digital giants' M&A on dotcom giants' value creation and dotcom giants' M&A on digital giants' value creation.

Chapter 3 examines the effect of mergers and acquisitions as competitive actions on the value creation for competitors in the digital technology industry. It analyzes three types of anticipated reactions of responders, two distinct rival sets and 373 transactions conducted by the group of digital giants. The results illustrate that the industry has special competitive dynamics, and that traditional market definition is not applicable. Digital giants' M&A activity transmits signals to other companies in the digital technology industry. Shareholders appear to expect rivals to react and mimic the competitive move. The effect is stronger for indirect rivals, which are other digital giants, despite these companies having different business focuses. Direct rivals, which are firms in the same industry, are impacted by other influences that can indicate increased efficiency on the part of the acquirer without signaling effects being fully outweighed.

Chapter 4 compares the M&A activity of digital technology giants and the activity of previous dotcom giants. In the late 1990s, the dotcom boom drove stock markets to new highs as the digital technology industry moved into the focus of investors and a group of six dotcom giants became part of the largest publicly traded companies worldwide. This chapter analyzes 365 transactions by these dotcom giants and compares the results with the M&A activity of digital giants in the same period. Two main effects can be observed. First, shareholders react differently to the M&A activity of dotcom giants depending on the firm's value growth. They seem to expect higher returns from the transactions by shrinking dotcom giants than those by growing dotcom giants, and appreciate diversifying deals by these firms which can indicate a potential reaction to industry change and a transition process. Higher levels of liquidity can support this process and increase the value creation for shrinking dotcom giants. Second, digital technology giants occupy a special position in the digital technology industry. They experience a unique relatedness effect and appear to have a distinct signaling power to firms in the industry.

Chapter 5 consolidates the main findings of the dissertation and provides an overall conclusion and discussion of the implications.

2 Digital Giants' Mergers and Acquisitions Activity: Drivers of Value Creation and Value Dilution[4]

2.1 Introduction

In 2012, the social platform Facebook acquired Instagram, a photo sharing application, for a purchase price of $1 billion. This was twice the valuation from the previous funding round paid for a company with 13 employees, no revenues but 35 million users (Raice et al., 2012). The acquisition is particularly remarkable because the considerably larger platform Facebook had already developed the concept for an own photo application one year earlier (Siegler, 2011) but decided instead to acquire Instagram. This raises the question of whether innovation and value creation for a successful digital platform is more likely to be driven by mergers and acquisitions or organically?

In a digital environment, industry and product boundaries are diminishing (Yoo et al., 2010; Yoo et al., 2012). Platforms evolve over time, and M&A can initiate value creation through the recombination of digital resources (Henfridsson et al., 2018; Staykova and Damsgaard, 2017). Different value perspectives exist (e.g., Ghazawneh and Mansour, 2015; Kujala and Väänänen, 2009), but the value that is appropriated by users of a platform (user value) and that appropriated by owners (owner value) are closely interlinked (e.g., Brousseau and Penard, 2007; Sirmon et al., 2007). High economies of scale and scope, network effects alongside multiple opportunities to access users shape the market environment of the digital technology industry, with many submarkets dominated by a single leading platform (e.g., Crémer et al., 2019; Furman et al., 2019; van Gorp and Batura, 2015). The digital technology giants operate the largest digital-enabled platforms. They have achieved the dominant position by interacting industry-specific factors with company-specific accelerators. A factor that clearly distinguishes them from the rest of the industry is a distinct financial strength that is reflected in the availability of vast economic resources,

---

4 An adapted version of this chapter has been published: Sternal, M., Schiereck, D., 2019. Do Digital Giants Create Value by Mergers and Acquisitions? in: Proceedings of the 40th International Conference on Information Systems (ICIS), Munich, Germany.

strong acquisition activities and high levels of financial liquidity (Dolata, 2018). The M&A activity enables the companies to grow inorganically and internalize capabilities. For example, Apple hired the former Goldman Sachs investment banker Adrian Perica as the new head of M&A in 2009. Up to this time, Apple's chief executive officer (CEO) Steve Jobs had major concerns that acquisitions could harm the corporate culture of Apple that was driven by the self-image of the technological leader being more effective at developing by its own efforts than by purchasing from outside (Burrows 2010). While research has extensively studied M&A value effects in traditional industries (e.g., Haleblian et al., 2009; King et al., 2004), the influences of market environment and financial strength distinguish the leading digital platforms from other businesses, and further research is required (Kohli and Grover, 2008). Previous studies do not establish any general value creation for acquirers, but these certain conditions can alter the effect for digital giants. Thus, boundary expansion of digital platforms can have different implications to inorganic growth of traditional businesses. This chapter fills this research gap and sheds light on the less covered owner's perspective of platforms (Ghazawneh and Mansour, 2015) by analyzing the value effect of digital technology giants' M&A activity. The guiding research question is, "Does platform boundary expansion with regard to mergers and acquisitions create value for digital technology giants?"

The chapter addresses this question by analyzing shareholder value as a forward-looking measure that directly reflects new information (Fama, 1970). Since M&A value creation for acquirers is contingent on subgroup-specific differences (King et al., 2004), six value drivers that are particularly relevant to digital technology giants can be derived based on the market environment and distinct financial strength. The chapter investigates the M&A success in an event study of 435 transactions by the seven digital giants between 2008 and 2017. On average, the results show no value creation or dilution. However, the analyses reveal significant effects for several value factors. First, acquisitions of firms that are related to the core business of digital technology giants create value, which can be driven by the market environment in terms of reinforcing network effects, complementarities and decreasing competition. Second, acquisitions of unrelated targets dilute value, a factor that can be attributed to limited value potential and opportunity costs with regard to other possible investments. Finally, high levels of free cash flow absorb some value creation in related and increase value dilution in unrelated deals. Financial liquidity decreases corporate control by capital markets and can encourage management to improve the own position through M&A instead of following shareholders' interests.

This study makes three primary contributions to the literature. First, it combines perspectives on value creation from different strands of literature. Building on the concepts of user value (e.g., Henfridsson et al., 2018; Kujala and Väänänen, 2009), user-based valuation (e.g., Damodaran, 2018; McCarthy et al., 2017) and resource-based view (e.g., Barney, 1991; Sirmon et al., 2007), this contribution analyzes user value and owner value empirically, employing a set of M&A transactions. The study utilizes information systems-related and market-specific concepts (e.g., economies of scale and scope, network effects, access to users) as well as finance-related and company-specific concepts (e.g., acquisition experience, managerial self-interest, managerial hubris). Second, this research contributes to the knowledge of M&A value creation for owners of leading digital technology platforms. Shareholder value creation becomes more important for digital platforms as the largest firms have all been listed on stock exchanges for several years, with further players followed in 2019 (e.g., Lyft, Uber). Additionally, previous studies discuss different groups of platform leaders (Gawer and Cusumano, 2002) or tech titans (Shapiro, 2019) without providing any strict definition. These companies have conducted a wide range of transactions, but for a large part of these deals, low levels of information exist. This chapter defines the group of digital technology giants based on replicable criteria. The analyzed deal sample is gathered from two databases (Datastream, Capital IQ) across the last ten years without limitations on acquisition size or target details, and is validated by further press research. To the best of the author's knowledge, there is no previous empirical analysis on the M&A value potential of a broader group of leading digital platforms. Finally, this research indicates that digital technology giants are in a field of tension between the positive influence of the market environment on the one hand and the negative influence of financial strength on the other. It forges a link between the distinct economic resources and dominant position of leading digital platforms (e.g., Cusumano et al., 2019; Dolata, 2018) and the literature on free cash flow and managerial self-interest (e.g., Jensen, 1986; Lang et al., 1991). While the financial liquidity of digital technology giants is beneficial for "winner-take-all" outcomes, it decreases control by capital markets and can drive managerial motives in related as well as unrelated transactions. Each of these opposing factors has been discussed in prior literature, but the factors have not been analyzed together as concurrent influences in the context of the digital technology industry. It sheds a new light on digital giants' massive economic endow-

2 Digital Giants' Mergers and Acquisitions Activity

ment and emphasizes the importance of corporate governance, a topic that is largely neglected in the discussion on value creation for digital giants.

The remainder of this chapter is organized as follows. Section 2.2 reviews the research on the digital technology industry, the group of digital giants and value creation as well as value dilution drivers. Section 2.3 describes the data sample and applied research methodology. Section 2.4 presents and discusses the empirical results. The final section summarizes and derives implications for future research.

2.2 Literature Review and Research Hypotheses

Platforms are not stable over time, but follow an evolutionary path that is determined by the presence and reconfiguration of certain attributes (Staykova and Damsgaard, 2017).[5] For example, Facebook evolved from a university network to a worldwide messaging and advertising platform within 15 years of firm history and might become a provider of financial services in the next years. Digital technology has broken down product and industry boundaries. A product can be both product and platform at the same time, and the same companies can compete and collaborate at different layers of the platform in a combined ecosystem (Yoo et al., 2010). This drives innovation that is characterized by a convergence of user experiences, products and industries as well as generativity in terms of unfinished products and continuing innovation (Yoo et al., 2012). Based on Yoo et al.'s (2010) definition of digital innovation as a recombination of physical and digital components into new products, Henfridsson et al. (2018) synthesize that value creation and capture in the digital technology environment is enabled through the recombination of digital resources. Firms design new value offerings or channel users through own resources, but individuals also create and capture value by using different digital resources. The firm-initiated recombination can be driven internally (e.g., Like-button), through cooperation (e.g., Libra cryptocurrency) or by means of M&A (e.g., Messenger application; all examples of Facebook's activity). Research puts the focus on value creation for platform users (e.g., Kujala and Väänänen, 2009) or complementors (e.g., Ghazawneh and Mansour, 2015). However from a business model perspective, the owner value in terms of profitability is important to ensure sustainability of user value through

---

5 See McIntyre and Srinivasan (2017) for a comprehensive review of platforms and networks.

platform survival (Brousseau and Penard, 2007). Bharadwaj et al. (2013) emphasize that digital technology enables value creation by leveraging resources, information and multisided platforms as well as value capture due to coordination of business models in networks and control of digital ecosystems. Multisided platforms enable additional ways for creating and capturing value here, and for monetizing products and services. Charges can be made for different sides of a platform instead of payment for actual usage (Eisenmann et al., 2006). Henfridsson et al. (2018) refer to monetization and pricing of innovation as an important implication for future IS research.

Building on the resource-based view (e.g., Barney, 1991; Wernerfelt, 1995), the two value concepts and M&A activity are interlinked: resource management in the form of acquisitions enables a firm to provide value to customers and thus generate a competitive advantage. In combination with positive profitability, this creates value for the owner (Sirmon et al., 2007). Sirmon et al. (2007) summarize that "value creation occurs when a firm exceeds its competitors' ability to provide solutions to customers' needs, while maintaining or improving its profit margins" (p. 273–274). However, companies in high technology industries are driven by high growth and high uncertainty (Kohers and Kohers, 2000). This makes determining value creation and valuation more challenging. Trueman et al. (2000, 2001) link the usage of web pages to the valuation of digital technology companies. Similarly, in the concept of customer lifetime value in marketing literature, the value of a user is the starting point for estimating the owner value (e.g., Berger et al., 2006; Gupta et al., 2004; McCarthy et al., 2017; Schulze et al., 2012; Stahl et al., 2003). In recent years, finance literature has adopted the concept of user-based valuation of digital companies (e.g., Damodaran, 2018). This study bases the analysis of value creation on the event study methodology as, following the efficient market hypothesis (Fama, 1970), deal announcements have a direct effect on acquirer share prices. The advantage of this methodology is that the impact on owner value can be instantly observed and isolated from corporate actions in comparison with the impact on user value. While empirical results on acquirers' shareholder value across industries and companies are mixed, specific subgroups of firms are able to create value in mergers and acquisitions (King et al., 2004). In line with this, Haleblian et al. (2009) identify a range of acquisition conditions alongside acquisition causes that can drive value creation, grouping them into four categories: deal characteristics, managerial effects, firm characteristics and environmental factors. These groups can be extended by other dimensions, for example the technological context (Zhu et al., 2003) or cultural fit and integration (Bauer and Matzler, 2014). The value drivers of this study are derived and discussed in the next subsections. An overview of the factors is presented in table 2.2.1.

Table 2.2.1: Digital Technology Giants' M&A Value Drivers

Characteristic	Construct	Variable	Hypothesis	Expected Effect
Market Environment	Economies of scale and scope	*CAAR* for total sample	H1	+
	Network effects and complementarities	*CAAR* for related transactions, *Relatedness*	H2	+
	Access to users and opportunity costs	*CAAR* for unrelated transactions	H4	-
Financial Strength	Acquisition experience	*Acquirer Experience*	H3	+
	Managerial self-interest	*Free Cash Flow*	H5, H6	-
	Managerial hubris	*Firm Size*	H7	-

Table 2.2.1 presents the M&A value drivers of digital technology giants' mergers and acquisitions.

2.2.1 Digital Giants' Characteristics and Value Drivers

The study analyzes the predominant group of leading platform owners, the digital technology giants. Literature uses different names for these companies including tech titans (Shapiro, 2019) and giant tech firms (Lamoreaux, 2019) and several acronyms such as FAANG for Facebook, Amazon, Apple, Netflix and Google, GAFA for Google, Amazon, Facebook and Apple or BAT for Baidu, Alibaba and Tencent (Schlesinger et al., 2019; Wang and Hui, 2017). However, no clear definition exists, the range of selected companies differs and primarily reflects a United States of America (US) centered perspective. This study concentrates on the largest publicly listed players in order to follow a replicable approach and provide a global view. Digital technology giants are defined as the largest companies worldwide that focus on digital-enabled platforms, with seven firms (Alibaba, Alphabet, Amazon, Apple, Facebook, Microsoft and Tencent) from the global top twenty list identified in terms of the market capitalization as of December 31, 2017 (see table 2.2.2). A certain size threshold is to some extent random, but the next largest digital player has less than half the market capitalization of the smallest identified firm, which influences the sub-group-specific characteristics.[6] The selected digital technology giants differ in their product and service offering as well as geographical focus, but have all established innovation and transaction platforms (Cusumano et al., 2019). Gawer and Cusumano (2002) identify influences on platform leadership and name the relationship with external complementors and the scope of the firm in terms of internal share alongside product technology and internal organization. Dolata (2018) emphasizes the interaction of market-specific factors, including network effects as well as company-specific accelerators, as the financial strength for achieving the dominant position.

Table 2.2.2: Largest Publicly Traded Companies Worldwide by Market Capitalization in 2017

Rank	Company	Founded	Headquarters	Market Capitalization
1	Apple Inc.	1976	United States	868,879
2	Alphabet Inc.	1998 *	United States	729,457
3	Microsoft Corp.	1975	United States	659,906
4	Amazon.com Inc.	1994	United States	563,535
5	Facebook Inc.	2004	United States	512,757
6	Tencent Holding Ltd.	1998	China	493,340
7	Berkshire Hathaway Inc.	1955	United States	489,249
8	Alibaba Group Holding Ltd.	1999	China	441,620
9	Johnson & Johnson Inc.	1886	United States	375,361
10	JPMorgan Chase & Co.	1799 *	United States	371,052
11	Exxon Mobil Corp.	1870 *	United States	354,392
12	Samsung Electronics Co. Ltd.	1969	South Korea	343,312
13	Industrial and Commercial Bank of China Ltd.	1984	China	326,798
14	Bank of America Corp.	1784 *	United States	307,912
15	Wells Fargo & Co.	1852	United States	298,755
16	Walmart Inc.	1945 *	United States	292,535
17	Royal Dutch Shell PLC	1890 *	Netherlands	280,180
18	Nestle SA	1866 *	Switzerland	267,678
19	Visa Inc.	1958 *	United States	258,392
20	China Construction Bank Corp.	1954 *	China	248,171

Table 2.2.2 presents the market capitalization per company of the largest publicly traded companies worldwide. Digital technology giants are marked bold. Market capitalization is measured in $ million as of December 31, 2017. * indicates that the predecessor was founded at this date.

The digital technology industry as part of the high technology sector features high levels of growth potential and uncertainty (Kohers and Kohers,

---

6 The only exception is Samsung, but the business includes large parts of household appliances and electronic components.

2000). The environment is influenced by three main market dynamics. First, global markets as well as relatively low marginal costs in most submarkets lead to strong economies of scale and scope and create an advantage for large players (e.g., Furman et al., 2019). Companies can rapidly achieve or strengthen a dominant position as well as maintain high levels of growth through M&A (Mchawrab, 2016). Second, the digital technology environment is influenced by strong direct and indirect network effects which decrease competition and increase market concentration (e.g., Crémer et al., 2019). Direct network effects arise if additional users increase the value of a product or service for all other users. Indirect network effects enhance the value of a product or service due to other connected products or services. Direct and indirect network effects decrease competition and increase market concentration. This is the main reason for "winner-take-all" outcomes in many product and service categories of the industry and creates first-mover advantages (Farrell and Saloner, 1985; Katz and Shapiro, 1985; Shapiro and Varian, 1999). Third, players in the digital technology industry have multiple direct access points to end users and most products and services are easily imitable (e.g., van Gorp and Batura, 2015). Additionally, the use of similar product and services in parallel decreases switching costs (Chen and Hitt, 2002). These factors lead to low entry barriers for new entrants in each submarket and intensify competition. The dominant player's position is frequently challenged and creative destruction and Schumpeterian competition can be observed (Haucap and Heimeshoff, 2014). In addition to the threat of new entrants, competition among the digital technology giants is intense. Even though the product and service offerings of these companies differ to some extent, they continuously compete with each other for the attention of consumers (Evans, 2013).

Overall, the market environment seems to have two effects on M&A value creation. The economies of scale and scope increase attractiveness of growth through higher efficiency. Deals in the industry can generally create value by designing new value offers. Similarly, strong direct and indirect network effects have a positive impact on acquisitions of related businesses as they reward early leaders and fast growth within a specific submarket due to higher user value. Complementarities and relatedness of target and acquirer can be another potential value driver. In contrast, direct access points to end users and low switching costs ease access to new business opportunities for all firms, increase competition and counteract the reinforcing effects of the dominant position. Diversification can negatively influence the owner value creation for digital technology giants due to investments in projects that do not enhance user value and block financial resources for other value offers.

A distinct financial strength distinguishes the digital giants from the rest of the industry. The group contains the largest publicly traded companies worldwide and the high valuation of these firms has direct impact on the firm size. In addition, the economic endowment allows the companies to invest internally and externally on a large scale (Dolata, 2018). Spending on capital expenditure as well as research and development of the digital technology giants has grown strongly in the last 10 years (see table 2.2.3). It also influences the total number of transactions and the size of major acquisitions. A first data extract from the Securities Data Company (SDC) database and the Capital IQ database lists 1,980 deals for all giants between 2008 and 2017, which averages out at 28.3 deals per company per year. Prominent deals include Microsoft's acquisitions of LinkedIn for $27 billion in 2016 and Facebook's takeover of WhatsApp for $19 billion in 2014.[7] The investments allow the digital technology giants to test new business opportunities and build up M&A capabilities. In addition, financial liquidity enables management to conduct transactions without the control of capital markets, which is usually assured through transparency and costs of capital in keeping with the risk level of investments. The group of digital technology giants has generated significant levels of free cash flow over the last decade (see table 2.2.3). Thus, the high levels of internal resources can make the giants prone to corporate governance issues in terms of conflicts of interests between management and shareholders. Returning to the case mentioned in the introduction, Facebook CEO Mark Zuckerberg privately negotiated the $1 billion Instagram deal without the knowledge of the board and involvement of law firms and banks (Raice et al., 2012). The broader scope of actions can lead to unmonitored transactions. Mchawrab (2016) notes that the excess cash of digital technology giants offers flexibility but might lead to wrong investment decisions. Acquisitions can be driven by managerial motives based on self-interest or hubris instead of user value and shareholder value.

---

7 Transaction values are based on the SDC and Capital IQ databases.

Table 2.2.3: Digital Technology Giants' Characteristics

	Capital Expenditures	Research and Development	Free Cash Flow	Total Assets	Market Capitalization
2008*	1	3	6	31	98
2009*	1	3	6	36	134
2010*	2	3	7	49	154
2011*	3	4	8	66	180
2012**	3	4	10	75	224
2013**	4	5	10	89	256
2014**	6	7	11	110	299
2015	5	8	15	117	357
2016	6	9	16	135	381
2017	8	11	19	169	557

Table 2.2.3 presents the means of *Capital Expenditures, Research and Development, Free Cash Flow, Total Assets* and *Market Capitalization* across the digital technology giants per year. *Free Cash Flow* is calculated as operating income before depreciation and amortization minus income tax minus interest expenses minus dividends, deflated by book value of total assets. The figures are presented in $ billion. * indicates that the figures do not include Facebook and Alibaba data, ** indicates that the figures do not include Alibaba data.

Overall, the distinct financial strength can affect value creation in two ways. The number of transactions trigger learning effects and can create user and owner value in subsequent deals based on acquisition experience. On the other hand, the economic resources in terms of financial liquidity and firm size can also lead to corporate governance issues and value dilution due to managerial self-interest or managerial hubris.

2.2.2 Value Creation Drivers

Digital technology giants use acquisitions to defend their current market position as well as penetrate new markets. Players aim to strengthen the core business and integrate other businesses across platforms to create value for shareholders (van Gorp and Batura, 2015). Strong *economies of scale and scope* favor growth in the digital technology industry here. Both dynamics increase concentration and enable leading digital platforms to build ecosystems across different submarkets (e.g., Furman et al., 2019). Uhlenbruck et al. (2006) emphasize the relevance of market power and creation of entry barriers by economies of scale in the rapidly changing digital technology environment. This is particularly important as most products and services are standardized and easily imitable, and the business models are more transparent than in traditional industries. They observe highly significant positive abnormal returns to internet firms that buy other internet firms, with synergies being generated through acquisition of knowledge and capabilities as well as an increased customer base. In line with this, Kohers and Kohers (2000) argue that acquirers have attractive investment opportunities in a high growth and high uncertainty environment. They establish that high technology firms can generate highly significant positive abnormal returns through M&A. Rhéaume and Bhabra (2008) identify positive value creation for acquirers in information-based industries, including photography, publishing, telecommunications, computing and entertainment, which they link to synergistic gains. Schief et al. (2013) conduct a meta-analysis examining the M&A activity in the software industry. They analyze five studies that investigate acquisitions in this industry between 1980 and 2008. The observed acquirer return varies and they attribute it to opposing influences. The expected positive value can be offset by several factors including large transaction premiums. Wilcox et al. (2001) analyze one specific high technology industry, transactions in the telecommunications industry in the US, and find positive acquirer returns. Jope et al. (2010) analyze value effects in the technology, media and telecommunications industry and point out that technology convergence and deregulation give rise to new product and service combinations that can create value. The acquisition of knowledge and resources becomes more important as platform and industry boundaries continue to diminish in the digital technology industry. However, they observe negative abnormal returns in relation to acquirers which they attribute to overpayment in order to remain competitive in the context of a changing environment. This is in line with the rational overpayment hypothesis by Akdoğu (2009) who shows that acquirers can gain a competitive edge through transactions, despite negative abnormal returns.

This study therefore expects acquisitions to have a positive influence on value creation in the digital technology industry due to increased efficiency through strong economies of scale and scope as well as access to capabilities and knowledge. It can digital technology giants enable to recombine resources and design new value offers.

Hypothesis 1. *Transactions by digital technology giants result in positive abnormal returns to the acquirer.*

High levels of direct and indirect *network effects* can amplify the synergistic potential of transactions as well as increase user value and market power. New users can connect with more people via Facebook's services in western countries and Tencent's services in Asia than via any other network. Sellers prefer Amazon's marketplace and Alibaba's platforms because of the large user basis, which in turn increases the product assortment and attracts further customers. Developers offer more software for a popular operating system, which again makes the system more attractive. A wide range of studies analyze relatedness and synergistic potential of M&A activity (e.g., Devos et al., 2009; Lubatkin, 1983; Rumelt, 1974; Seth, 1990). Empirical research on the digital technology industry provides evidence of market and technology synergies in related transactions. Rhéaume and Bhabra (2008) divide their sample by transactions within and across information sectors, and analyze per group and sector the effect of relatedness in terms of the shared 2-digit Standard Industrial Classification (SIC) code. Related acquisitions lead to significant positive abnormal returns, independent of the specific information sector. They argue that these transactions enable synergies and create more value than unrelated transactions, leading to insignificant value gains. Additionally, they find that most acquiring companies buy related targets within the same sector and thus maximize shareholder value. Wilcox et al. (2001) analyze the effect of diversification in the telecommunications industry on the basis of the shared 2-digit SIC code. They show higher value gains for companies conducting related transactions and attribute this to market and technology synergies that are incorporated by shareholders. Yang et al. (2018) show significant positive abnormal returns for related acquisitions conducted by Alphabet, but find no significance for transactions by Apple. Uhlenbruck et al. (2006) and Akdoğu (2009) find positive but insignificant effects of relatedness on acquirer shareholder value.

In line with this, Amit and Zott (2001) argue that *complementarities* in terms of product and service bundles as well as integrated operational and technological solutions are a source of value creation in the digital technology industry. They link this to revenue synergies and increased efficiency for firms and users. Network effects amplify synergies and have two other effects on platforms. First, offering bundles of related products or services not only strengthens the dominant position in the base good market but can also challenge the position of rivals in the supplemental good markets (Lee, 2000). Second, Gallaugher and Wang (2002) and Gao and Iyer (2006) show that complements to a product or service in software markets enable lock-in effects and increase the intensity of indirect network effects which in turn fuel market concentration. Increasing innovation of complements also influences user value positively and fosters a dominant platform (Gawer and Cusumano, 2014). Gao and Iyer (2006) conclude that acquisitions of firms with complementary but not similar products or services are a valid source of value creation. This also applies to the rest of the digital technology industry (McIntyre and Chintakananda, 2014). Thus, acquiring a related target reinforces the core business and platform ecosystems, enables synergies and increases market power and user value due to strong network effects and complementarities.

Besides this, the distinct financial strength helps digital technology giants to decrease competition in the market through related deals. The current strength of the digital giants thus fosters the future market position (McIntyre and Chintakananda, 2014). First, firms buy related competitors before these pose a threat to their own position. These preemptive investments lower future innovation in the market and foster "winner-take-all" outcomes in each submarket dominated by one leading player (Kuchinke and Vidal, 2016; van Gorp and Batura, 2015). Second, the digital technology giants can actively increase switching costs and reduce customer attrition not only by means of complementary products but also by enhancing quality through the recombination of resources by acquiring a related company with the required resources and capabilities (Chen and Hitt, 2002). In line with this, Yang et al. (2018) argue that firms can strengthen their own platforms with relevant innovation and gain a competitive advantage by acquiring related targets.

To summarize, this study expects a positive effect of relatedness on value creation for digital technology giants. Related transactions can profit from favorable market dynamics in terms of network effects and complementarities as well as financial strength that reduces competition.

Hypothesis 2. *Related transactions by digital technology giants result in positive abnormal returns to the acquirer.*

The influence of financial strength on M&A activity is reflected directly in the number of transactions. *Acquisition experience* is based on the idea that completed deals lead to learning effects and the increased acquirer experience is beneficial for future M&A. Haleblian and Finkelstein (1999) argue that the relation between both variables is U-shaped, with firms with no prior acquisition and very experienced acquirers noting the best financial performance. Additionally, target relatedness to prior acquired targets also increases the acquisition performance. They conclude that inexperienced acquirers inappropriately generalize on the basis of a small number of prior deals, leading to lower performance while firms with a high number of prior transactions appropriately discriminate between different acquisitions. Hayward (2002) emphasizes that experience of acquirers not only includes the amount of prior deals but also qualitative factors. Similarity with previous acquisitions, prior performance and timing have an impact on the success of a transaction and need to be considered by buyers. Uhlenbruck et al. (2006), similar to Haleblian and Finkelstein (1999), control the number of previous acquisitions and find a significant negative relation with acquisition performance. They do not test for a non-linear relationship but instead argue that internet firms are part of the inexperienced acquirer group and that the effect might be attributable to decreasing marginal acquisition benefits or integration capacity limits. In line with this, some giants are quite young, thus having lower levels of organizational experience and lacking long-term learning effects. This can partly influence the effect of acquirer experience (Haleblian and Finkelstein, 1999).

Nevertheless, the group of digital technology giants has conducted a large number of transactions in prior years. This study expects acquirer experience to enhance the quality of resource recombination with regard to the M&A activity and positively influence the shareholder value of digital technology giants through increased efficiency.

Hypothesis 3. *Acquirer experience has a positive influence on the abnormal returns to digital technology giants.*

2.2.3 Value Dilution Drivers

The discussion of the previous subsection indicates that related transactions by digital technology giants create value. Taking this a step further, unrelated deals seem to be less beneficial. In general, empirical evidence on diversification is ambiguous.[8] The motive for diversifying actions can be traced back to the attributes of the digital technology industry. The market environment is characterized by multiple direct *access points to end users* and low level of switching costs. The potential for multi-homing varies between submarkets, but can increase competition and ease access for new entrants (e.g., Crémer et al., 2019; Furman et al., 2019; van Gorp and Batura, 2015). On the one hand, these factors encourage unrelated acquisitions to take new business opportunities and fulfill growth expectations when facing competition in the core market. The reorganization of Google as Alphabet points in this direction and shows management's strong commitment to diversification. The company has consolidated its core businesses in one "alpha" segment, while another segment contains

---

8 See Martin and Sayrak (2003) for a comprehensive review of diversification and value creation.

unrelated other "bets" which are subsidized and expected to generate future profits (Cusumano, 2017). On the other hand, the conditions exist for any rival in the submarket, and the digital technology giants are unable to similarly utilize the dominant core market position as they can with related transactions. While the market environment in terms of network effects, complementarities and decreasing competition strengthens related transactions, unrelated transactions have a higher inherent uncertainty (Wilcox et al., 2001). Firms try to reduce operating risk and use unrelated deals as a hedging strategy for technological uncertainty in rapidly changing industries, while value creation is not exhibited (Rhéaume and Bhabra, 2008). In line with this, Seth (1990) argues that risk reduction can be equivalently done at shareholder level. Additionally, unrelated deals involve *opportunity costs* in terms of blocked financial resources and lower focus on value-enhancing related deals. Taking into account economies of scale and scope as well as network effects as discussed above, the market position of a combined firm in the unrelated submarket is challenging unless a dominant player is acquired.

The innovation potential and creation of user value seems to be limited, and financial resources that could be invested elsewhere are blocked. This study therefore expects unrelated deals by digital technology giants to dilute value, especially in the context of "winner-take-all" outcomes.

Hypothesis 4. *Unrelated transactions by digital technology giants result in negative abnormal returns to the acquirer.*

The insights into digital technology giants and the effect of relatedness raise the question of why the companies conduct diversifying deals, despite the limited value potential. The second main influence on digital technology giants, the distinct financial strength, requires further analysis here. On the one hand, the financial strength gives them latitude to test new business opportunities, and enables investments that might be difficult to finance by debt (Furman et al., 2019). On the other hand, the strong financial liquidity broadens the scope of action for digital giants in terms of decreased corporate control, a key function of capital markets. However, low levels of control can lead to corporate governance issues and value dilution. For example, Morck et al. (1990) identify diversification driven by managerial motives as one type of acquisitions that leads to lower acquirer returns. Managers are more committed to unrelated transactions as a way of reducing corporate risk, ensuring corporate survival or testing new businesses provided this secures their own position, even though this might not be in the shareholders' interest. Hereby, high levels of liquidity allow management to conduct these transactions without the control of capital markets. The massive financial resources of Apple in particular are unprecedented, both relatively and in absolute terms. The company reported more than $250 billion in cash, cash equivalents, and marketable securities in 2017 (Mickle, 2017). In general, the average free cash flow per digital giant per year has risen from $6 billion in 2008 to $19 billion in 2017 (see table 2.2.3). Literature on the effect of financial strength on M&A activity supports the potential of corporate governance issues. The free cash flow theory by Jensen (1986, 1988) describes *managerial self-interest* in terms of agency conflicts between management and shareholders. Management prefers a high level of controlled resources to reduce monitoring by capital markets, whereas shareholders desire the payout of excess cash to increase performance. In this situation, acquisitions are an attractive method for management to spend cash and increase own power and compensation even though the transactions might not increase shareholder value. He argues that it is prevalent in firms with high free cash flow and low monitoring by capital markets. Several studies test this hypothesis empirically. Lang et al. (1991) analyze acquirer returns in relation to cash flow for companies with good and poor investment opportunities. They show a significant negative influence of cash flow on the shareholder value for acquirers with poor investment opportunities. This is not the case for companies with good investment opportunities. Similar results are obtained by Schlingemann (2004), who presents a significant negative effect of internally generated free cash flow on acquirer three-day abnormal return. This relation is stronger for companies with below median investment opportunities. Smith and Kim (1994) analyze the performance of acquirers with a high level of free cash flow and find negative abnormal returns. They conclude that this group of bidders overpay for transactions, and link the overinvestment problem to the free cash flow theory. A different approach is used by Harford (1999) who analyzes the effect of excess cash on acquisition performance. He shows that firms with excess cash are more likely to acquire other companies and that these acquisitions result in lower abnormal return and lower operating performance. The study establishes a connection between excess cash and the sum of prior free cash flow, and provides support for the free cash flow theory.

Summarizing the discussions on digital technology giants' financial strength, managerial motives and diversification, high levels of free cash flow can lead to investments which do not enable innovation or create new value offers but which dilute user and owner value. Jensen (1986) directly relates diversification mergers to the agency problems of free cash flow. "Diversification programs generally fit this category, and the theory predicts they will generate lower total gains" (Jensen, 1986, p. 328). This study expects unrelated transactions to be motivated by managerial self-interest and free cash flow to have a negative influence on the abnormal return.

Hypothesis 5. *Free cash flow has a negative influence on the abnormal returns to digital technology giants for unrelated transactions.*

Even though literature primarily links diversifying actions to managerial motives (e.g., Morck et al., 1990), the financial strength of digital technology giants can also decrease value creation in related transactions. The negative effect of high levels of liquidity in terms of limited corporate control exists in all deal types, with management able to conduct related acquisitions that are beneficial to the own position and not to shareholder or user value. Hypothesis H2 suggests that, in general, related transactions can benefit from favorable dynamics as discussed above.

However, this study expects part of these transactions to be driven by managerial self-interest and to have negative returns, thus decreasing the overall positive effect. The influence of free cash flow in related transactions can differ from the influence in unrelated transactions, due to the positive impact in related deals in terms of network effects, complementarities and competition-decreasing actions that are also partly driven by the distinct financial endowment.

Hypothesis 6. *Free cash flow has a negative influence on the abnormal returns to digital technology giants for related transactions. The influence of free cash flow for related transactions is different to the influence for unrelated transactions.*

The group of digital technology giants dominates the list of the largest companies worldwide. Empirical research in high technology industries indicates that not only the level of available financial resources but also the firm size in terms of market valuation can negatively affect management's M&A decisions and value creation (e.g., Kohers and Kohers, 2000; Schief et al., 2013). In a broad cross-industrial study, Moeller et al. (2004) show that larger acquirers pay higher premiums and complete a larger number of transactions. They attribute this to *managerial hubris* and conclude that this behavior is more relevant in transaction decisions of larger acquirers. Similarly, Malmendier and Tate (2005, 2008) show management of companies with substantial financial resources to be more susceptible to managerial hubris in terms of overconfidence and to diversifying and less profitable acquisitions. This context sheds another light on the high number of transactions by digital technology giants, and on the negotiations of the Facebook-Instagram-deal. Management of leading platforms can overestimate their own capabilities, focus less on offers that create user and shareholder value and spend resources for value diluting investments.

Even though Fuller et al. (2002) argue that the relative acquirer size in comparison with the target absorbs shareholder value effects to some degree, this study expects that managerial hubris is a motive for value diluting deals by digital technology giants. It can influence the M&A activity in terms of a negative effect of firm size.

Hypothesis 7. Firm size has a negative influence on the abnormal returns to digital technology giants.

2.3 Data and Research Methodology

2.3.1 Data Sample

The mergers and acquisitions sample for the event study is gathered from the Securities Data Company database and the Capital IQ database. The analyzed event is defined as a merger or acquisition with change in majority stake completed by one of the digital technology giants (Alibaba Group Holding Ltd., Alphabet Inc., Amazon.com Inc., Apple Inc., Facebook Inc., Microsoft Corp., Tencent Holding Ltd.) and announced between January 1, 2008 and December 31, 2017. The SDC transaction list includes all worldwide M&A deals in the announcement period in which the acquirer ultimate parent equals one company of the peer group. The Capital IQ transaction list includes all worldwide M&A deals and private placements in the announcement period in which buyer or investor parent equals one company of the peer group. Both lists are matched and cleaned for double or wrong entries.[9]

The final transaction sample is determined by applying the following selection criteria:

1. The transaction is a merger or acquisition and not a strategic partnership, joint venture, option purchase, patent acquisition, real estate deal,

---

9 For example, the acquirer is not part of the parent company at the time of acquisition, or acquirer and seller of the target are part of the same parent company.

renewable energy project, license agreement, share buyback, recapitalization or similar type of transaction.

2. The acquiring company buys a controlling stake and the transaction leads to a change in majority holding in the target company, i.e., transactions based on minority investments or venture capital investments are excluded.

3. At least one second source exists that can verify the transaction, i.e., transactions that are only covered in one database are verified using Factiva, TechCrunch or other digital technology specific information services.

4. The announcement date can be clearly determined, i.e., a company statement or news coverage was made on a specific date.

5. All necessary information (e.g., target SIC code) is available for the transaction.

6. The transaction is successfully completed.

7. The acquiring company has been listed for at least 150 trading days prior to the deal announcement date.

8. The transaction is the only M&A deal by the acquirer ultimate parent on the event date.

9. There is no significant confounding event (e.g., Alphabet stock split in 2014) in the event window that biases the results, i.e., the Wall Street Journal is scanned for five days before and five days after each announcement.

The data gathering from both databases leads to a first matched and cleaned sample of 1,980 deals. The final selection criteria reduce the sample to a list of 435 transactions conducted by the digital giants between 2008 and 2017. The impact of the selection criteria is presented in table 2.3.1. The reductions per step vary between the digital technology giants and steps. Alphabet leads the first data sample with 838 transactions followed by Tencent, Microsoft and Alibaba with 321, 240 and 232 deals, respectively. Tencent's high amount of transactions without a change in majority holding in the target company is striking. 91 % of all deals are minority investments, venture capital investments or consortium deals with no majority stake. Apple and Facebook contrast strongly in this respect, with only 2 % and 7 % of their first data sample deals in this category. The high share of deals with missing data for Alibaba, Apple and Facebook is driven by transactions without additional verification and rumored deals. The further restrictions for Facebook and Alibaba are mainly associated with missing share price data before the initial public offering (IPO) in

2012 and 2014, respectively. The other companies' restrictions are multiple acquisitions on one day and further confounding events.

Table 2.3.1: Data Sample Selection Funnel

Number of Deals by	First Data Sample	Other Deal Type (# 1)	No Majority Change (# 2)	Missing Information (# 3-5)	Further Restrictions (# 6-9)	Final Data Sample
Alibaba	232	6	164	25	19	18
Alphabet	838	20	605	33	33	147
Amazon	169	10	82	12	0	65
Apple	85	4	2	17	4	58
Facebook	95	3	7	11	35	39
Microsoft	240	9	114	20	1	96
Tencent	321	5	293	11	0	12
Total	1,980	57	1,267	129	92	435

Table 2.3.1 presents the number of transactions per company in the first data sample, the sample selection steps # 1-9 and the final data sample.

Table 2.3.2 provides a detailed view of the final data sample with the remaining 435 transactions. The main share of transactions is included in both databases, with the SDC database listing 23 and the Capital IQ database 62 exclusive acquisitions. The data shows that the total number of transactions is not equally distributed over the years and companies but has grown in the last ten years and peaked in 2015. Alphabet leads the list with 147 transactions in the review period, while Tencent only conducted 12 transactions that meet the selection criteria.

The transaction list is validated by press research using Factiva, company websites and digital technology specific information services, e.g., TechCrunch and VentureBeat, to ensure that announcement dates and other transaction details are correct. This is necessary because the data sample is not restricted to large transactions, and deals in the digital technology industry are generally not well covered in the databases. A similar approach is applied by Benson and Ziedonis (2010) and Lerner et al. (2011) for validating data on corporate venture capital and leveraged buyout deals, respectively. If there is a difference in the announcement date of both databases and other sources, the date is set at the first date at which the deal was covered by the press as confirmed (officially or unofficially) and not rumored, similar to Wilcox et al. (2001). Following MacKinlay (1997), the event day moves to the next trading date if the announcement date is on a weekend. Furthermore, the Datastream database is used to gather the relevant daily share prices and market indices. The Datastream Total Return Index, which includes price movements, dividend payments and changes in the share structure, is used to calculate the stock and benchmark returns. Company financials are provided by the Worldscope database, and the Fama-French factors are obtained from Kenneth R. French's website.

Table 2.3.2: Distribution of Deals by Acquirer, Database and Year

Number of Deals by			Acquirer							Database		
	Total	in %	Alibaba	Alpha-bet	Ama-zon	Apple	Face-book	Micro-soft	Tencent	Both Data-bases	Only SDC	Only Capital IQ
2008	29	7%	0	3	7	1	0	18	0	24	2	3
2009	17	4%	0	4	4	2	0	7	0	15	1	1
2010	37	9%	0	23	5	5	0	3	1	36	0	1
2011	35	8%	0	20	7	2	0	5	1	30	0	5
2012	31	7%	0	13	4	4	0	6	4	22	3	6
2013	44	10%	0	12	7	8	10	7	0	34	1	9
2014	62	14%	0	27	5	10	11	9	0	56	1	5
2015	66	15%	7	14	8	11	6	19	1	51	7	8
2016	61	14%	6	19	7	6	8	11	4	42	4	15
2017	53	12%	5	12	11	9	4	11	1	40	4	9
Total	435	100%	18	147	65	58	39	96	12	350	23	62

Table 2.3.2 presents the number of transactions per acquirer, database and year.

2.3.2 Definition of Variables

This study uses the SIC code framework to determine *Relatedness* between acquirer and target. It is a well-established and frequently used approach in the relatedness and diversification literature. The method is sometimes criticized for being unable to reflect the full complexity of relatedness (e.g., Lubatkin, 1987; Wilcox et al., 2001). However, Montgomery (1982) analyzes the differences between continuous SIC-based product-count measures and qualitative measures and finds high degrees of overlap. In this study, the primary SIC code of target and acquirer is directly compared on a 3-digit level, similar to Uhlenbruck et al. (2006). The 4-digit code is extremely narrow, especially for the digital industry, whereas the 2-digit level is very broad. For example, Alibaba, Alphabet, Facebook and Tencent have the primary SIC code 7375, information retrieval services. A major share of products and services (e.g., marketplace platforms for Alibaba, advertising platforms for Alphabet, social networks for Tencent and Facebook) are captured by the 4-digit SIC code, but the business segments are also linked to the 3-digit industry group 737, which includes computer programming, data processing and other computer related services. However, the major group 73, business services, which includes for example personnel supply and dwelling services, is too broad. The same argument applies to the other digital giants. The primary SIC code by SDC database is utilized if possible. For the 62 Capital IQ only transactions, the primary industry according to the Global Industry Classification Standard is matched to the respective SIC code by employing a mapping framework provided by Capital IQ. All transactions for which the SIC code differs between both databases, or which have only one SIC code, are checked manually and validated. The Capital IQ SIC code is used if the SDC SIC code does not fit.

Jensen (1986, 1988) describes agency costs of free cash flow, but does not provide a definition or measurement of free cash flow. Many different measures are used in the literature as proxies for free cash flow and the implications can differ considerably. The formulas start mostly from the operating income or the operating cash flow. This study applies two different definitions of free cash flow (FCF). The first approach (*Free Cash Flow 1*) is based on Lehn and Poulsen (1989) and used by Smith and Kim (1994) and Schlingemann (2004) as presented in formula (2.3.1):

$$FCF_1 = OPI + DEP - TAX - INT - DIV, \tag{2.3.1}$$

where *OPI* represents the operating income, *DEP* the depreciation and amortization, *TAX* the total income tax minus change in deferred taxes, *INT* the gross interest expenses on debt and *DIV* the sum of dividends paid on preferred and common stocks. The second approach (*Free Cash Flow 2*) starts from the operating cash flow and is based on Brealey et al. (2017). Formula (2.3.2) shows the calculation:

$$FCF_2 = CFO - CAP, \tag{2.3.2}$$

where *CFO* represents the operating cash flow and *CAP* the capital expenditures. Both measures are normalized by the book value of total assets.

Other analyzed acquirer characteristics are firm size and acquirer experience. *Firm Size* is calculated according to Moeller et al. (2004) as the natural logarithm of the total equity market capitalization. Free cash flow as well as firm size are measured at the fiscal year prior to the event. The variable *Acquirer Experience* is defined as the total number of completed acquisitions by the acquirer up to the analyzed transaction. All deals from the SDC database are analyzed. The selection criteria are deal status completed or pending and deal type merger, acquisition of majority interest or acquisition of assets. A sanity check is conducted and all transactions from the final event study data set as well as deals with further restrictions (# 6–9) are included while the unsuccessful acquisitions are excluded. The acquirer experience list includes 670 deals from 1987 to 2017. Furthermore, this study applies target-specific and deal-specific characteristics that have demonstrated predictive power over acquirer returns in previous research as control variables. These dummy variables include *Domestic Deal* that indicates if the acquirer and target are located in the same country (e.g., Danbolt and Maciver, 2012), *Chinese Deal* that indicates if the acquirer and target are both located in China (e.g., Chari et al., 2010; Chi et al., 2011), and *Public Target* that indicates if the target is a public company (e.g., Chang, 1998; Laamanen et al., 2014). Two additional control variables are created for the three years with the highest and the three years with the lowest number of transactions per company across the sample (e.g., Croci et al., 2010; Mcnamara et al., 2008). The dummy variable *High Year* indicates if the announcement date of the transaction is in the year 2014, 2015 or 2016 and *Low Year* indicates if the announcement date of the transaction is in the year 2008, 2009 or 2012.

The detailed statistics of the final data sample in table 2.3.3 show differences between the digital giants. While Alphabet, Facebook, Microsoft and Tencent mostly conduct related transactions, the other three companies have at least 66 % unrelated acquisitions. Average *Firm Size* varies between a market capitalization of $111 billion for Tencent and $494 billion for Apple. Average free cash flow is only weakly dominated by Apple, with 15 % for *Free Cash Flow 1* and 21 % for *Free Cash Flow 2*. *Acquirer Experience* shows a slightly different picture. Microsoft has the most completed transactions with on average 169 deals, but the firm is also the oldest company in the sample. Alphabet is catching up with Microsoft and has on average across the sample 125 completed transactions, but in 2017 it already had on average 195 deals compared with 205 deals for Microsoft. Across the sample, the larger share of transactions is domestic, with acquirer and target based in the same country.[10] Additionally, most targets of the digital technology giants are privately held companies. Only 3 % of all acquired companies are publicly traded, which concurs with other studies on targets in the digital technology industry (e.g., Uhlenbruck et al., 2006). The share of acquisitions in the three years with high and low M&A activity divides up as expected, with 43 % and 18 % for all transactions, respectively.[11]

---

10 The only exception is Tencent, which has conducted less than half of its acquisitions in China.

11 Only Alibaba and Facebook deviate due to the later IPOs.

Table 2.3.3: Characteristics of Transactions and Acquirers by Digital Technology Giant

| | Acquirer | | | | | | | |
	Alibaba	Alphabet	Amazon	Apple	Facebook	Microsoft	Tencent	Total
Related Deals	6	127	6	2	28	83	11	263
Unrelated Deals	12	20	59	56	11	13	1	172
Free Cash Flow 1	7	16	9	15	11	13	16	13
Free Cash Flow 2	14	14	11	21	11	19	19	15
Acquirer Experience	24	125	51	48	45	169	6	99
Firm Size	214	315	162	494	182	313	111	294
Domestic Deal	61	73	69	62	67	64	33	67
Chinese Deal	61	0	0	0	0	0	33	3
Public Target	11	3	3	2	0	3	0	3
High Year	72	41	31	47	64	41	42	43
Low Year	0	14	23	12	0	32	33	18

Table 2.3.3 presents the number of related and unrelated deals as well as the means of both *Free Cash Flow* measures, *Acquirer Experience*, *Firm Size* and of the control dummy variables *Domestic Deal*, *Chinese Deal*, *Public Target*, *High Year* and *Low Year* per acquirer. *Free Cash Flow 1* is calculated as operating income before depreciation and amortization minus income tax minus interest expenses minus dividends, deflated by book value of total assets. *Free Cash Flow 2* is calculated as operating cash flow minus capital expenditures, deflated by book value of total assets. *Acquirer Experience* is defined as number of completed acquisitions until the analyzed transaction. *Firm Size* is the natural logarithm of total equity market capitalization and presented in $ billion without the natural logarithm transformation. *Domestic Deal* is equal to 1 if the acquirer and target are located in the same country and 0 otherwise. *Chinese Deal* is equal to 1 if the acquirer and target are located in China and 0 otherwise. *Public Target* is equal to 1 if the target is public and 0 otherwise. *High Year* is equal to 1 if the transaction is announced in 2014, 2015 or 2016 and 0 otherwise. *Low Year* is equal to 1 if the transaction is announced in 2008, 2009 or 2012 and 0 otherwise. *Free Cash Flow 1* and *Free Cash Flow 2* as well as the dummy variables are shown in percentage.

2.3.3 Event Study Methodology

The aim of the study is to understand the short-term value effect of M&A on the acquirer and examine the impact of value creation and value dilution drivers. The first part of the study analyzes the value effect of transactions overall and for each digital giant separately. The second part focusses on the influence of relatedness effects, with the events per company grouped into transactions related to acquirer business and transactions that are not related. Finally, the robustness of the results is verified and the value drivers including relatedness, free cash flow, acquirer experience and firm size are further analyzed in a multivariate regression.

The event study methodology is widely used in the finance as well as information system literature (e.g., Acquisti et al., 2006; Dehning et al., 2003;

Dos Santos et al., 1993; Oh and Kim, 2001). The study follows the standard event study methodology (see figure 2.3.1) as described by Brown and Warner (1980, 1985) and discussed intensively in literature (e.g., Binder, 1998; Corrado, 2011; Kothari and Warner, 2007; MacKinlay, 1997; McWilliams and Siegel, 1997). Different return generating models are used to calculate the abnormal return in an event study. This study mainly focuses on the market return model as the advantages of more sophisticated estimation methods are limited (Campbell et al., 1997). The robustness subsection also includes results with the market-adjusted return model and the three-factor model by Fama and French (1993).

Figure 2.3.1: Event Study Methodology

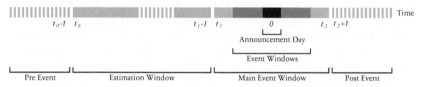

Figure 2.3.1 presents the event study methodology including the arrangement of estimation window and event windows.

The realized stock and market portfolio returns are calculated as log returns as recommended by Corrado and Truong (2008), based on the Datastream Total Return Index. Formula (2.3.3) shows the abnormal return calculation for any event j of stock i at time t:

$$AR_{j,t} = R_{i,t} - \left(\widehat{\alpha}_j + \widehat{\beta}_j * R_{M,t}\right), \tag{2.3.3}$$

where $R_{i,t}$ represents the realized log return to stock i at time t and $R_{M,t}$ the realized log return to the respective market portfolio at time t. The coefficients $\widehat{\alpha}_j$ and $\widehat{\beta}_j$ are computed for each event j by applying an ordinary least squares (OLS) regression on the market model, as shown in formula (2.3.4), and respective estimation window t_0 to t_1-1:

$$R_{i,t} = \alpha_i + \beta_i * R_{M,t} + \varepsilon_{i,t}. \tag{2.3.4}$$

For each stock i the appropriate market portfolio is determined and applied. For the US-based and US-listed companies[12] this study utilizes the commonly used S&P 500 index as benchmark, which includes all five stocks for the analyzed period.[13] The five firms are all listed at the NASDAQ stock exchange. Therefore, the NASDAQ Composite index might be an alternative, but the dominance of the digital technology giants in terms of market capitalization can influence the index and bias the results. For the two China-based and Hong Kong-listed (Tencent Holding Ltd.) or US-listed (Alibaba Group Holding Ltd.) companies, another index is more suitable. As discussed by MacKinlay (1997), the R^2 of the OLS regression of formula (2.3.4) is calculated for Tencent over the total period and for Alibaba since IPO with different benchmarks (MSCI World Index, MSCI ACWI Index, NYSE Composite, Hang Seng Index and MSCI China Index). Alibaba has the highest R^2 for both MSCI World indices and Tencent for the Hong Kong and China-focused indices. However, Tencent dominates both indices with 10–20 % share, which can bias the results. Therefore, the MSCI ACWI index is used as the respective market portfolio for Alibaba and Tencent. It includes not only developed but also emerging markets, and thus China as the home market of both companies.

The length of the estimation window t_0 to t_1-1 differs widely among empirical studies. For example, Corrado (2011) suggests 250 trading days as a typical estimation window, which equals approximately one year. However, Park (2004) shows in a multi-country context that event study results in the airline industry are not sensitive to the length of the estimation window as long as it exceeds 100 days. Two companies of the peer group do not have stock returns over the full length of the event study as Facebook's IPO was on May 18, 2012 and that of Alibaba on September 19, 2014. Thus, the estimation window length is set at 145 trading days [-150;-6] to keep as many events as possible in the sample and to ensure an estimation window length of at least 100 trading days.

The abnormal returns per event are summed up to cumulative abnormal returns (CAR) according to formula (2.3.5):

$$CAR_{j,[t_1;t_2]} = \sum_{t_1}^{t_2} AR_{j,t}, \qquad\qquad (2.3.5)$$

---

12 This group includes Alphabet Inc., Amazon.com Inc., Apple Inc., Facebook Inc. and Microsoft Corp.
13 Facebook is part of the S&P 500 index since December 23, 2013.

where t_1 and t_2 represent the start and end of the event window. Following the recommendations of McWilliams and Siegel (1997), the main event window of the event study is set at two weeks, more specifically eleven-day [-5;+5], to keep it short and all relevant stock movements included. Other analyzed event windows include the event week [-2;+2], the days around the event [-1;+1], [-1;0], [0;+1] and the event day [0]. The one-day window allows observation of the isolated announcement day effect, whereas the two-day windows ensure inclusion of the effect of earlier information leakage or transactions announced after close of trading. Depending on the analysis, the cumulative average abnormal return (CAAR) is calculated by aggregating and averaging the $CAR_{j,[t_1;t_2]}$ on a company or other level as defined by formula (2.3.6):

$$CAAR_{[t_1;t_2]} = \frac{1}{n}\sum_j^n CAR_{j,[t_1;t_2]}, \qquad\qquad (2.3.6)$$

where n represents the number of event observations per analysis. The cumulative average abnormal returns are tested for statistical significance by employing four different test statistics, two parametric and two non-parametric tests. The two parametric tests are the Patell's Z-test (1976) and the standardized cross-sectional test (BMP-test) developed by Boehmer et al. (1991). Patell's Z-test is widely used as standard event study methodology, but is not well specified in the presence of cross-sectional correlation and event-induced volatility (Marks and Musumeci, 2017). The BMP-test accounts for event-induced volatility and the applied version is adjusted for cross-correlation as described by Kolari and Pynnönen (2010). Non-parametric test statistics do not rely on normally distributed abnormal returns and are more powerful than parametric tests (Campbell and Wesley, 1993). In this event study, the Rank-test as developed by Corrado (1989) and Corrado and Zivney (1992) and the generalized Sign-test (Cowan, 1992) are used. All four tests are applied to ensure that the results are not biased, and discrepancies between the test statistics need to be treated with caution (Campbell et al., 2010).

For robustness checks, different benchmarks (equal weighted indices and Datastream Level 1 Total Market indices), alternative return generating models (market-adjusted return model and Fama-French three-factor model) and a further reduced transaction sample are employed. The abnormal return according to the market-adjusted return model is calculated as in formula (2.3.7):

$$AR_{j,t} = R_{i,t} - R_{M,t},$$ (2.3.7)

and formula (2.3.8) shows the abnormal return calculation according to the three-factor model:

$$AR_{j,t} = R_{i,t} - \left(\widehat{\alpha}_j + \widehat{\beta}_{1,j}*MKT_t + \widehat{\beta}_{2,j}*SMB_t + \widehat{\beta}_{3,j}*HML_t\right),$$ (2.3.8)

where MKT_t represents the excess market return over risk-free rate, SMB_t the return difference between a small and a large cap stocks portfolio and HML_t the return difference between a high and a low book-to-market stocks portfolio. The three factors and stock returns for this return generating model are calculated as discrete and not as log returns following the approach of Fama and French (1992, 1993).

2.3.4 Multivariate Regression Methodology

The cumulative abnormal returns are further analyzed with multivariate regressions to determine the impact of the value drivers. The panel analysis is based on a fixed-effect regression model, which is determined as in formula (2.3.9):

$$CAR_{j,[-5;\,+5]} = \alpha_i + \sum_k^y \left(\beta_k*VAR_{k,j}\right) + u_j,$$ (2.3.9)

where $CAR_{j,[-5;\,+5]}$ represents the cumulative abnormal return for the event j in the main eleven-day [-5;+5] event window, α_i the firm-specific intercept of stock i, β_k the regression coefficients of the independent variables, $VAR_{k,j}$ the independent variables, y the number of independent variables per model and u_j the error term. A regression model with firm-fixed effects is used because the event study analysis reveals differences between the digital giants which might be attributable to individual time-invariant characteristics. This conjecture is supported by the Durbin-Wu-Hausman test between a random-effects and a fixed-effects specification. The test shows the unique errors to be correlated with the regressors so that the fixed-effects model is preferred. Year dummies are not included as the joint F-test shows that the dummies are not statistically different from zero and that time fixed-effects are not needed. Finally, a modified Wald test is conducted which indicates heteroscedasticity and the usage of robust standard errors. Robust Huber-White standard errors are calculated and compared with time-cluster as well as firm-cluster standard errors. No large difference is observed and following the recommendations of Petersen (2009), the Huber-White standard errors are used.

This study tests three different multivariate regressions. The first two setups (model I and II) analyze mainly hypotheses H2, H3, H4 and H7 and shed light on the influence of acquirer characteristics and relatedness. The independent variables include *Firm Size, Acquirer Experience, Relatedness* and *Free Cash Flow*. The second model differs from the first by the inclusion of *(Acquirer Experience)²*, a squared term of acquirer experience following the approach of Haleblian and Finkelstein (1999). Model III focuses on hypotheses H5 and H6 and the interaction of relatedness and free cash flow (*Free Cash Flow * Relatedness*). The variable *Free Cash Flow* is centered to its mean in model III to ease the interpretation. All models are calculated separately, with *Free Cash Flow 1* and *Free Cash Flow 2*. The target-specific and deal-specific characteristics are applied as controls including the dummy variables *Domestic Deal, Chinese Deal, Public Target, High Year* and *Low Year*.

2.4 Empirical Results

2.4.1 Value Creation in Digital Giants' Transactions

The share price reactions for the total sample of all digital giants and per company are shown in table 2.4.1. On an aggregated level, only the [0;+1] and [-1;+1] event windows are statistically significant with a slightly positive abnormal return of 0.06 % and 0.01 %, respectively. The share price reaction on the event day and the day after is significant at the 10 % level for both non-parametric tests but not for the parametric tests. The [-1;+1] window is only significant for the Corrado-test. Overall, this sample provides mostly insignificant results which are in line with prior studies analyzing acquirer returns on an aggregated level (e.g., Andrade et al., 2001; Bruner, 2002; King et al., 2004; Martynova and Renneboog, 2008). However, the results contradict previous studies of high technology acquirers that observe value creation (e.g., Kohers and Kohers, 2000; Uhlenbruck et al., 2006; Rhéaume and Bhabra, 2008). Hypothesis H1 is not supported. It seems that shareholders of digital technology giants react in general cautiously to M&A as a strategy to maintain a dominant position and to ensure future growth. On the one hand, the digital technology giants might not be able to benefit from favorable market dynamics. The digital giants

Table 2.4.1: CAARs for the Total Sample on Aggregated and Company Level

	(1) CAAR	(2) Patell-test	(3) BMP-test	(4) Sign-test	(5) Corrado-test	(6) Positive	(7) Sample
Panel A: Total Sample							
[-5;+5]	-0.03%	0.55	0.54	0.86	0.51	50%	435
[-2;+2]	-0.17%	-0.44	-0.44	0.19	0.00	49%	435
[-1;+1]	0.01%	0.37	0.44	1.15	1.81 *	51%	435
[-1;0]	-0.10%	-0.77	-0.91	0.38	0.62	49%	435
[0;+1]	0.06%	0.75	0.89	1.92 *	1.86 *	53%	435
[0]	-0.05%	-0.67	-0.81	1.06	0.36	51%	435
Panel B: Alibaba							
[-5;+5]	-0.39%	-0.25	-0.28	0.14	-0.02	50%	18
[-2;+2]	-0.78%	-0.69	-0.65	0.14	-0.35	50%	18
[-1;+1]	-0.16%	-0.15	-0.14	0.61	0.45	56%	18
[-1;0]	-0.47%	-0.78	-0.72	0.61	-0.11	56%	18
[0;+1]	-0.55%	-0.91	-1.01	0.14	-0.58	50%	18
[0]	-0.86%	-2.13 **	-2.04 **	-0.33	-1.75 *	44%	18
Panel C: Alphabet							
[-5;+5]	0.86%	3.05 ***	2.66 ***	2.88 ***	2.17 **	62%	147
[-2;+2]	0.47%	2.47 **	2.19 **	2.05 **	1.98 **	59%	147
[-1;+1]	0.34%	2.03 **	2.60 ***	1.23	2.72 ***	55%	147
[-1;0]	0.06%	0.39	0.48	0.24	0.99	51%	147
[0;+1]	0.35%	2.59 ***	3.20 ***	3.21 ***	3.50 ***	63%	147
[0]	0.07%	0.69	0.83	2.22 **	1.64	59%	147
Panel D: Amazon							
[-5;+5]	-1.69%	-2.11 **	-2.12 **	-1.75 *	-1.45	37%	65
[-2;+2]	-0.79%	-1.37	-1.35	-0.26	-0.91	46%	65
[-1;+1]	0.06%	0.02	0.02	0.48	0.73	51%	65
[-1;0]	-0.10%	-0.39	-0.35	0.73	0.40	52%	65
[0;+1]	0.29%	0.90	0.94	1.23	1.41	55%	65
[0]	0.13%	0.69	0.69	0.73	1.31	52%	65
Panel E: Apple							
[-5;+5]	0.54%	0.95	1.16	0.76	0.36	52%	58
[-2;+2]	0.06%	0.11	0.12	-0.03	0.53	47%	58
[-1;+1]	0.00%	0.02	0.03	1.02	0.38	53%	58
[-1;0]	-0.04%	0.00	-0.01	0.50	0.42	50%	58
[0;+1]	0.04%	0.24	0.33	1.02	0.14	53%	58
[0]	0.00%	0.29	0.40	0.76	0.14	52%	58
Panel F: Facebook							
[-5;+5]	-0.44%	-0.65	-0.57	0.49	-0.25	49%	39
[-2;+2]	-1.40%	-1.96 **	-2.36 **	-1.76 *	-1.84 *	31%	39
[-1;+1]	-0.67%	-1.39	-1.47	0.17	-0.50	46%	39
[-1;0]	-0.25%	-0.72	-1.14	0.17	0.09	46%	39
[0;+1]	-0.46%	-1.51	-1.57	0.17	-1.02	46%	39
[0]	-0.05%	-0.74	-1.07	0.17	-0.46	46%	39
Panel G: Microsoft							
[-5;+5]	-0.55%	-1.40	-1.54	-2.11 **	-1.01	38%	96
[-2;+2]	-0.32%	-1.50	-1.53	-1.30	-1.07	42%	96
[-1;+1]	-0.23%	-0.91	-1.12	-0.68	-0.82	45%	96
[-1;0]	-0.27%	-1.16	-1.40	-0.89	-0.84	44%	96
[0;+1]	-0.21%	-1.19	-1.45	-1.71 *	-1.27	40%	96
[0]	-0.26%	-1.74 *	-2.04 **	-1.71 *	-1.57	40%	96
Panel H: Tencent							
[-5;+5]	1.53%	0.89	1.97 **	2.45 **	0.91	83%	12
[-2;+2]	0.28%	0.26	0.38	1.30	0.23	67%	12
[-1;+1]	0.28%	0.34	0.52	0.14	0.45	50%	12
[-1;0]	0.27%	0.47	1.10	0.14	0.54	50%	12
[0;+1]	0.08%	0.04	0.05	-0.43	0.13	42%	12
[0]	0.07%	0.14	0.31	0.14	0.17	50%	12

Table 2.4.1 presents the abnormal share price reaction for all transactions (panel A) and per company (panel B-H) in different event windows. Column (1) displays the cumulative average abnormal return, column (2)-(5) the test statistics, column (6) the share of transactions

with a positive abnormal return and column (7) the sample size per analysis. Statistical significance at 1 %, 5 % and 10 % levels is indicated with ***, ** and *, respectively.

might have reached some level of maturity or size and not be able to exploit the industry conditions. This could prompt shareholders to take a neutral stance towards acquisitions by these companies. On the other hand, there might be a positive influence of the digital technology environment on the M&A activity, with this being outweighed by other effects, for example as result of managerial motives. The influence of relatedness and acquirer experience as well as firm size and free cash flow as indication of managerial hubris and managerial self-interest is analyzed in the multivariate regression.

The results at company level differ. For all event windows, Alphabet shows highly significant positive CAARs.[14] The CAAR in the [-5;+5] event window is 0.86 %, whereas the combined abnormal share price reaction on the event day and the day after is still 0.35 %. In contrast, Amazon and Facebook have a significant negative abnormal share price reaction for one event window each. Amazon's CAAR in the main event window is negative at -1.69 %, and Facebook has a negative CAAR of -1.40 % in the event week. Alibaba and Microsoft have a significant but less negative abnormal return on the event day of -0.86 % and -0.26 %, respectively. Positive abnormal returns with no consistent significance are observed for Apple and Tencent. Even though most observations can be explained by the results on aggregated level, Alphabet's highly significant positive abnormal returns are striking. Another potential explanation for performance variance among digital giants, besides differing intensity of managerial motives, can be found in industry relatedness of acquirer and target. The descriptive statistics indicate variation in the number of related and unrelated deals. Alphabet has 86 % related transactions, while the total sample has 60 % related transactions. Thus, an effect of relatedness would also influence the performance on firm level.

2.4.2 Relatedness Effects on Aggregated Level

Table 2.4.2 presents CAARs on aggregated level for related and unrelated transactions separately. Relatedness is measured based on a shared 3-digit SIC code. Panel A shows the results for the 263 related and panel B for the

---

14 Only exceptions are the event windows of the event day and the day before.

172 unrelated transactions. The cumulative average abnormal return for related transactions is significant positive in the two-week event window and in the days around the event. The [-5;+5] event window has a positive CAAR of 0.53 % and is significant at the 5 % level for the parametric and 10 % level for the non-parametric test statistics. The respective two-week event window for unrelated transactions is significant negative at the 10 % level for the parametric tests with an abnormal return of -0.88 %. The event week window has a CAAR of -0.58 % at the 5 % significance level for the parametric tests. All other event windows also show negative returns, but these are not significant.

Table 2.4.2: CAARs for Related and Unrelated Transactions on Aggregated Level

	(1) CAAR	(2) Patell-test	(3) BMP-test	(4) Sign-test	(5) Corrado-test	(6) Positive	(7) Sample
Panel A: Related Transactions							
[-5;+5]	0.53%	2.23 **	2.06 **	1.92 *	1.72 *	55%	263
[-2;+2]	0.09%	1.06	1.02	1.06	1.01	52%	263
[-1;+1]	0.20%	1.56	1.96 *	1.43	2.33 **	53%	263
[-1;0]	0.03%	0.18	0.24	0.69	0.97	51%	263
[0;+1]	0.15%	1.57	1.90 *	1.92 *	2.26 **	55%	263
[0]	-0.02%	-0.22	-0.27	0.93	0.52	52%	263
Panel B: Unrelated Transactions							
[-5;+5]	-0.88%	-1.88 *	-1.92 *	-1.00	-1.55	44%	172
[-2;+2]	-0.58%	-2.01 **	-1.98 **	-1.00	-1.39	44%	172
[-1;+1]	-0.28%	-1.33	-1.37	0.07	-0.30	48%	172
[-1;0]	-0.29%	-1.45	-1.46	-0.24	-0.34	47%	172
[0;+1]	-0.09%	-0.75	-0.80	0.68	-0.13	50%	172
[0]	-0.11%	-0.80	-0.86	0.52	-0.13	49%	172

Table 2.4.2 presents the abnormal share price reaction for related transactions (panel A) and unrelated transactions (panel B) on aggregated level in different event windows. Column (1) displays the cumulative average abnormal return, column (2)-(5) the test statistics, column (6) the share of transactions with a positive abnormal return and column (7) the sample size per analysis. Statistical significance at 1 %, 5 % and 10 % levels is indicated with ***, ** and *, respectively.

The results provide supporting evidence for hypothesis H2 as related transactions create value for shareholders. Shareholders seem to expect network effects, complementarities and reduced competition as described in the previous section. Furthermore, the results show that unrelated transactions dilute value for shareholders, which supports hypothesis H4. A larger share of these acquisitions seems to be driven by negatively influencing factors and not by synergistic benefits. A potential explanation can be managerial motives in terms of managerial hubris or managerial self-interest. This is investigated in the multivariate regressions in a later subsection. The comparison of both types of acquisitions shows an increasing spread in the abnormal returns over the different event windows. Although the significance for unrelated deals is low, it serves as an indication and is further tested. Overall, Rhéaume and Bhabra (2008) find similar results for transactions across different information sectors and Wilcox et al. (2001) for diversification in the telecommunication industry. Additionally, the analysis shows that digital giants acquire more related than unrelated targets. This is also in line with the results of Rhéaume and Bhabra (2008) and indicates that companies maximize shareholder value creation. However, taking into account the results from subsection 2.4.1 on company level it is questionable whether the effect can be observed for all firms.

2.4.3 Related Transactions on Company Level

Table 2.4.3 and table 2.4.4 present the share price reactions grouped by related and unrelated transactions on company level. Related transactions in table 2.4.3 conducted by Alphabet, Apple and Amazon show significant positive abnormal returns. Alphabet's sample size comprises 127 events and most event windows are significant. The [-5;+5] window is significant at the 1 % significance level and has a CAAR of 1.12 %.[15] Yang et al. (2018) find a similar and also significant positive abnormal return of 0.93 % for transaction that are related to Alphabet's main business. For Amazon and Apple some event windows are significant positive, but the sample size of 6 and 2 events, respectively limits the general validity of these results. Even though Corrado and Zivney (1992) state that the parametric t-test as well as non-parametric rank test and Sign-test are sufficiently specified for smaller samples, they also emphasize that the distribution characteristics for the parametric test deviate for a sample size of 10 events and smaller. Thus, significance levels for small samples need to be interpreted carefully. Alibaba's, Facebook's, Microsoft's and Tencent's CAARs for related transactions provide no consistent significance.

The analysis on company level provides some implications for related transactions by digital giants. First, the results for Alphabet, Amazon and Apple indicate that shareholders appreciate acquisitions of targets which are related to digital giants. Thus, in this type of transaction, the acquirers appear to benefit from the digital technology market environment and related transactions can utilize network effects, complementarities and reduce competition. However, the level of value creation differs between the

---

15 The Corrado-test is significant at the 5 % level.

companies. It seems that shareholders have different expectations regarding synergies or allocation of the potential to acquirer and target driven by varying characteristics. Dolata (2018) emphasizes that "Apple, Google or Amazon proved to be very adaptable in the last decade" (p. 15), which differentiates them from other digital technology giants and might be valued by shareholders. The companies have successively bought related targets to strengthen their own dominant position. Apart from that, Gao and Iyer (2006) emphasize the difference between acquisitions of targets with similar and complementary offerings that cannot be depicted with the relatedness measure. Different M&A strategies in terms of target focus might influence the value creation and lead to varying results.

Second, the significant positive effect on total level is strongly driven by one company. Across the event windows, Alphabet shows a significant positive abnormal return and contributes with 127 acquisitions to the total sample size of 263 related events. Shareholders appear to value any related transaction by the company and expect positive returns from inorganic growth. Kuchinke and Vidal (2016) note that Alphabet has frequently used transactions to expand the product and service offerings in past years and that the major reorganization in 2015 facilitates the acquisition and integration of targets. In addition, Cusumano (2017) emphasizes that acquisitions have always taken on a key role in the firm's strategy. He further argues that the corporate transformation enables a clear distinction between core and non-core businesses. Alphabet is also transparent on publishing official transaction announcements and further information. Shareholders might distinguish between Alphabet and the other giants and are willing to pay a premium for related transactions based on Alphabet's M&A strategy and provided transparency on transactions. The transparency can also limit the influence of corporate governance issues and managerial motives.

Table 2.4.3: CAARs for Related Transactions on Company Level

	(1) CAAR	(2) Patell-test	(3) BMP-test	(4) Sign-test	(5) Corrado-test	(6) Positive	(7) Sample
Panel A: Alibaba							
[-5;+5]	1.35%	0.52	0.50	0.88	0.23	67%	6
[-2;+2]	-0.33%	-0.21	-0.29	0.06	-0.35	50%	6
[-1;+1]	0.39%	0.28	0.30	0.06	0.34	50%	6
[-1;0]	0.08%	0.04	0.05	0.88	0.10	67%	6
[0;+1]	-0.25%	-0.26	-0.32	0.06	-0.28	50%	6
[0]	-0.55%	-0.81	-1.17	0.06	-0.85	50%	6
Panel B: Alphabet							
[-5;+5]	1.12%	3.67 ***	3.07 ***	2.89 ***	2.55 **	63%	127
[-2;+2]	0.66%	3.16 ***	2.80 ***	2.53 **	2.56 **	61%	127
[-1;+1]	0.40%	2.16 **	2.80 ***	1.47	2.76 ***	57%	127
[-1;0]	0.06%	0.28	0.34	0.05	0.82	50%	127
[0;+1]	0.38%	2.63 ***	3.30 ***	3.06 ***	3.34 ***	64%	127
[0]	0.04%	0.38	0.45	1.65 *	1.11	57%	127
Panel C: Amazon							
[-5;+5]	-2.83%	-0.97	-0.75	-0.73	-0.48	33%	6
[-2;+2]	-1.66%	-0.79	-0.95	0.09	0.03	50%	6
[-1;+1]	0.89%	0.75	1.35	0.91	1.26	67%	6
[-1;0]	0.14%	0.22	0.53	0.09	0.70	50%	6
[0;+1]	1.27%	1.32	2.19 **	1.72 *	1.66 *	83%	6
[0]	0.52%	0.87	1.57	0.91	1.15	67%	6
Panel D: Apple							
[-5;+5]	-1.61%	-0.70	-0.76	0.16	-0.53	50%	2
[-2;+2]	1.71%	0.91	9.98 ***	1.58	1.30	100%	2
[-1;+1]	1.83%	1.27	30.11 ***	1.58	1.66 *	100%	2
[-1;0]	1.35%	1.06	1.47	1.58	1.39	100%	2
[0;+1]	1.49%	1.34	2.42 **	1.58	1.77 *	100%	2
[0]	1.01%	1.19	7.50 ***	1.58	1.60	100%	2
Panel E: Facebook							
[-5;+5]	1.20%	0.85	0.80	0.85	0.57	54%	28
[-2;+2]	-0.94%	-1.02	-1.16	-1.05	-1.07	36%	28
[-1;+1]	-0.09%	-0.27	-0.28	0.85	0.31	54%	28
[-1;0]	0.12%	0.01	0.02	1.22	0.61	57%	28
[0;+1]	-0.21%	-0.61	-0.61	0.85	-0.28	54%	28
[0]	0.00%	-0.38	-0.50	0.09	-0.07	46%	28
Panel F: Microsoft							
[-5;+5]	-0.42%	-1.08	-1.19	-1.53	-0.57	40%	83
[-2;+2]	-0.25%	-1.25	-1.27	-1.31	-0.92	41%	83
[-1;+1]	-0.07%	-0.27	-0.35	-0.21	-0.28	47%	83
[-1;0]	-0.12%	-0.46	-0.59	-0.21	-0.29	47%	83
[0;+1]	-0.10%	-0.50	-0.65	-1.31	-0.62	41%	83
[0]	-0.15%	-0.89	-1.08	-0.87	-0.79	43%	83
Panel G: Tencent							
[-5;+5]	0.99%	0.65	1.46	2.25 **	0.68	82%	11
[-2;+2]	-0.36%	-0.13	-0.21	1.04	-0.17	64%	11
[-1;+1]	0.03%	0.14	0.20	-0.16	0.29	45%	11
[-1;0]	0.34%	0.54	1.18	0.44	0.69	55%	11
[0;+1]	-0.25%	-0.28	-0.33	-0.77	-0.23	36%	11
[0]	0.06%	0.12	0.26	-0.16	0.15	45%	11

Table 2.4.3 presents the abnormal share price reaction for related transactions per company (panel A-G) in different event windows. Column (1) displays the cumulative average abnormal return, column (2)-(5) the test statistics, column (6) the share of transactions with a positive abnormal return and column (7) the sample size per analysis. Statistical significance at 1 %, 5 % and 10 % levels is indicated with ***, ** and *, respectively.

Third, a further effect might overlap the benefits of related acquisitions and distort the results. Hypotheses H6 and H7 expect a negative influence of free cash flow and firm size based on managerial self-interest and managerial hubris, respectively. The sample shows insignificant returns for related transactions by Alibaba, Facebook, Microsoft and Tencent. Thus, for these firms some related transactions that create value might be appreciated by shareholders while other transactions that are driven by managerial self-interest or hubris might be penalized, offsetting the potential gains. This is further analyzed later.

2.4.4 Unrelated Transactions on Company Level

Table 2.4.4 presents a different picture for unrelated transactions on company level. The digital giants show negative abnormal share price returns. Facebook has a strong negative CAAR of -2.58 % in the event week window, which is significant at the 5 % (parametric tests) and 10 % (Sign-test) significance levels. Other windows are also significant negative. Microsoft has a CAAR of -0.96 % on the event day, which is significant at the 5 % level across all test statistics. The [-1;0] event window is significant negative with a CAAR of -1.26 %. Amazon and Alibaba show significant abnormal returns only in one event window each. Alibaba's abnormal return on the event day is -1.01 % and significant at the 5 % (Patell-test) and 10 % (BMP-test and Corrado-test) significance level, while Amazon has a CAAR of 1.57 % in the two-week event window, which is significant at the 5 % level (parametric tests). The CAARs for unrelated transactions conducted by Apple are not significant across the different event windows. Alphabet has negative but not significant CAARs in the multi-day event windows, whereas the two-day windows have slightly positive but insignificant abnormal returns. The event day has a small positive return that is significant at the 10 % level for the non-parametric tests.

The results show value dilution for unrelated acquisitions, but the effect differs among companies. This might be driven by the varying share of value creating and value diluting transactions per digital giant. Dolata (2018) argues that Facebook and Microsoft, which show large negative abnormal returns, are in a weaker competitive position in comparison with the other digital technology giants. He further states that Microsoft has difficulties in adapting to a changing environment, and Kuchinke and Vidal (2016) describe Facebook's expansion strategy as focused on a dominant role in social networks. Thus, shareholders might be more critical in general with

Table 2.4.4: CAARs for Unrelated Transactions on Company Level

	(1) CAAR	(2) Patell-test	(3) BMP-test	(4) Sign-test	(5) Corrado-test	(6) Positive	(7) Sample
Panel A: Alibaba							
[-5;+5]	-1.26%	-0.68	-0.87	-0.45	-0.20	42%	12
[-2;+2]	-1.01%	-0.69	-0.62	0.13	-0.22	50%	12
[-1;+1]	-0.43%	-0.39	-0.36	0.71	0.36	58%	12
[-1;0]	-0.74%	-0.98	-0.88	0.13	-0.23	50%	12
[0;+1]	-0.70%	-0.93	-1.05	0.13	-0.59	50%	12
[0]	-1.01%	-2.04 **	-1.85 *	-0.45	-1.78 *	42%	12
Panel B: Alphabet							
[-5;+5]	-0.83%	-0.97	-0.98	0.53	-0.73	55%	20
[-2;+2]	-0.73%	-1.25	-0.97	-0.81	-1.37	40%	20
[-1;+1]	-0.03%	0.06	0.06	-0.37	0.37	45%	20
[-1;0]	0.06%	0.34	0.40	0.53	0.67	55%	20
[0;+1]	0.12%	0.39	0.37	0.97	1.11	60%	20
[0]	0.21%	0.91	0.97	1.87 *	1.88 *	70%	20
Panel C: Amazon							
[-5;+5]	-1.57%	-1.90 *	-1.95 *	-1.61	-1.35	37%	59
[-2;+2]	-0.70%	-1.18	-1.13	-0.30	-0.95	46%	59
[-1;+1]	-0.03%	-0.22	-0.22	0.22	0.35	49%	59
[-1;0]	-0.13%	-0.48	-0.41	0.74	0.19	53%	59
[0;+1]	0.19%	0.52	0.53	0.74	0.93	53%	59
[0]	0.09%	0.45	0.43	0.48	0.98	51%	59
Panel D: Apple							
[-5;+5]	0.61%	1.09	1.30	0.74	0.45	52%	56
[-2;+2]	0.00%	-0.07	-0.07	-0.33	0.29	45%	56
[-1;+1]	-0.07%	-0.22	-0.26	0.74	0.07	52%	56
[-1;0]	-0.09%	-0.20	-0.24	0.21	0.16	48%	56
[0;+1]	-0.02%	-0.01	-0.02	0.74	-0.19	52%	56
[0]	-0.03%	0.07	0.09	0.48	-0.16	50%	56
Panel E: Facebook							
[-5;+5]	-4.61%	-2.59 ***	-1.66 *	-0.43	-1.26	36%	11
[-2;+2]	-2.58%	-2.07 **	-2.16 **	-1.65 *	-1.37	18%	11
[-1;+1]	-2.15%	-2.19 **	-1.96 *	-1.04	-1.27	27%	11
[-1;0]	-1.21%	-1.37	-1.86 *	-1.65 *	-0.77	18%	11
[0;+1]	-1.12%	-1.87 *	-1.58	-1.04	-1.23	27%	11
[0]	-0.17%	-0.80	-0.99	0.18	-0.63	45%	11
Panel F: Microsoft							
[-5;+5]	-1.41%	-1.07	-1.02	-1.89 *	-1.33	23%	13
[-2;+2]	-0.75%	-0.92	-0.85	-0.22	-0.55	46%	13
[-1;+1]	-1.24%	-1.80 *	-1.70 *	-1.33	-1.61	31%	13
[-1;0]	-1.26%	-1.99 **	-1.82 *	-1.89 *	-1.66 *	23%	13
[0;+1]	-0.94%	-1.96 **	-1.77 *	-1.33	-1.98 **	31%	13
[0]	-0.96%	-2.48 **	-2.51 **	-2.44 **	-2.36 **	15%	13

Table 2.4.4 presents the abnormal share price reaction for unrelated transactions per company (panel A-F) in different event windows. For Tencent, no data is shown as the respective sample includes only one transaction. Column (1) displays the cumulative average abnormal return, column (2)-(5) the test statistics, column (6) the share of transactions with a positive abnormal return and column (7) the sample size per analysis. Statistical significance at 1 %, 5 % and 10 % levels is indicated with ***, ** and *, respectively.

diversifying transactions by the two companies and therefore discount them. In addition, the level of corporate governance issues can differ and a large share of these acquisitions might be driven by managerial self-interest instead of value creation, which is analyzed in the multivariate regression. Alphabet's positive event day reaction can be influenced by shareholders' expectations. Dolata (2018) points out that Alphabet is actively engaged in several expansion trends, and Cusumano (2017) underlines the "company's commitment to experimentation" (p. 25). Shareholders seem to appreciate the expansion across platform boundaries as Alphabet might have extraordinary capabilities to recombine resources and create value offers. Additionally, the high level of transparency can limit corporate governance issues and the share of value diluting transactions.

Figure 2.4.1: CAARs for Related and Unrelated Transactions on Aggregated Level

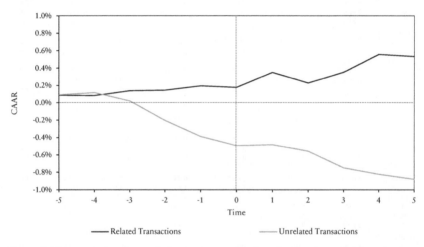

Figure 2.4.1 presents the abnormal share price reaction for related and unrelated transactions on aggregated level over the two-week main event window.

A comparison of the results from table 2.4.3 and table 2.4.4 shows a strong contrast between related and unrelated transactions across digital giants (see also figure 2.4.1). The companies have positive (Alphabet, Amazon, Apple) or non-significant (Alibaba, Facebook, Microsoft, Tencent) CAARs for related transactions, and negative (Alibaba, Amazon, Facebook, Microsoft) or non-significant (Alphabet, Apple) CAARs for unrelated transactions. The results indicate that shareholders of digital giants penalize unrelated transactions, whereas they expect value gains from related transactions. The extent of the effects differs, but a spread between both types of transactions can be observed across the sample. It seems that Alphabet and Apple are able to benefit from revenue and concentration synergies and network effects, while Alibaba, Facebook and Microsoft are prone to value diluting antecedents, for example managerial motives.

Amazon shows both value effects. The variation can be driven by differing characteristics or strategies and is further analyzed in the multivariate regressions. No significant abnormal return is measured for Tencent, which might be attributed to a lower relevance of the transactions for shareholder value or the low sample size for this acquirer. Overall, the results are in line with prior findings in literature and a good indication to support hypotheses H2 and H4. The relatedness effect is also tested in the multivariate regressions for further support.

2.4.5 Robustness Analysis

In order to verify that the results are not driven by the event study methodology, the analysis is repeated with different benchmarks, alternative return generating models and an adapted event list. The results of these robustness tests on company level are presented in table 2.4.5, table 2.4.6 and table 2.4.7.

The first robustness test focuses on the applied benchmarks. Corrado and Truong (2008) suggest the usage of an equal weighted index for a most robust test specification. Panel A of table 2.4.5 shows the event study results with the equal weighted version of the MSCI ACWI and S&P 500. Additionally, the Datastream Level 1 Total Market indices, which are broad value weighted market indices for different countries and regions, are used as benchmarks in another analysis similar to the approach by Campbell et al. (2010). The results are presented in panel B of table 2.4.5. Alibaba's and Tencent's abnormal returns are calculated with the Datastream Total Market Index World and the Datastream Total Market Index US is used for Alphabet, Amazon, Apple, Facebook and Microsoft. The abnormal returns as well as test statistics provide results similar to those of table 2.4.3 and table 2.4.4, and show that the event study methodology is robust to the usage of different benchmarks.

The event study is repeated with different return generating models to further test the abnormal returns. Fuller et al. (2002) suggest the usage of the market-adjusted return model for firms with multiple acquisitions as earlier deals might bias the estimation window and estimated market parameters. In an additional test, the Fama-French three-factor model is applied which provides a more sophisticated view of the abnormal return calculation by including size and book-to-market effects. The three factors provided by Kenneth R. French are used here, specifically the US factors for the US-based firms and the global factors for Alibaba and Tencent. Table 2.4.6 presents the results. Both return generating models calculate similar abnormal returns to those of the market return model. It indicates no general bias in the estimation window as well as no distorting influence of the growth and value factors.

Table 2.4.5: Robustness Analysis with Alternative Benchmarks

	(I) Related Transactions				(II) Unrelated Transactions			
	(1) CAAR	(2) BMP-test	(3) Sign-test	(4) Corrado-t.	(1) CAAR	(2) BMP-test	(3) Sign-test	(4) Corrado-t.
Panel A: Equal Weighted Benchmark								
Alibaba								
[-5;+5]	1.89%	0.75	0.92	0.58	-1.31%	-1.02	-1.02	-0.09
[0]	-0.62%	-1.28	0.10	-0.87	-1.10%	-2.09 **	-0.44	-1.78 *
Alphabet								
[-5;+5]	1.16%	3.02 ***	2.64 ***	2.40 **	-0.84%	-0.98	1.01	-0.83
[0]	0.07%	0.77	2.28 **	1.44	0.24%	1.14	1.91 *	1.81 *
Amazon								
[-5;+5]	-2.41%	-0.57	-0.68	-0.37	-1.49%	-1.77 *	-1.33	-1.09
[0]	0.47%	1.43	0.96	1.10	0.10%	0.44	0.24	1.08
Apple								
[-5;+5]	-1.46%	-0.67	0.15	-0.46	0.51%	1.06	0.95	0.42
[0]	1.32%	6.68 ***	1.57	1.85 *	-0.05%	-0.07	-0.12	-0.25
Facebook								
[-5;+5]	1.25%	0.86	0.01	0.66	-4.64%	-1.73 *	-0.56	-1.22
[0]	0.02%	-0.35	0.01	0.10	-0.12%	-0.91	0.05	-0.59
Microsoft								
[-5;+5]	-0.45%	-1.23	-0.77	-0.54	-1.82%	-1.29	-2.40 **	-1.52
[0]	-0.13%	-0.87	-0.55	-0.68	-0.93%	-2.24 **	-1.29	-2.03 **
Tencent								
[-5;+5]	0.45%	0.77	0.37	0.20				
[0]	0.04%	0.24	-0.24	0.15				
Panel B: Value Weighted Benchmark								
Alibaba								
[-5;+5]	1.54%	0.59	0.92	0.39	-1.32%	-0.96	-0.45	-0.17
[0]	-0.59%	-1.26	0.11	-0.87	-1.00%	-1.87 *	-0.45	-1.71 *
Alphabet								
[-5;+5]	1.13%	3.05 ***	2.93 ***	2.58 ***	-0.84%	-1.00	0.60	-0.77
[0]	0.04%	0.45	1.33	1.08	0.22%	1.01	1.95 *	1.89 *
Amazon								
[-5;+5]	-2.75%	-0.73	-0.72	-0.45	-1.53%	-1.91 *	-1.30	-1.34
[0]	0.52%	1.55	0.92	1.13	0.09%	0.44	0.53	0.89
Apple								
[-5;+5]	-1.59%	-0.74	0.17	-0.58	0.60%	1.29	1.00	0.55
[0]	1.05%	8.81 ***	1.59	1.67 *	-0.03%	0.12	0.73	-0.11
Facebook								
[-5;+5]	1.17%	0.78	0.86	0.54	-4.63%	-1.70 *	-1.06	-1.25
[0]	0.01%	-0.47	0.10	0.03	-0.15%	-0.95	0.16	-0.66
Microsoft								
[-5;+5]	-0.40%	-1.14	-1.19	-0.60	-1.38%	-0.97	-1.86 *	-1.27
[0]	-0.14%	-0.94	-0.53	-0.74	-0.97%	-2.50 **	-1.86 *	-2.36 **
Tencent								
[-5;+5]	0.88%	1.33	1.02	0.58				
[0]	0.06%	0.28	-0.18	0.26				

Table 2.4.5 presents the abnormal share price reaction for related (I) and unrelated (II) transactions per company in different event windows. The robustness analysis applies alternative benchmarks. Panel A shows the results with an equal weighted benchmark and panel B with a value weighted benchmark. For Tencent, no data is shown for unrelated transactions as the

respective sample includes only one transaction. Column (1) displays the cumulative average abnormal return and column (2)-(4) the test statistics. Sample size per analysis is equal to the figures in the main event study setup. Statistical significance at 1 %, 5 % and 10 % levels is indicated with ***, ** and *, respectively.

Table 2.4.6: Robustness Analysis with Alternative Return Generating Models

	(I) Related Transactions				(II) Unrelated Transactions			
	(1) CAAR	(2) BMP-test	(3) Sign-test	(4) Corrado-t.	(1) CAAR	(2) BMP-test	(3) Sign-test	(4) Corrado-t.
Panel A: Market-Adjusted Return Model								
Alibaba								
[-5;+5]	1.44%	0.63	0.99	0.42	-0.56%	-0.32	-0.45	0.30
[0]	-0.60%	-1.24	0.17	-0.88	-1.08%	-2.02 **	-1.02	-1.96 *
Alphabet								
[-5;+5]	1.15%	3.32 ***	2.67 ***	2.79 ***	-0.72%	-0.88	-0.04	-0.66
[0]	0.05%	0.56	1.78 *	1.10	0.22%	1.01	2.19 **	2.06 **
Amazon								
[-5;+5]	-1.73%	-0.34	-0.96	-0.46	-0.72%	-0.80	-1.01	-1.01
[0]	0.63%	1.94 *	1.49	1.14	0.12%	0.60	0.29	0.96
Apple								
[-5;+5]	-0.48%	-0.38	-0.15	-0.82	1.31%	2.96 ***	0.74	0.43
[0]	0.88%	1.93 *	1.27	1.35	0.05%	0.77	0.20	0.00
Facebook								
[-5;+5]	2.60%	1.69 *	0.89	0.46	-2.82%	-1.07	-0.36	-1.05
[0]	0.03%	-0.35	-0.62	-0.32	-0.12%	-0.86	-0.36	-0.70
Microsoft								
[-5;+5]	-0.11%	-0.34	-0.44	-0.64	-1.73%	-1.56	-1.33	-1.45
[0]	-0.11%	-0.68	-0.44	-0.78	-0.92%	-2.46 **	-1.88 *	-2.21 **
Tencent								
[-5;+5]	1.62%	2.18 **	1.49	0.41				
[0]	0.13%	0.49	-0.32	0.16				
Panel B: Fama-French Three-Factor Model								
Alibaba								
[-5;+5]	1.27%	0.46	0.99	0.18	-1.26%	-1.22	-1.50	-0.76
[0]	-0.75%	-1.91 *	-0.64	-1.41	-0.96%	-1.77 *	-1.50	-2.08 **
Alphabet								
[-5;+5]	1.16%	3.09 ***	2.76 ***	2.62 ***	-1.04%	-0.95	0.59	-0.74
[0]	0.04%	0.32	0.63	0.69	0.23%	1.05	1.49	1.58
Amazon								
[-5;+5]	-3.15%	-0.92	-0.67	-0.54	-1.27%	-1.78 *	-1.81 *	-1.06
[0]	0.33%	1.02	0.15	0.74	0.09%	0.33	0.54	0.57
Apple								
[-5;+5]	-0.15%	-0.16	0.12	-0.02	0.61%	1.34	1.25	0.66
[0]	0.99%	6.83 ***	1.54	1.71 *	0.06%	0.70	0.44	0.60
Facebook								
[-5;+5]	0.68%	0.71	-0.15	0.02	-3.13%	-1.51	-1.16	-0.83
[0]	-0.17%	-0.90	-0.15	-0.48	-0.16%	-1.20	0.05	-0.78
Microsoft								
[-5;+5]	-0.24%	-0.82	-0.99	-0.14	-1.52%	-1.09	-1.83 *	-1.38
[0]	-0.26%	-1.86 *	-0.55	-1.41	-0.95%	-2.54 **	-2.38 **	-2.54 **
Tencent								
[-5;+5]	0.56%	0.98	0.43	0.61				
[0]	0.19%	0.70	-0.17	0.57				

Table 2.4.6 presents the abnormal share price reaction for related (I) and unrelated (II) transactions per company in different event windows. The robustness analysis applies alternative return generation models. Panel A shows the results with the market-adjusted return model and panel B with the Fama-French three-factor model. For Tencent, no data is shown for un-

related transactions as the respective sample includes only one transaction. Column (1) displays the cumulative average abnormal return and column (2)-(4) the test statistics. Sample size per analysis is equal to the figures in the main event study setup. Statistical significance at 1 %, 5 % and 10 % levels is indicated with ***, ** and *, respectively.

The last robustness analysis investigates whether the sample is biased by confounding events (see table 2.4.7). The selection criteria are therefore extended, and the analyzed data sample includes only transactions that are the only M&A deal by the acquirer ultimate parent in the two weeks around the event. This leads to the exclusion of 157 events that are close to another transaction in the main [-5;+5] event window. The abnormal returns are similar to the results presented in table 2.4.3 and table 2.4.4. The statistical significance is for some transactions higher and for others lower. Only Facebook's unrelated transactions show no significance after reducing the sample size by more than one-third.

Table 2.4.7: Robustness Analysis with Alternative Sample

	(I) Related Transactions				(II) Unrelated Transactions			
	(1) CAAR	(2) BMP-test	(3) Sign-test	(4) Corrado-t.	(1) CAAR	(2) BMP-test	(3) Sign-test	(4) Corrado-t.
Alibaba		Sample Size: 4				Sample Size: 10		
[-5;+5]	1.73%	0.41	1.09	0.16	-1.22%	-0.69	0.16	-0.02
[0]	-0.95%	-1.46	-0.91	-1.32	-1.26%	-1.97 **	-1.11	-2.12 **
Alphabet		Sample Size: 60				Sample Size: 10		
[-5;+5]	1.64%	2.43 **	2.15 **	2.38 **	-1.44%	-1.16	-0.58	-1.01
[0]	0.19%	1.44	2.40 **	2.11 **	0.09%	0.27	1.31	1.01
Amazon		Sample Size: 6				Sample Size: 52		
[-5;+5]	-2.83%	-0.75	-0.73	-0.48	-1.85%	-2.11 **	-1.70 *	-1.59
[0]	0.52%	1.57	0.91	1.15	0.10%	0.36	0.22	0.91
Apple		Sample Size: 2				Sample Size: 38		
[-5;+5]	-1.61%	-0.76	0.16	-0.53	0.62%	1.05	0.75	0.39
[0]	1.01%	7.50 ***	1.58	1.60	0.02%	0.46	0.75	0.48
Facebook		Sample Size: 15				Sample Size: 7		
[-5;+5]	3.91%	1.58	1.67 *	1.76 *	0.12%	0.57	0.70	0.47
[0]	0.63%	1.21	1.15	1.25	0.18%	-0.18	-0.06	-0.14
Microsoft		Sample Size: 52				Sample Size: 9		
[-5;+5]	-0.19%	-0.35	-0.62	-0.53	-1.69%	-0.82	-1.55	-1.35
[0]	-0.09%	-0.45	-0.07	-0.52	-1.39%	-2.82 ***	-2.88 ***	-2.76 ***
Tencent		Sample Size: 11						
[-5;+5]	0.99%	1.46	2.25 **	0.68				
[0]	0.06%	0.26	-0.16	0.15				

Table 2.4.7 presents the abnormal share price reaction for related (I) and unrelated (II) transactions per company in different event windows. The robustness analysis applies an alternative sample which excludes deals that are next to another transaction in the main event window. For Tencent, no data is shown for unrelated transactions as the respective sample includes only one transaction. Column (1) displays the cumulative average abnormal return and column (2)-(4) the test statistics. Sample size per analysis is shown above results. Statistical significance at 1 %, 5 % and 10 % levels is indicated with ***, ** and *, respectively.

Overall, the checks support the robustness of the presented abnormal returns relative to alternative specifications of the event study methodology, and the results are a good reflection of the short-term shareholder value changes.

2.4.6 Analysis of Value Drivers

The results of the multivariate regressions are presented in table 2.4.8. Column (1) shows the results of model I-III calculated with *Free Cash Flow 1*, and column (2) the results calculated with *Free Cash Flow 2*.

Table 2.4.8: Multivariate Regression Analysis

	Model I		Model II		Model III	
	(1)	(2)	(1)	(2)	(1)	(2)
Relatedness	0.017 **	0.018 **	0.018 **	0.019 **	0.017 **	0.018 **
	(2.29)	(2.43)	(2.33)	(2.47)	(2.29)	(2.44)
Acquirer Experience	0.000	0.000	0.000	0.000	0.000	0.000
	(-0.33)	(-0.35)	(0.97)	(0.96)	(-0.29)	(-0.68)
(Acquirer Experience)^2			0.000	0.000		
			(-1.11)	(-1.11)		
Free Cash Flow	-0.244 ***	-0.197 ***	-0.245 ***	-0.196 ***	-0.262 **	-0.143 *
	(-2.75)	(-3.03)	(-2.74)	(-3.03)	(-2.26)	(-1.93)
FCF * Relatedness					0.027	-0.093
					(0.210)	(-1.04)
Firm Size	0.009	0.006	0.006	0.003	0.009	0.007
	(1.370)	(0.89)	(0.88)	(0.43)	(1.370)	(1.17)
Controls						
Domestic Deal	0.001	0.000	0.001	0.000	0.001	0.000
	(0.11)	(0.02)	(0.13)	(0.04)	(0.11)	(0.08)
Chinese Deal	0.032 *	0.033 *	0.032 *	0.033 *	0.032 *	0.033 *
	(1.76)	(1.8)	(1.76)	(1.790)	(1.76)	(1.81)
Public Target	-0.003	-0.004	-0.002	-0.002	-0.002	-0.005
	(-0.23)	(-0.29)	(-0.120)	(-0.18)	(-0.2)	(-0.37)
High Year	-0.019 ***	-0.021 ***	-0.020 ***	-0.021 ***	-0.019 ***	-0.021 ***
	(-3.64)	(-3.73)	(-3.65)	(-3.73)	(-3.63)	(-3.70)
Low Year	-0.001	-0.002	-0.002	-0.003	-0.001	-0.002
	(-0.08)	(-0.29)	(-0.23)	(-0.44)	(-0.08)	(-0.38)
Firm-fixed Effects	Yes	Yes	Yes	Yes	Yes	Yes
Constant	-0.171	-0.099	-0.121	-0.050	-0.201	-0.156
	(-1.32)	(-0.76)	(-0.91)	(-0.37)	(-1.59)	(-1.28)
Sample Size	435	435	435	435	435	435
Adjusted R^2	0.07	0.08	0.07	0.08	0.07	0.08

Table 2.4.8 presents the impact of value drivers on the abnormal share price reaction for all transactions in different regression setups (model I-III). The dependent variable is the CAR over the main [-5;+5] event window. Column (1) displays the results calculated with *Free Cash Flow 1* for *Free Cash Flow* and the interaction variable and column (2) with *Free Cash Flow 2*. *Relatedness* is equal to 1 if the acquirer and target share the same 3-digit SIC code and 0 otherwise. *Acquirer Experience* is defined as number of completed acquisitions until the analyzed transaction and *(Acquirer Experience)^2* is the squared term. *Free Cash Flow 1* is calculated as operating income before depreciation and amortization minus income tax minus interest expenses minus dividends, deflated by book value of total assets. *Free Cash Flow 2* is calculated

as operating cash flow minus capital expenditures, deflated by book value of total assets. *FCF* * *Relatedness* is the interaction variable of *Free Cash Flow* with *Relatedness*. *Firm Size* is the natural logarithm of total equity market capitalization. *Domestic Deal* is equal to 1 if the acquirer and target are located in the same country and 0 otherwise. *Chinese Deal* is equal to 1 if the acquirer and target are located in China and 0 otherwise. *Public Target* is equal to 1 if the target is public and 0 otherwise. *High Year* is equal to 1 if the transaction is announced in 2014, 2015 or 2016 and 0 otherwise. *Low Year* is equal to 1 if the transaction is announced in 2008, 2009 or 2012 and 0 otherwise. Firm-fixed effects are included in all specifications. Significance is based on robust Huber-White standard errors and t-statistics are shown in parentheses. Statistical significance at 1 %, 5 % and 10 % levels is indicated with ***, ** and *, respectively.

Model I and II analyze the impact of relatedness and free cash flow on shareholder value. A related transaction by a digital technology giant has on average a 1.7-1.9 percentage points higher abnormal return over the two-week event window. This effect is significant at the 5 % level across the different specifications. In comparison, Moeller et al. (2004) observe a 0.5 percentage points higher CAR for related transactions by large acquirers over a three-day event window, significant at 5 % level. The spread between CAARs for related and unrelated transactions, which is described in subsection 2.4.2, is 1.41 % in the two-week event window. The multivariate regression models control for firm-fixed effects and show that the presented relatedness effect is not driven by Alphabet or another company but is observable across the group of digital technology giants. Thus, the results validate the spread and give further support for hypotheses H2 and H4. Shareholders differentiate between related and unrelated acquisitions.

The influence of *Free Cash Flow* contrasts with the effect of *Relatedness*. The variable has a negative influence on the CAR, which is significant at 1 % level. An increase in relative free cash flow by 1 percentage point decreases the cumulative abnormal return by 0.2 percentage points across both models and free cash flow measures. The effect concurs with the results of other empirical studies. Lang et al. (1991) present a decrease of 0.6 percentage points over a two-week event window, and Schlingemann (2004) shows an influence of 0.1 percentage points over a three-day event window. The significant negative influence of free cash flow across transactions provides support for hypothesis H5 and for the alternative explanation of hypothesis H6 that two effects overlap. Financial flexibility seems to amplify the negative effect for unrelated deals and be an explanation for varying results for related deals on company level. Lower control by capital markets can lead to deals that are motivated by managerial self-interest and not by value creation.

Model III investigates the interaction of relatedness and free cash flow. The variable *Free Cash Flow* is centered to its mean to ease the interpretation. Thus, the coefficient of the variable that interacts with the centered variable describes the effect for an acquirer with average level of *Free Cash Flow*. In both specifications of model III, column (1) and (2), a related transaction leads to a 1.7 – 1.8 percentage points higher abnormal return, which is significant at 5 % level, as in model I and II. In addition to this, the model shows that free cash flow has a negative effect on related and unrelated deals as the interaction variable reveals that the effect does not differ significantly between both deal types. The economic impact of *Free Cash Flow 2* matches the results of model I and II, and *Free Cash Flow 1* has a slightly higher impact. The variables are significant at 10 % level and at 5 % level, respectively. All in all, this supports hypothesis H5. Free cash flow has a statistically significant negative influence on unrelated transactions. There is also a negative effect of free cash flow on related acquisitions, but it is not significantly different from the effect on unrelated deals. Thus, there is no evidence that the influence of managerial self-interest differs between related and unrelated transactions; hypothesis H6 is partly supported.

The coefficients of *Acquirer Experience* as well as *Firm Size* show no significance across the different models. It seems that the number of previous acquisitions as well as the size of digital technology giants have no effect on shareholder value. Model II examines the inferences by Haleblian and Finkelstein (1999), and tests a U-shaped relation between acquirer experience and acquisition performance in contrast with a linear relation in model I. *Acquirer Experience* as well as *(Acquirer Experience)^2* show no significance in either model. This study cannot replicate the results by Haleblian and Finkelstein (1999) and Uhlenbruck et al. (2006) so that hypothesis H3 is not supported. Acquirer experience might be influenced by other factors than the isolated number of completed deals, as suggested by Hayward (2002). For buyer size, two opposing explanations appears to be possible. On the one hand, acquirer size has no influence for digital technology companies in general and does not indicate managerial hubris in this context. On the other hand, acquirer size has no influence within the sub-segment of large companies, specifically between the digital technology giants. This does not contradict Moeller et al. (2004). They show a significant positive abnormal return of the subsample of small acquirers, but an insignificant return to large firms. The direct effect of *Firm Size* is only analyzed across the total sample and not within the different size segments.

Thus, managerial hubris cannot be rejected as M&A motive, but the results do not support hypothesis H7.

The control variables *Domestic Deal*, *Public Target* and *Low Year* show no significance across the different regression models and free cash flow measures. However, *Chinese Deal* and *High Year* are consistently significant at the 10 % and 1 % significance level, respectively. It shows that the Chinese digital technology companies Alibaba and Tencent profit from domestic deals in comparison with all other acquirers and transactions by an on average 3.2 – 3.3 percentage points higher abnormal return. This might be traced back to expectations about increase in corporate governance practices by the stock-listed digital giants and generally lower M&A competition for Chinese targets (Chari et al., 2010; Chi et al., 2011). Furthermore, the multivariate regression models show that low M&A activity has no influence on the abnormal returns while high activity is strongly negatively related. Transactions in the years 2014, 2015, 2016 lead on average to a 1.9 – 2.1 percentage points lower abnormal return in comparison with deals in other years. This is in line with the literature on M&A activity and merger waves. Mcnamara et al. (2008) show that transactions at the peak of acquisition activity have the lowest performance and link this to bandwagon effects that influence the later buyers while early acquirers can benefit from first mover advantages.

To summarize the results across the subsections, acquisition experience and firm size do not indicate value creation or managerial hubris. In contrast, a positive impact of relatedness as well as a negative impact of free cash flow are observed. The results support that related transactions create value and diversifying transactions dilute value. The value creation in related deals can be traced back to network effects, complementarities and increased market concentration. However, increasing levels of free cash flow can fuel managerial self-interest and counteract shareholder value creation in related as well as unrelated acquisitions. Thus, the digital technology giants appear to profit from the industry environment and synergies in both types of transactions, but managerial self-interest lowers the value creation in related acquisitions and fully offsets the value creation in unrelated acquisitions. There might be a different motive for diversifying transactions besides shareholder value creation and managerial self-interest. Alternatively, traditional finance methods might not be appropriate for determining the M&A value creation for digital platforms (e.g., Herzog, 2018; Mchawrab, 2016). Nevertheless, the results support that the digital technology giants are influenced by two opposing factors – the industry environment that fosters network effects, complementarities as well as synergistic potential on the one hand, and the financial strength that drives corporate governance issues and managerial self-interest on the other.

2.5 Discussion

This study examines the value effects of boundary expansion on the owners of leading digital platforms, and investigates the question of whether M&A activity creates value for digital technology giants. Therefore, 1,980 deals are gathered from two databases, and 435 deals between 2008 and 2017 are finally selected for the analyses. The effects for the total sample are hardly significant, whereas related acquisitions lead to significant positive abnormal returns and unrelated deals to significant negative abnormal returns. While the value creation differs between the transaction types and digital technology giants, free cash flow has a significant negative influence on the abnormal returns for both transaction types. Acquisition experience and firm size show no significant effect.

The results provide two main insights. First, the study indicate that digital technology giants use related acquisitions to reshape platform boundaries and recombine digital resources. They can create user value through innovation and profit from reinforcing network effects, complementarities and decreasing competition. This has a direct positive effect on shareholder value and shows that it is not M&A activity in general but rather the subset of these deals that contributes to the giants' success story. In contrast, unrelated acquisitions dilute value. Digital technology giants can use these deals to find new opportunities when facing competition, but cannot profit from favorable market conditions. The value potential seems to be limited and the diversifying actions block financial resources that could be invested in other projects. Research needs to focus not only on user value, but also consider owner value. This study shows the close link between both value concepts. The market can recognize changes in user value and the benefits of market environment directly through owner value. Shareholder value can be utilized as an early indicator for expected user value, and sustainable user value requires that an owner is able to operate a platform with the level of profitability required by shareholders. In practice, the study suggests that digital technology giants should focus on related M&A for creating user and shareholder value. This means that a platform should aim at targets that are close to the core business (e.g., a social platform should focus on connecting mobility services and users instead of operating mobility services). Furthermore, owners should critically monitor unrelated deals. If the transactions fail to provide any user value or increased efficiency that can be translated into shareholder value, the owners should limit the activity. While platform boundary expansion across submarkets can be successful, it also bears opportunity costs. Additionally, a different motive besides value creation might influence diversification efforts. In contrast, regulators need to critically monitor related deals as the market dynamics foster decreasing competition and "winner-take-all" outcomes. In recent years, the reactions of antitrust authorities globally reflect a policy change and can lead to stronger future regulation of digital technology giants' M&A activity.

Second, this research indicates that the digital technology giants are in a field of tension between the positive influence of the market environment on the one hand and the negative influence of financial strength on the other. On average, shareholders have neither a positive nor a negative valuation of M&A activity of digital technology giants across related and unrelated transactions. However, the distinct financial strength can drive managerial self-interest in both deal types and negatively influence shareholder value. The digital giants' strong growth and the increase in available financial resources decrease control of capital markets and allow management to conduct risky investments and follow objectives other than value creation. While transaction motives are difficult to evaluate on the basis of transaction data, the significant and strong market reaction to the level of free cash flow is a good indicator. Research needs to analyze management as an agent that can have its own interests besides user and shareholder value. This study indicates that corporate governance issues are an important topic that research has to consider when dealing with dominant platforms. In addition, research should concentrate on market and company characteristics when analyzing M&A activity of digital technology giants instead of searching for overarching value drivers, and studies should differentiate between subgroups and deal types as the effects vary. In practice, firm owners should ensure stronger capital markets control of digital technology giants. To this end, they can increase the level of debt or reduce financial resources by share buyback and dividend programs as well as demand greater transparency on acquisitions, at least subsequent to the completion of deals.

This research has some limitations. First, available information on digital technology giants' transactions is very limited. Targets are mostly private firms, with information on the deals often not being disclosed. This means that only some control variables can be included. Additionally, the sample might have a selection bias (e.g., Gaspar et al., 2005). However, it is not possible to build an extended data set as a way of correcting this bias as data on firms in the industry is also limited. Second, the relatedness measure has some drawbacks. Boundaries in the digital technology industry are changing dynamically, and the SIC code framework does not fully reflect the structure of the submarkets. Nevertheless, the approach is comprehensible, frequently used in the context of the digital technology industry, while alternative measures such as the categories of the Crunchbase database have other weaknesses. Finally, a high share of transactions is driven by Alphabet and Microsoft which can influence the results. The event study is therefore also conducted on company level to understand the dynamics and the regressions apply firm-fixed effects in order to control for differences among digital technology giants. The study indicates that further research is required. Future work should continue to investigate the connection of user and shareholder value and potential corporate governance issues of dominant platforms. In this context, different approaches to analyze the impact of M&A activity on user value and to determine acquisition motives seem to be promising fields of study. Additionally, further insight could be gained from understanding the impact of M&A activity on competition in the digital technology submarkets and the long-term influence on the acquirers.

3 Competitive Dynamics in the Digital Technology Industry: Rival Effects in the Light of Digital Giants' Mergers and Acquisitions Activity[16]

3.1 Introduction

"Don't be evil" – Preface of Google's Code of Conduct until it was discreetly removed in April 2018.[17]

Little is known about competitive moves of firms in the digital technology industry. The impact of platform boundary expansion across ecosystems and the special role of the large digital technology giants require further research (e.g., Constantinides et al., 2018; Ferrier et al., 2010). Anecdotal evidence indicates that digital giants' transactions influence price movements of other companies in the industry. In February 2019, the share price of Sonos rose by 7 % because an analyst report mentions the company as a potential target of Apple. In February 2014, the share prices of Facebook and Tencent increase after the acquisition of WhatsApp by Facebook.[18] In recent years, the economical and societal impact of the largest digital technology companies has changed and with it the perception of them. Between 2017 and 2019, the European competition authority imposed three fines on Alphabet for abusing market power in advertising, mobile operating system and search engine markets (Schechner and Pop, 2019). In 2019, a report commissioned by the UK government recommended that the antitrust assessment of mergers and acquisitions activity in the digital technology industry should be adapted, and even the US antitrust regulators are preparing investigations of key digital giants (Furman et al., 2019; Schlesinger et al., 2019). This raises the question, "How do other firms react to digital technology giants' competitive actions in terms of

---

16 An adapted version of this chapter is in the journal submission process: Sternal, M, Schiereck, D. & Benlian, A. Competitive Dynamics in the Digital Technology Industry: Rival Effects in the Light of Digital Giants' M&A Activity.

17 The Google webpage with the Code of Conduct shows an adjusted version from the beginning of May, 2018 (Conger, 2018).

18 Share price data is based on the Datastream database.

mergers and acquisitions?" More specifically, "Does digital giants' platform boundary expansion influence industry rivals and other digital giants?"

Platforms evolve over time, and firms expand platform boundaries through innovation by way of mergers and acquisitions (Staykova and Damsgaard, 2017; Yoo et al., 2010). These competitive actions are driven by the interplay between technological change and competition (Clemons and Madhani, 2010; Kim et al., 2016). Digital technology giants operate the largest digital-enabled platforms and have influence on other firms in the market (e.g., Lamoreaux, 2019; Shapiro, 2019). The giants compete within their core businesses, but compete also with other giants across sub-markets for customer attention, new markets and capabilities (Evans, 2013; van Gorp and Batura, 2015). The special market dynamics in the digital technology industry in terms of strong economies of scale and scope, high levels of direct and indirect network effects as well as easy market access influence the competition (e.g., Crémer et al., 2019; Furman et al., 2019). The response of rivals to competitive actions can range from imitation, no response to other aggressive or defensive move (Smith et al., 2001). First, no or insufficient reaction of the rival interlinks with the Market Concentration Hypothesis that expects rivals and acquirer to benefit by increased industry concentration (e.g., Eckbo, 1983), and the Efficiency Hypothesis that expects rivals to suffer in relation to the acquirer due to a competitive advantage (e.g., Akdoğu, 2009). Second, the rival can conduct other moves in terms of value cocreation and benefit as a potential future target as described in the Acquisition Probability Hypothesis (e.g., Song and Walkling, 2000). Finally, the rival can imitate the competitive action and profit from information signals as discussed in the Growth Probability Hypothesis (e.g., Gaur et al., 2013).

The study is based on the analysis of 373 transactions by the group of digital technology giants between 2008 and 2017 and the reaction of two different types of rival sets, the direct rivals (industry rivals) and the indirect rivals (other digital giants). This research indicate that digital technology giants' competitive actions in terms of mergers and acquisitions have a distinct influence across the platform ecosystems and transmit signals to rivals' shareholders. On a granular level, shareholders of digital giants as indirect rivals receive strong signals and expect their companies to mimic the competitive action, despite no product or service rivalry. The effect is larger than for industry rivals. For these direct rivals, an influence of efficiency increase can be observed that offsets the positive signals for value creating transactions (positive deals; deals with positive acquirer return). The effect is inversed for value diluting transactions (negative deals; deals with negative acquirer return) and decreases the negative impact of signaling. Thus, shareholders appear to expect direct rivals to imitate the competitive action, but only to a limited extent. In line with previous literature, the study finds no impact of collusion on rival returns and also no evidence of value cocreation.

The contribution of this study is threefold. First, it analyzes the effect of platform boundary expansion of a focal firm on the value creation for rivals in the digital technology industry. It examines the impact of digital giants' transactions on different groups of competitors. Previous studies in the information systems literature link the level of network effects and competition in the digital industry to competitive reactions in terms of internal and external investments (e.g., Kim et al., 2016; Pan et al., 2019) or analyze the effect of competitive actions on the focal firm's performance (e.g., Gnyawali et al., 2010; Li et al., 2010). Other empirical studies analyze rival effects across high technology industries neglecting competitive moves (e.g., Kohers and Kohers, 2004), or focus on an external influence such as a regulatory change (e.g., Jope et al., 2010). This contribution extends the analyses in the information systems literature and integrates competitive dynamics literature with rival effects literature (e.g., Eckbo, 1983; Song and Walkling, 2000) to examine the effect of competitive moves across platform ecosystems. Second, the study focusses on competitive actions of the group of digital technology giants that consists of the largest publicly traded companies worldwide. These firms exert significant economical and societal influence on firms and people across economies, and they create new challenges for competitive law and regulators, while further research on competitive dynamics and platform businesses is required (Constantinides et al., 2018). Previous information systems literature analyzes the effect of competitive behavior on a case-by-case basis and draw general conclusions. For example, Foerderer et al. (2018) investigate Google's entry into a complementary market with a photo application, and Clemons and Madhani (2010) discuss the antitrust implications of Google's business model as an example for a platform on which one side subsidizes the usage of the other side. This contribution is based on research on information systems (e.g., Gnyawali et al., 2010; Kim et al., 2016), economics (e.g., Evans and Schmalensee, 2015; van Gorp and Batura, 2015) and finance (e.g., Akdoğu, 2009; Cai et al., 2011) that discusses competitive behavior. It examines the aggregated effect of digital giants' competitive actions on other giants and other firms in the industry. Finally, this study applies an extended methodology, analyzes rival effects on different competitor groups and distinguishes between various rival effects theories. Most research focuses on one rival group and shows one rival perspective. However, different groups of rivals exist, buyer-side rivals react differently to target-side rivals (Gaur et al., 2013), and early rival effects literature already discusses the potential overlap of different influencing factors (Chatterjee, 1986; Eckbo, 1983). This research analyzes the effect on mixed target-side and buyer-side rivals (direct rivals) and pure buyer-side rivals (indirect rivals) and tests different response types and rival stories. It indicates mixed effects of signaling and efficiency increase on direct rivals and signaling on indirect rivals. Shareholders evidently expect direct rivals to show a limited reaction and indirect rivals to imitate the competitive action. Rival characteristics are less important here, and the acquirer and deal characteristics have higher relevance for rival effects.

The rest of this chapter is structured as follows. Section 3.2 determines the theoretical background on competition in the digital technology industry and on rival effects. The research hypotheses are also explored in this context. Section 3.3 describes the data sample, rival sets and applied research methodology. Section 3.4 reports the results of the event study and multivariate regression models. The final section discusses the findings and concludes this chapter.

3.2 Literature Review and Research Hypotheses

Digital technology giants have conducted several hundred transactions over the last decade. The previous chapter shows that shareholders value digital giants' mergers and acquisitions activity differently, depending on the type of transaction. Related acquisitions are positively recognized by shareholders and unrelated transactions lead to a significant negative effect. The value increase of related deals can be attributed to reinforcing network effects, complementarities and decreasing competition while the value dilution is linked to low value potential and high opportunity costs.

The announcement of a transaction not only has a direct effect on the share price of the acquirer; the new information is also reflected in the rivals' share prices (Binder, 1998). It is not sufficient to solely analyze mergers and acquisitions on the basis of individual short-term shareholder value changes. It is also necessary to conduct an analysis in the context of the industry environment and competitors. The analysis of abnormal returns of mergers and acquisitions with the help of the event study methodology is based on the semi-strong form of the efficient market hypothesis

(McWilliams and Siegel, 1997).[19] This implies that market share prices reflect all publicly available information. The digital technology giants with distinct financial strength and broad media coverage have a special role in the industry. The activities of these companies can reveal relevant information and have a potential impact on other digital technology companies, including other digital giants.

3.2.1 Digital Giants and Competition in the Digital Technology Industry

Rapid technological development and competition drive innovation in the digital technology industry (Kim et al., 2016; Pan et al., 2019). Yoo et al. (2010) define digital innovation as a recombination of digital and physical resources into new products and services. Firms can initiate this recombination and the expansion of platform boundaries internally through research and development or externally through acquisition or cooperation. Clemons and Madhani (2010) conclude that "technology determines what is possible for firms to do, and the interaction of economics and technology guides the behavior" (p. 44). Thus, the rapid technological development in the digital technology industry changes the scope of actions for companies, but the interaction of technological change and economics with regard to competition determines innovation and competitive actions, for example internal and external spending. Kim et al. (2016) observe that companies in markets with high competition increase R&D spending and external investments in terms of corporate venture capital. They argue that the acquisition of knowledge to create a competitive advantage is a key benefit of external innovation in comparison with R&D, especially in the volatile and competitive digital technology market environment. Pan et al. (2019) show that firms decrease research and development investments when facing the potential threat of new entry, but relatively increase the spending in submarkets with high network effects. They link network effects to the effectiveness of this preemptive R&D. Likewise, companies in the digital technology industry, which is characterized by high network effects, conduct preemptive investments in terms of M&A to minimize potential threats (Kuchinke and Vidal, 2016). Pan et al. (2019) also observe that firms in environments with a higher threat of new entry are more likely to be acquired than firms in low threat environments and thus conclude

---

19 Fama (1970) distinguishes between three different forms of the efficient market hypothesis.

that the level of potential competition is closely linked to competitive dynamics.

The size of large platforms in the digital technology industry can increase efficiency and innovation, but also anticompetitive behavior in the market (Lamoreaux, 2019). Shapiro (2019) discusses the dominance of giant technology companies and calls for stronger antitrust enforcement. In line with this, Constantinides et al. (2018) argue that anti-competitive behavior is a new challenge for regulators and can have important implications for policy. The digital giants differ from other players on the basis of their distinct financial strength in terms of economic endowment, high liquidity as well as the large number of mergers and acquisitions. The combination of market-specific and company-specific factors fosters platform leadership and enable these firms to occupy a dominant position in their respective submarkets (Dolata, 2018; Gawer and Cusumano, 2002). However, digital-enabled platforms are constantly evolving through innovation, and products as well as submarkets in the digital technology industry have no stable boundaries (Staykova and Damsgaard, 2017; Yoo et al., 2010). Therefore, the economics in the digital industry with regard to competition need to be analyzed not only within submarkets (product and service rivalry) but also across markets and platforms (platform rivalry).

Three main market dynamics drive competition within submarkets in the digital technology industry. First, strong economies of scale and scope favor larger players and rapid growth (e.g., Furman et al., 2019; Mchawrab, 2016). Second, high levels of direct and indirect network effects foster market concentration and can lead to "winner-take-all" outcomes in submarkets. Both factors decrease competition (e.g., Crémer et al., 2019; Shapiro and Varian, 1999). Third, low entrance barriers to digital technology submarkets drive competition as firms have direct customer contact, and products and services are easy to imitate. Similarly, multi-homing lowers switching costs which by extension increases competition (e.g., Chen and Hitt, 2002; van Gorp and Batura, 2015). These three main market dynamics can lead to a single dominant player in a submarket, but also to a frequent change of the market structure as a kind of Schumpeterian competition (e.g., Haucap and Heimeshoff, 2014). A sufficient size is required to compete successfully, and companies need to adapt to market changes to maintain their own position. The network effects can also have a reverse effect, with a leading player rapidly losing market size (Evans and Schmalensee, 2016). To prevent this, acquisitions are a viable approach towards quickly increasing the customer basis, obtaining new technical capabilities and acquiring additional knowledge (Uhlenbruck et al., 2006). Digital technology giants are in competition with these industry or direct rivals as buyer-side rivals, but the firms that operate in the same submarket can also be potential targets for the giants in related transactions as target-side rivals.

Shifting the focus from product and service rivalry to platform rivalry shows that the digital technology giants are not only in competition with direct rivals but also with the group of digital giants and further players across submarkets of the digital technology industry.[20] The digital giants dominate their own core business, but also compete in other submarkets (Evans, 2017). The market definition is a key challenge in the digital technology industry as companies often have more than one relevant market. Thus, competition authorities need to focus on the revenue model rather than the offered product and service (van Gorp and Batura, 2015). In line with this, Evans and Schmalensee (2015) point out that the market definition and scope of markets have immense impact on the assessment of competitive constraints and dominance. The market definition in the digital industry as well as the economics of multi-sided-platforms increase complexity and competition (Evans and Schmalensee, 2016). The work of Rochet and Tirole (2003, 2006) on competition and price allocation in two-sided markets highlights the strong interdependency between the different sides of a platform and discusses the impact of multi-homing on competition on all sides. Despite different products and services, the indirect rivals compete as pure buyer-side rivals for new markets, capabilities and customer attention (Evans, 2013; van Gorp and Batura, 2015). The same market dynamics as mentioned above are present, but multi-homing drives competition and "winner-take-all" outcomes do not exist. Indirect network effects are more important than direct ones, and companies need to focus on relevant size, not on overall size (Evans and Schmalensee, 2016).

The differentiation between the two rival sets and between the different roles of rivals is important as the effect of digital technology giants' competitive actions in terms of M&A activity can differ and explanations for target-side rivals are not necessarily valid for buyer-side rivals and vice versa (Gaur et al., 2013).

---

20 See Evans and Schmalensee (2015) for a comprehensive literature overview of multi-sided platforms and competition.

3.2.2 Competitive Dynamics and Rival Effects

The interaction between technological change and the distinct role of the digital giants, the effects of product and service rivalry and platform rivalry have a strong influence on the competitive dynamics and innovation. Two main groups of competitive dynamics with regard to increased internal and external investments can be distinguished. First, value cocreation actions that include codevelopment, partnerships and other alliances. Second, competitive actions that include new products, acquisitions and other actions (Gnyawali et al., 2010; Li et al., 2010). Smith et al. (2001) provide a comprehensive overview on the competitive dynamics literature and emphasize the link between action and reaction as well as argue that competitive actions are embedded in the competitive environment. The resulting *performance* of competitive dynamics depends on the *action* and *reaction* as well as the *actor*, *responder* and the *competitive context* (see figure 3.2.1).

Figure 3.2.1: Competitive Dynamics Model

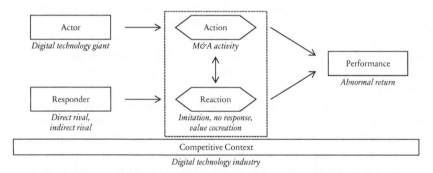

Figure 3.2.1 presents the competitive dynamics model based on components as described by Smith et al. (2001). The entities, actions and results that are analyzed in the study are written below in italics.

The previous subsection discusses digital technology giants as *actors*, direct and indirect rivals as *responders* and the *competitive context* of the digital technology industry. The study focusses on external investments in terms of mergers and acquisitions as *competitive actions*. Different types of *reactions* are possible. The response can be an imitation of the initial action, another defensive or aggressive competitive action or no response. Besides response type, literature also analyzes the likelihood, lag and order of responses (Smith et al., 2001). The interplay of action and reaction can be iterative and extended to sequences of competitive actions (e.g., Ferrier,

2001). In contrast, this contribution analyzes the short-term abnormal return as *performance* measure, and investigates the immediately anticipated reaction of competitors to the competitive action. The direct effect of mergers and acquisitions on rivals' value creation has been analyzed on a general level in different studies (e.g., Chatterjee, 1986; Eckbo, 1983; Song and Walkling, 2000). The first work in this area was conducted by Eckbo (1983) and Stillman (1983) who examine the influence of horizontal acquisitions on rivals and discuss market concentration. The rival effects literature has also analyzed transactions in the context of the high technology sector (e.g., Akdoğu, 2009; Bittlingmayer and Hazlett, 2000; Kohers and Kohers, 2004), but not specifically in the digital technology industry.

The short-term value creation can reflect three anticipated reactions of rivals that concur with different rival effects stories and hypotheses. First, the direct and indirect rivals do not react or react insufficiently. The digital giant can generate a competitive advantage due to the acquisition and create value for the owners and users of a platform (Brousseau and Penard, 2007; Sirmon et al., 2007). The strong "winner-take-all" effects in the digital technology industry foster market concentration and strengthen the position of the dominant players (Shapiro and Varian, 1999; van Gorp and Batura, 2015). This is reflected in two different hypotheses. On the one hand, the *Market Concentration Hypothesis* which is based on the idea that acquirer and rivals benefit from increased market concentration due to related transactions. On the other hand, the *Efficiency Hypothesis* which argues that rivals are negatively affected by increased efficiency in comparison with the acquirer. Second, the rival firm pursues a value cocreation strategy and positions itself as a potential future target. Similar to the codevelopment and relational capability actions as discussed in Gnyawali et al. (2010), the responder aims for closer interaction with the actor. In line with this, the *Acquisition Probability Hypothesis* suggests that rivals benefit as they can become future targets. Third, the responder identically imitates the action and acquires a similar target or passively mimics the move by focusing on further growth in the submarket. They can benefit from attention spillover and signaling effects (e.g., Foerderer et al., 2018). This is linked to the *Growth Probability Hypothesis* which assumes that rivals are positively or negatively affected as transactions reveal new information in terms of changed growth probability.

The next subsections discuss the theories and implications separately, and the study defines isolated hypotheses. However, it does not imply that only one effect can be present in the results or only one theory is supported. The results most likely reflect a mix of different theories and effects.

3.2.3 "Winner-Take-All" Markets and Market Concentration Hypothesis

The Market Concentration Hypothesis is based on the idea that a related transaction fosters market concentration and collusion between rivals in the industry. The acquirer and rivals can benefit from related transactions as consolidation leads to lower product output and higher customer prices (Eckbo, 1983). Market concentration in terms of collusion and increased monopoly power as a potential benefit for all remaining competitors in an industry is frequently discussed in literature, but substantial empirical evidence is missing. Eckbo (1983, 1985) and Stillman (1983) analyze market concentration and the effect of horizontal transactions and antitrust investigations on the value of competitors. They are not able to find support that acquirer and rivals can profit from anticompetitive effects due to acquisitions. In a similar approach, Bittlingmayer and Hazlett (2000) investigate the impact of market concentration in one of the digital technology submarkets. They observe the industry and competitor reactions to antitrust actions against Microsoft, but do not find any value gains. Fee and Thomas (2004) and Shahrur (2005) extend the work of Eckbo (1983) and examine the effect of horizontal transactions on rivals as well as suppliers and customers. Both studies find no evidence for monopolistic collusion from the rival perspective. Fee and Thomas (2004) determine market concentration in terms of increased buying power as a M&A motive only for the acquirer, and Shahrur (2005) finds some support for this. Song and Walkling (2000) and Akhigbe and Madura (1999) analyze rival effects across industries. They find significant negative effects of market concentration in terms of the Herfindahl index on rival returns and reject the Market Concentration Hypothesis. A different perspective is presented by Kim and Singal (1993) who observes positive rival effects with airline mergers. They analyze product price data instead of share price data and link it to increased market power. However, the influence on shareholder value is not tested in this study.

In the context of the digital technology giants, market concentration appears to have no significant influence on rival return if the companies do not react. The strong direct and indirect network effects in the digital technology industry foster "winner-take-all" outcomes in the submarkets (e.g., Crémer et al., 2019).[21] Thus, each submarket is dominated by one leading

---

21 See Farrell and Saloner (1985), Katz and Shapiro (1985) and Shapiro and Varian (1999) for further information on network effects and "winner-take-all" outcomes.

player. If an acquisition leads to increased market power, the market leader can strengthen its own position while the benefits for other players in the market remain limited. If market concentration had a positive effect on competitors, the direct rivals would slightly profit from the increased market power in related transactions similar to the acquiring digital technology giant, while the indirect rivals would most likely not be affected. However, this study does not expect an impact of market concentration on rivals in the context of the digital technology industry and strong network effects.

3.2.4 Competitive Advantages and Efficiency Hypothesis

The Efficiency Hypothesis is based on the idea that a transaction creates a competitive advantage for the acquirer compared to its competitors. This is relevant for direct rivals as they compete as buyer-side rivals in the same market as the acquirer. However, the increased efficiency can have also an effect on platform rivalry and competition for capabilities, new markets and customer attention and thus affect indirect rivals. Akdoğu (2009) describes two types of Efficiency Hypothesis. The Tough Competitor Hypothesis assumes that an acquisition provides a competitive advantage for the buyer and penalizes the rivals. The Rational Overpayment Hypothesis describes the situation of an acquirer buying a target although it is value diluting. However, the alternative state of no deal is worse for the buyer than the acquisition. The outcome leads to losses for the acquirer and rivals.

The previous chapter shows that related transactions by digital technology giants lead to on average positive abnormal returns to the acquirer. It can be traced back to reinforced direct and indirect network effects, complementarities and decreasing competition. Additionally, increased market concentration in a "winner-take-all" market with strong network effects can be seen as a competitive advantage for the acquirer. Thus, the buying digital giant appears to maintain the dominant position in its core market by utilizing a competitive advantage that creates value for the acquirer and dilutes value for the rivals. Yang et al. (2018) investigate the competition between Alphabet and Apple within the mobile ecosystem and find support for the Tough Competitor Hypothesis for Alphabet's related acquisitions. However, they observe no significant acquirer returns and rival effects of Apple's related transactions.

The value effect for unrelated transactions by digital technology giants differs. The previous chapter shows that, on average, this deal type dilutes value for the acquirer. The Rational Overpayment Hypothesis states that a negative abnormal return does not necessarily imply an irrational action. It can be a sign of high opportunity costs and shareholders' critical view. However, the transaction might still lead to a better outcome in comparison with competitors than no deal. Molnar (2007) and Akdoğu (2011) develop theoretical models that support the Rational Overpayment Hypothesis. Additionally, Molnar (2007) tests the hypothesis empirically with a sample of horizontal acquisitions and finds supporting evidence. High levels of creative destruction and Schumpeterian competition in the digital technology industry support the theory as well. Strong competition and new entrants frequently challenge the dominant positions of key players and replace the market leaders in the submarkets (Haucap and Heimeshoff, 2014; Spulber and Yoo, 2015). Kohers and Kohers (2004) describe competitive moves across high-technology industries that support the Rational Overpayment Hypothesis and can explain value diluting transactions. They assume that some high-technology companies, as a reaction to competition and growth expectations, only conduct transactions to prevent a competitor from acquiring the specific target. Akdoğu (2009) analyzes transactions in the telecommunications industry after a regulatory change in 1996 in the US which resulted in a strong increase in M&A activity. She finds no significant positive acquirer return but significant negative rival effects of diversifying actions, and explains this by rational overpayment. Closer rivals in terms of same service offerings and size show stronger rival effects than other competitors, with rival return positively related to the abnormal return to the acquirer. She synthesizes that acquisitions can lead to a competitive advantage for the acquirer which is reflected in negative rival effects. Jope et al. (2010) analyze different transactions and rival sets in the telecommunication industry and reveal negative returns to acquirers and rivals. They reject managerial hubris as a motive and argue that acquirers might overpay but that it is necessary to gain a competitive advantage. They find no significant difference between related and unrelated transactions for acquirer and rivals. However, overall rival effects on indirect competitors are lower as the competitive advantage might be less relevant for them as in the study of Akdoğu (2009).

The literature on rival effects and the digital technology industry shows that efficiency increase can be a driver for digital giants' acquisitions but is questionable as explanation for the rival reaction. Shareholders might expect the rivals not to wait before reacting and to be quickly able to imitate the competitive advantage through M&A. Furthermore, transactions from the telecommunication industry are not fully applicable as they are also driven by changes in regulation. Nevertheless, this study expects efficiency increase to explain to some extent the return to direct and indirect rivals. Digital giants benefit from network effects, complementarities as well as market concentration in related transactions, and use unrelated acquisitions to ensure future growth. Shareholders of rivals can critically monitor the competitive advantage, and the rivals' share prices reflect the anticipated insufficient reactions of the companies.

Hypothesis 1a. *Transactions by digital technology giants result in negative abnormal returns to direct rivals.*

Rivalry between indirect rivals differs from competition within the submarket. The digital giants operate in different submarkets, but compete for new markets, capabilities and customer attention with other players across platform ecosystems (Evans, 2013; van Gorp and Batura, 2015). In this competitive context, they do not have the same predominant position. Network effects do not lead to "winner-take-all" outcomes, and multi-homing can drive competition (Evans and Schmalensee, 2016). In addition, Dolata (2019) points out that the companies only have monopoly power over the non-commercial side. On the traditional business side, the competitive situation is different.

In consideration of the competition between digital technology giants despite different core businesses, an increase in efficiency appears to have a smaller effect on indirect rivals as direct rivals. This study expects an effect, but the impact is most likely smaller.

Hypothesis 2a. *Transactions by digital technology giants result in negative abnormal returns to indirect rivals.*

Morck et al. (1990) show that past performance can indicate success in transactions for the acquirer. In the digital technology industry, network effects increase market concentration, and a good current position helps to achieve a strong future position (McIntyre and Chintakananda, 2014). Similarly, van Gorp and Batura (2015) describe that dominant players in the digital technology industry tend to lever their market power. It can therefore be expected that a stronger acquirer in terms of higher historical sales growth, profitability and market power benefits more in comparison with the competitors, and that these factors amplify the negative effect on rival return. In addition, relatedness can also strengthen the impact of the competitive advantage as related transactions benefit more from network effects. Finally, Akdoğu (2009) argues that the acquirer abnormal return has a significant impact on rival return depending on the version of the Efficiency Hypothesis. A positive impact indicates the Rational Overpayment version, and a negative relation indicates the Tough Competitor version.

This study expects relatedness, industry concentration, acquirer profitability and acquirer sales growth to have a negative influence on the rival return across deal types. In addition, the study expects acquirer return to have a negative effect in transactions that create value for the acquirer and a positive effect in transactions that dilute value for the acquirer.

Hypothesis 3. *Acquirer characteristics (profitability, sales growth) and deal characteristics (relatedness, industry concentration) have a negative influence on the abnormal returns to direct rivals. Acquirer return has a negative influence for value creating transactions and a positive influence for value diluting transactions.*

In accordance with the argumentation for hypotheses H1a and H2a, this study expects the acquirer and deal characteristics to also have an impact on the indirect rival return which, however, is most likely to be weaker. Furthermore, the study expects relatedness between rival and target to have an impact on the indirect rival return. The competitive advantage of the acquirer can increase if target and indirect rival are related and the rival is not able to buy the potentially attractive target similar as discussed by Kohers and Kohers (2004).

Hypothesis 4. *Acquirer characteristics (profitability, sales growth) and deal characteristics (relatedness, industry concentration, rival target relatedness) have a negative influence on the abnormal returns to indirect rivals. Acquirer return has a negative influence for value creating transactions and a positive influence for value diluting transactions.*

3.2.5 Potential Targets and Acquisition Probability Hypothesis

The Signaling Hypothesis is already discussed by Eckbo (1983) and Chatterjee (1986) in terms of an information effect that can offset negative implications of increased efficiency on rival returns. They argue that an efficiency increasing transaction can lead to positive rival effects if the positive information effect is larger than the negative effect of the efficiency gain. In general, the Signaling Hypothesis states that the share price reaction of rivals reflects new information about the rivals or the whole industry. A distinction can be made between the two main versions, the Acquisition Probability Hypothesis and the Growth Probability Hypothesis.

The Acquisition Probability Hypothesis suggests that the share price of a rival increases in response to an acquisition as shareholders expect the firm to become a future target, even if the initial transaction is value diluting (Song and Walkling, 2000). This hypothesis is less relevant for indirect rivals as each digital technology giant seems to be too large and to require too many resources to be acquired by another giant, but it offers a different perspective on direct rivals as target-side rivals in related transactions.[22] Clougherty and Duso (2009) analyze large horizontal transactions and present positive target and rival returns. However, they are not able to find a trend or merger wave impact on positive rival effects, and observe rival effects to be robust to merger and rival characteristics in terms of rival geography and proximity, absolute and relative rival size as well as product-market type and number of rivals. Thus, they reject information effects and the Acquisition Probability Hypothesis. In contrast, Song and Walkling (2000) investigate target rivals and find significant positive target and rival returns which they connect to the Acquisition Probability Hypothesis. They show that future targets feature higher returns than non-targets, with the probability of being a target as well as the level of surprise of an acquisition having a positive influence on rival returns.

The expected effect of the Acquisition Probability Hypothesis contradicts the expected effect of the Efficiency Hypothesis on direct rivals. Direct rivals can position themselves as potential future targets and experience positive returns for related transactions. The study tests this theory as an alternative to Hypothesis H1a.

Hypothesis 1b. *Related transactions by digital technology giants result in positive abnormal returns to direct rivals.*

Song and Walkling (2000) identify different rival characteristics that can be linked to the probability of takeover and have an influence on rival returns. They use this as evidence for the Acquisition Probability Hypothesis. These variables include sales growth, managerial ownership, leverage and Tobin's Q. Throughout all regressions, sales growth and managerial ownership have significant negative effects. Firms with higher historical growth and a higher share of managerial ownership are more difficult and thus less likely to be acquired. However, the economic impact of the managerial ownership variable is minor. Leverage and Tobin's Q have a positive effect, which means that firms with a higher level of debt and, follow-

---

22 Akhigbe and Madura (1999) show that larger rivals in terms of the market capitalization are less likely to be acquired.

ing the interpretation of Lang et al. (1991), with more growth potential are more likely to be acquired. Both variables are only significant in some regression models. Akhigbe and Madura (1999) find no effect of Tobin's Q on a sample of large US mergers, but a significant negative influence of rival firm size and a significant positive impact of rival free cash flow. They link the result for both variables to a lower level of required internal resources for financing the transaction. Kohers and Kohers (2004) also test the Acquisition Probability Hypothesis. They expect rivals with low managerial ownership, high book-to-market ratio and a high level of free cash flow to show a stronger rival return reaction. However, they are not able to find significant effects. Literature on the digital technology industry describes on the basis of preemptive investments an acquisition strategy that supports the Acquisition Probability Hypothesis. Firms buy direct rivals before they become a threat to their own business (Kuchinke and Vidal, 2016; van Gorp and Batura, 2015). This suggests that the likelihood of takeover and by extension the level of rival return under the Acquisition Probability Hypothesis can increase if a firm becomes more relevant.

To conclude, some rival characteristics can indicate the attractiveness of a potential future target in the digital technology industry. This study expects rival leverage, rival Tobin's Q as well as rival free cash flow to have a positive effect, and rival sales growth and rival firm size to have a negative effect on direct rival returns.[23]

Hypothesis 5. *Rival characteristics have a positive (leverage, Tobin's Q, free cash flow) or negative (sales growth, firm size) influence on the abnormal returns to direct rivals.*

3.2.6 Signaling Effects and Growth Probability Hypothesis

This study distinguishes between two types of Signaling Hypothesis due to the possibility of separating the information effect of a transaction, particularly in the digital technology industry, from a potential takeover motive. While the Acquisition Probability Hypothesis is not relevant for the group of digital technology giants, the Growth Probability Hypothesis is appropriate for indirect rivals as well as both deal types of direct rivals. The hy-

---

23 The influence of rivals' book-to-market ratio and managerial ownership has not been tested, as book-to-market can interfere with Tobin's Q and managerial ownership shows no significant economic impact in previous studies.

pothesis suggests that a transaction signals future industry growth expectations (Gaur et al., 2013). This can result in positive returns to acquirers and rivals, but both can also experience negative returns if shareholders value the initial acquisition critically and the deal transmits a warning signal. Thus, M&A activity can transmit positive and negative signals. The Future Acquirer Anticipation Hypothesis as presented by Cai et al. (2011) is closely related to the Growth Probability Hypothesis. It considers that the market already anticipates potential future acquisitions by rivals as a response to the action at the time an initial bid is made. The hypothesis suggests that bidding for a target is on average value creating not only for acquirers but also for rivals, with future subsequent acquirers benefiting more.

Cai et al. (2011) analyze acquirer rivals and show that these firms already benefit at the time of the initial transaction while the level of value creation differs between subsequent acquirers and non-acquirers. They conclude that sufficient information is available in advance to distinguish between both rival groups and that acquisitions send anticipation signals to all rivals. Gaur et al. (2013) analyze acquisitions by Chinese companies and observe positive share price reactions to acquirer rivals. They explain it with the signaling power of the transaction and market expectations on future growth in the specific industry. The focus on the rapidly changing Chinese market provides similar growth dynamics to those of the digital technology industry. Kohers and Kohers (2004) argue that transactions in the high technology industries have a stronger amplifying effect since the industries are characterized by high levels of uncertainty and information asymmetry. The information effect can be more prominent for rivals of digital technology giants since the giants have an outstanding position in the industry that is driven by the distinct financial strength (Dolata, 2018). The previous chapter shows that these companies conduct many transactions, continuously increase investments and have high levels of liquidity. They can also influence other companies' reactions with regard to their M&A activity (Mattioli, 2017). Thus, an acquisition by a digital technology giant can transmit a positive or negative signal to other companies in the industry. Rivals' shareholders receive the signal and expect their companies to imitate the action and experience comparable positive or negative value effects.

For the high technology sector, Kohers and Kohers (2004) assume that acquisitions reveal information about the industry as a whole and show shareholders of competitors to react sensitively to transactions in a high growth, high uncertainty and high competition environment. They analyze the reactions of competitors in different high technology industries based on the same 4-digit SIC code as the target, and find significant positive rival effects. In contrast, Yang et al. (2018) discuss bidder-specific signaling and assume that non-main business acquisitions signal limited internal growth potential. They partly support this by documenting positive rival effects of Alphabet's diversifying transactions on Apple, while the rival effects of Apple's M&A activity on Alphabet is not significant. The authors link the missing significance to overlapping effects in the case of Alphabet and higher uncertainty as well as limited announcement information in the case of Apple.

The explanations allow for the conjecture that direct and indirect rivals can benefit from value creation for digital technology giants. Digital giants' acquisitions can be interpreted as signals for future growth in the industry in general, with rivals' shareholders anticipating future takeovers by their firms and expecting similar growth. In contrast, value diluting transactions by digital technology giants can signal lower growth potential to rivals. Thus, the Growth Probability Hypothesis and Future Acquirer Anticipation Hypothesis offer another potential explanation for the reaction of rivals. The expected direction is a mix of the effects of the Efficiency Hypothesis and Acquisition Probability Hypothesis.

Hypothesis 1c. Value creating transactions by digital technology giants result in positive abnormal returns and value diluting transactions in negative abnormal returns to direct rivals.

Hypothesis 2b. Value creating transactions by digital technology giants result in positive abnormal returns and value diluting transactions in negative abnormal returns to indirect rivals.

The relation between acquirer return and rival return can be further investigated in order to understand the dynamics behind rival effects and distinguish between the different theories. Several studies analyze this link in detail. Akdoğu (2009) applies it to distinguish between bidder-specific and industry-specific signals. She finds a positive relation of positive as well as negative acquirer returns which she connects to industry-specific signaling of growth potential or the Rational Overpayment Hypothesis. Other studies find similar effects of positive and negative acquirer returns as support for the Signaling Hypothesis (Cai et al., 2011; Gaur et al., 2013).

Following the previous literature, this study expects a positive relation for value creating and value diluting transactions and both types of rivals, and no bidder-specific signaling.

Hypothesis 6. *Acquirer return has a positive influence on the abnormal returns to direct rivals for both types of transactions.*

Hypothesis 7. *Acquirer return has a positive influence on the abnormal returns to indirect rivals for both types of transactions.*

Kohers and Kohers (2004) find no support for the Acquisition Probability Hypothesis in the high-technology industries sample, but evidence for industry-wide signaling with regard to the Growth Probability Hypothesis. They identify a range of information variables that can lead to stronger signaling effects and higher rival returns. These include high rival portfolio Tobin's Q, low average rival portfolio firm size as well as a high degree of surprise which is measured by target abnormal return, low target dividend payout and high industry concentration in unrelated transactions. They conclude that the shareholders react more sensitively to new information due to the high levels of uncertainty and asymmetric information in the high-technology industries. The results regarding concentration contradict the negative impact presented by Song and Walkling (2000) as evidence against the Market Concentration Hypothesis, but concur with Gaur et al. (2013). The latter also suggest that industry concentration has a positive effect on rival returns which is weaker for related transactions. They emphasize that rivals can have a less favorable position in a highly concentrated industry after a related transaction while a diversifying acquisition can signal further growth to them outside the core market. The study tests this empirically, and shows a negative concentration effect in related and a positive effect in unrelated transactions.

Overall, the study expects a set of information variables to have impact on the rival return and amplify or dampen signaling effects. On the one hand, future growth expectations in terms of Tobin's Q of rivals as well as acquirers can interact with the value creation or dilution signal and emphasize the positive or negative return. On the other hand, higher market concentration indicates a strong industry leader that can have higher information power for rivals and thus amplify signals. In addition to this, the return to a smaller rival is more likely to be driven by higher uncertainty and information asymmetries and can react more strongly to signals.[24]

---

24 Target abnormal return and target dividend payout are not tested due to limited data.

Hypothesis 8. *Information variables amplify (Tobin's Q, industry concentration) or dampen (rival firm size) the abnormal returns to direct rivals for both types of transactions.*

Hypothesis 9. *Information variables amplify (Tobin's Q, industry concentration) or dampen (rival firm size) the abnormal returns to indirect rivals for both types of transactions.*

3.2.7 Overview of Hypotheses

A summary of the discussed hypotheses and expected rival effects by transaction type is presented in table 3.2.1. It should be emphasized that the theories and hypotheses reflect isolated perspectives on rival returns, while the empirical results most likely reflect mixed effects that are driven by a partial overlap of influences. Different rival reactions can be anticipated by shareholders at the same time, with the overlap possibly reducing the

Table 3.2.1: Overview of Rival Effects Hypotheses and Expected Empirical Results

Hypothesis	Description	Expected Effect per Digital Giants' Deal				Influencing Factors
		Value Creating Deal		Value Diluting Deal		
		Direct Rivals	Indirect Rivals	Direct Rivals	Indirect Rivals	
Market Concentration Hypothesis	Rivals benefit from higher market concentration due to related transactions	Not relevant	Not relevant	Not relevant	Not relevant	Not relevant
Efficiency Hypothesis	Rivals are negatively affected by increased efficiency of the acquirer	Negative effect (H1a, H3)	Slightly negative effect (H2a, H4)	Negative effect (H1a, H3)	Slightly negative effect (H2a, H4)	- *Relatedness* - *Industry Concentration* - *Acquirer CAR* - *Acquirer Profitability* - *Acquirer Sales Growth* - *Rival Target Relatedness*
Acquisition Probability Hypothesis	Rivals benefit in related transactions as they can become future targets	Positive effect* (H1b, H5)	Not relevant	Positive effect* (H1b, H5)	Not relevant	- *Rival Firm Size* - *Rival Tobin's Q* - *Rival Leverage* - *Rival Free Cash Flow* - *Rival Sales Growth*
Growth Probability Hypothesis	Rivals are affected in both directions as transactions reveal new information about the industry	Positive effect (H1c, H6, H8)	Positive effect (H2b, H7, H9)	Negative effect (H1c, H6, H8)	Negative effect (H2b, H7, H9)	- *Industry Concentration* - *Acquirer CAR* - *Acquirer Tobin's Q* - *Rival Firm Size* - *Rival Tobin's Q*

Table 3.2.1 presents the four discussed rival effects hypotheses with a short description, the expected effect per digital giants' transaction type on direct and indirect rivals and factors that can influence the rival return. * indicates that the effect is expected only in related transactions.

magnitude of the results (Chatterjee, 1986; Eckbo, 1983). It therefore does not seem appropriate to examine the rival stories and hypotheses separately but rather in combination, as has been done in this study.

3.3 Data and Research Methodology

3.3.1 Data Sample and Rival Selection

The transaction sample for the analysis is gathered from two different sources, the Securities Data Company database and the Capital IQ database. This study investigates rival effects of a transaction completed by one of the digital technology giants (Alibaba Group Holding Ltd., Alphabet Inc., Amazon.com Inc., Apple Inc., Facebook Inc., Microsoft Corp., Tencent Holding Ltd.) and announced between January 1, 2008 and December 31, 2017. The data selection, cleaning and preparation process for the final sample is based on the study in the previous chapter. In addition, all M&A deals with overlapping event dates across the total sample are eliminated from the transaction sample. The final data sample with the remaining 373 transactions is validated by press research to identify potential confounding events in terms of interactions between digital technology giants. Table 3.3.1 presents the transaction sample divided by acquirer and year. The number of transactions increases across the years, peaking in 2016 with 53 deals. Alphabet is the largest acquirer with 131 transactions, followed by Microsoft with 80 deals and Amazon with 56 deals. Facebook and Alibaba have fewer acquisitions due to the late IPOs in 2012 and 2014, respectively. Other data sources employed are the Datastream database for the relevant daily share prices as well as market indices, and the Worldscope database for company financials. The study uses the Datastream Total Return Index for stock and benchmark returns which includes price movements, dividend payments and share structure changes.

The literature suggests different approaches for rival selection.[25] The methodology of this study is designed to investigate competitors' reaction to digital technology giants' M&A activity, and therefore focuses on acquirer rivals and not on target rivals. Two separate rival sets are created to

---

25 For example, Akhigbe and Madura (1999) use industry classification to identify target rivals, Jope et al. (2010) use industry classification and region to create different acquirer and target rival sets, and Clougherty and Duso (2011) use an expert assessment to identify rivals.

Table 3.3.1: Distribution of Deals by Acquirer and Year

	Number of Deals by		Acquirer						
	Total	in %	Alibaba	Alphabet	Amazon	Apple	Facebook	Microsoft	Tencent
2008	29	8%	0	3	7	1	0	18	0
2009	15	4%	0	3	4	1	0	7	0
2010	33	9%	0	21	5	4	0	2	1
2011	35	9%	0	20	7	2	0	5	1
2012	26	7%	0	12	3	3	0	4	4
2013	38	10%	0	11	5	7	9	6	0
2014	49	13%	0	23	5	6	9	6	0
2015	50	13%	7	11	6	7	5	13	1
2016	53	14%	5	16	6	5	7	10	4
2017	45	12%	4	11	8	8	4	9	1
Total	373	100%	16	131	56	44	34	80	12

Table 3.3.1 presents the number of transactions per acquirer and year.

analyze the competitors' shareholder value reaction, the direct and the indirect rival set. Both rival sets offer a different perspective. Direct rivals shed light on the competitive dynamics within the submarkets while the indirect rivals show the effects across markets and platforms. The direct rival set comprises competitors that operate in the same industry as the acquirer. The relevant data for all public and active acquirer rivals in terms of same 3-digit SIC code as the acquirer has therefore been collected. Companies without relevant data (e.g., share price data, financial data) and digital technology giants are eliminated from the rival set. In total, three different direct rival subgroups are created (SIC group 357, 596, 737). The final rival set includes the 30 largest rivals per 3-digit SIC code group to ensure that the effect on the main parts of the submarkets is captured. The size is measured in terms of the market capitalization at the 2017 calendar year-end. The indirect rival set consists of the seven digital technology giants and additionally Softbank Group Corp. as the owner of the worldwide largest digital technology investment fund. For the main analysis, only rivals with available share price data for the full time period are used.[26] To ensure that the number of rivals is equal across the sample, Tencent as the smallest digital giant in terms of the market capitalization at the 2017 calendar year-end is excluded as rival for deals by Facebook and Alibaba.

---

26 Facebook and Alibaba do not have data for the full period as Facebook's IPO was on May 18, 2012 and Alibaba's IPO on September 19, 2014.

3.3.2 Definition of Variables

Different acquirer, deal and rival characteristics are used as independent variables in the multivariate regression models of this study in order to understand the value drivers behind the rival returns. These characteristics include *Relatedness, Rival Target Relatedness, Industry Concentration (Normal and Adjusted), Acquirer CAR, Positive Deal, Tobin's Q, Leverage, Free Cash Flow, Firm Size, Sales Growth* and *Acquirer Profitability*. The variables are computed in accordance with prior literature to allow comparison across studies.

Following the study in the previous chapter, this research uses the SIC code framework to distinguish between related and unrelated transactions (*Relatedness*). An acquisition is related if the acquirer and target share the same 3-digit SIC code in accordance with Song and Walkling (2000) and Uhlenbruck et al. (2006). Transactions that have only one or different SIC codes in both databases are validated manually. The relatedness of indirect rivals is tested with another dummy variable (*Rival Target Relatedness*) which indicates if the rival shares the same 3-digit SIC code with the target. This study uses the Herfindahl Index to determine the degree of competition (*Industry Concentration*). A sales-based version is computed each year for each 3-digit SIC code submarket. Therefore, all public companies in the respective 3-digit SIC code submarket are determined similar to the direct rival set. However, for this purpose the analyzed data set also includes inactive players with available net sales data in at least one relevant year from 2006 to 2017. The variable is calculated as in formula (3.3.1):

$$HI = \sum_{i=1}^{N} \left(\frac{SAL_i}{\sum_{i=1}^{N} SAL_i} \right)^2, \tag{3.3.1}$$

where SAL_i represents the net sales per company i. This study uses a three-years average in accordance with Hou and Robinson (2006) to limit the effect of potential wrong entries. In addition, an adjusted version of the variable (*Industry Concentration, Adj.*) is computed without the influence of the digital technology giants per submarket.

The relation between rival return and acquirer return is tested by two different variables. First, the cumulative abnormal return to the acquirer in the main two-week event window (*Acquirer CAR*) is used following the approach by Akdoğu (2009). Second, a dummy variable (*Positive Deal*) indicates if the acquisition has a positive abnormal return over the two-week event window and is value creating in accordance with Gaur et al. (2013).

The variable *Tobin's Q* is approximated with a proxy suggested by Chung and Pruitt (1994) and also utilized by Kohers and Kohers (2004). The calculation is presented in formula (3.3.2):

$$Tobin's\ Q = \frac{MVE + PRS + (CLI - CAS) + LTD}{TAS},\qquad (3.3.2)$$

where *MVE* represents the market value of equity, *PRS* the liquidating value of preferred stock, *CLI* the current liabilities, *CLA* the current assets, *LTD* the long-term debt and *TAS* the total assets.[27] The variable is measured at the fiscal year prior to the acquisition announcement. The study also analyzes the financial structure of the acquirer and rivals. The variable *Leverage* is calculated by the long-term debt scaled to the total assets at the fiscal year prior to the event in accordance with Akdoğu (2009). *Free Cash Flow* is measured by the first approach of the study in the previous chapter, the proxy by Lehn and Poulsen (1989) as presented in formula (3.3.3):

$$FCF = OPI + DEP - TAX - INT - DIV,\qquad (3.3.3)$$

where *OPI* represents the operating income, *DEP* the depreciation and amortization, *TAX* the total income tax minus change in deferred taxes, *INT* the gross interest expenses on debt and *DIV* the sum of dividends paid on preferred and common stocks. The free cash flow measure is normalized by the book value of total assets and calculated at the fiscal year prior to the event. The variable *Firm Size* is defined as the natural logarithm of the total equity market capitalization at the fiscal year prior to the event in accordance with Moeller et al. (2004). *Sales Growth* is defined as the geometric average of the net sales growth of the last two fiscal years prior to the event, following the approach by Song and Walkling (2000). The variable *Acquirer Profitability* is measured by the operating income before depreciation and amortization scaled to total assets at prior fiscal year end in accordance with in Cai et al. (2011).

Additionally, several variables are applied as controls that have demonstrated predictive power over rival returns in literature. Similar to the previous study, *Acquirer Experience* is measured by the number of all relevant completed deals by the buyer in the SDC database until the analyzed event. Further dummy variables include *Domestic Deal* that indicates if the acquirer and target are located in the same country, and *Public Target* that

---

27 Negative values for Tobin's Q are set at 0.

indicates if the transaction target is a public company. *High Year* and *Low Year* indicate if the event date is in years with the highest (2014, 2015, 2016) or the lowest number (2008, 2009, 2012) of transactions per digital technology giant across the sample. The overview of the transaction sample shows a large share of deals conducted by Alphabet. The variable *Acquirer Alphabet* indicates if the buyer is Alphabet.

Table 3.3.2: Characteristics of Transactions and Firms by Digital Technology Giants and Rivals

	Mean			Median			Standard Deviation		
	Digital Giants	Direct Rivals	Indirect Rivals	Digital Giants	Direct Rivals	Indirect Rivals	Digital Giants	Direct Rivals	Indirect Rivals
CAR	0.1	-0.1	-0.1	0.1	0.0	-0.1	4.8	6.6	5.0
Tobin's Q	3.4	2.2	3.3	2.9	1.8	2.7	1.5	2.1	2.7
Profitability	19	16	19	19	15	18	7	9	7
Sales Growth	25	11	27	21	6	23	16	24	21
Firm Size	288	25	229	252	14	185	159	37	188
Leverage	7	13	16	3	9	13	8	14	16
Free Cash Flow	13	10	13	14	10	12	4	9	6

Table 3.3.2 presents the mean, median and standard deviation of the cumulative abnormal return as well as *Tobin's Q, Profitability, Sales Growth, Firm Size, Leverage* and *Free Cash Flow* of the group of digital giants, direct rivals and indirect rivals. CAR equals the cumulative abnormal return over the [-5;+5] event window. *Tobin's Q* is calculated as market value of equity plus liquidating value of preferred stock plus difference of current liabilities minus current assets plus long-term debt, deflated by book value of total assets. *Profitability* equals operating income before depreciation and amortization, deflated by book value of total assets. *Sales Growth* is defined as the geometric average of net sales growth of the last two years. *Firm Size* is the natural logarithm of total equity market capitalization and presented in $ billion without the natural logarithm transformation. *Leverage* equals long-term debt, deflated by book value of total assets. *Free Cash Flow* is calculated as operating income before depreciation and amortization minus income tax minus interest expenses minus dividends, deflated by book value of total assets. CAR, *Profitability, Sales Growth, Leverage* and *Free Cash Flow* are shown in percentage.

The descriptive statistics of the data sample are presented in table 3.3.2. Differences between the digital giants and rival sets exist. On the one hand, the means of *CAR, Tobin's Q, Profitability* and *Free Cash Flow* are on a similar level, but the standard deviations vary. On the other hand, the means and standard deviations of *Sales Growth, Firm Size* and *Leverage* differ strongly. Average *Sales Growth* varies between 11 % for direct rivals and 27 % for indirect rivals, and the mean of *Firm Size* shows an average market capitalization of $25 billion for direct rivals and $288 billion for digital giants. For both variables, the means of digital giants and indirect rivals are close to each other. *Leverage* is strongly dominated by the indirect rival set with an average of 16 %, while direct rivals have a mean of 13 % and digital giants of 7 %. In addition, the standard deviation of these variables is relatively high in comparison with the means. This differs for the other variables, except for *CAR*. The average *CAR* is between -0.1 % and 0.1 %, but the standard deviation is 4.8 % for digital giants, 5.0 % for indirect rivals and 6.6 % for direct rivals. The average *Profitability* is 16–19 % and average *Free Cash Flow* is 10–13 % for all three groups. The mean of *Tobin's Q* is 3.4 for the group of digital giants, 2.2 for direct rivals and 3.3 for the indirect rival set.

3.3.3 Research Methodology

This study's objective is to identify the implications of digital technology giants' mergers and acquisitions activity for direct and indirect rivals. In the first part of the study, the return reaction of both competitor groups is determined in an event study approach. In the second part, the value drivers of the rival effects are further analyzed with the help of multivariate regression models. The analyses also include tests for difference between both rival sets and a robustness subsection. Figure 3.3.1 illustrates the research model, analyzed variables and the underlying hypotheses.

Figure 3.3.1: Research Model

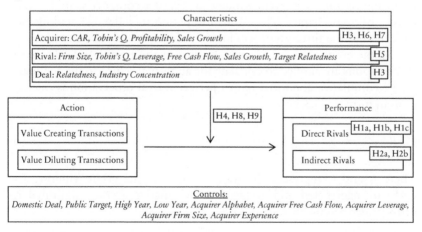

Figure 3.3.1 presents the research model with the analyzed variables and underlying hypotheses.

The event study is based on the standard methodology as described by Brown and Warner (1980, 1985). The rivals' abnormal returns are calculated on an individual level following the approach by Song and Walkling (2000). The calculation is conducted separately for both rival sets. The direct rival calculation consists of 30 competitors per event, and the indirect calculation of five competitors per event. This leads to 11,190 and 1,865 event-rival observations for the direct and indirect rival group, respectively. The market model is employed as return generating model, with log returns used for the realized stock returns and for the market portfolio returns in accordance with the previous study. The abnormal return is calculated for any event j and rival i at time t as presented in formula (3.3.4):

$$AR_{j,i,t} = R_{i,t} - \left(\widehat{\alpha}_{j,i} + \widehat{\beta}_{j,i} * R_{M,t}\right), \tag{3.3.4}$$

where $R_{i,t}$ represents the realized log return to rival i at time t and $R_{M,t}$ the realized log return to the respective market portfolio at time t. The return to rivals that are listed in Asia is lagged by one day to adjust for different trading times, as suggested by Park (2004). For each event-rival observation, $\widehat{\alpha}_{j,i}$ and $\widehat{\beta}_{j,i}$ are determined by an ordinary least square regression on the respective estimation window. The market portfolio is approximated by the S&P 500 index for US-listed firms, and the MSC ACWI index is used as benchmark for firms that are listed in other countries. The estimation window and main event window are set in accordance with the study in the previous chapter. The estimation period includes 145 trading days [-150;-6] and the three event windows are the two weeks around the event [-5;+5], the event week [-2;+2] and the days of the event [-1;+1]. The same specifications are applied to calculate the abnormal return to the acquirer.

The cumulative abnormal return per event-rival observation is calculated as in formula (3.3.5):

$$CAR_{j,i,[t_1;t_2]} = \sum_{t_1}^{t_2} AR_{j,i,t}, \tag{3.3.5}$$

where t_1 and t_2 represent the start and end of the event window. The CARs are aggregated and averaged to cumulative average abnormal returns, as defined by formula (3.3.6):

$$CAAR_{[t_1;t_2]} = \frac{1}{n}\frac{1}{m}\sum_j^n \sum_i^m CAR_{j,i,[t_1;t_2]}, \tag{3.3.6}$$

where *m* represents the number of rival observations and *n* the number of event observations per analysis. A set of four parametric and non-parametric test statistics is employed to test for statistical significance and ensure unbiased results. Differences between the test statistics need to be interpreted with caution (Campbell et al., 2010). The test statistics include the Patell's Z-test (1976), the standardized cross-sectional test developed by Boehmer et al. (1991), the Rank-test as developed by Corrado (1989) and Corrado and Zivney (1992) and the generalized Sign-test (Cowan, 1992). The cumulative average abnormal returns of the subsamples and rival sets are tested for differences by utilizing the parametric two-sided t-test for independent samples and the non-parametric Mann-Whitney U test (1947).

The drivers of the rival effects are identified in multivariate regression models. The analysis is separately conducted for direct and indirect rivals. The dependent variable is the direct or indirect rival return over the two-week event window. The analysis uses an OLS-regression model with robust Huber-White standard errors because the modified Wald test indicates heteroscedasticity. There is no evidence for invariant differences between the observations that require fixed-effects. This is also supported by the Durbin-Wu-Hausman test and the joint F-test on year dummies. The robust standard errors are compared with time-cluster and firm-cluster standard errors, but no large differences are observed so that the Huber-White standard errors are used, as recommended by Petersen (2009).

Three groups of regression models are tested in this study. The analysis differs between both rival sets. The models for direct rivals include the rival characteristics *Rival Leverage*, *Rival Free Cash Flow* and *Rival Sales Growth* to test for the Acquisition Probability Hypothesis, while the models for indirect rivals include *Rival Target Relatedness* so as to further test the Efficiency Hypothesis.[28] The first group of regression models separately analyzes the total transaction sample as well as the related and unrelated deals and contains no interaction variables. The second group contains the same basic regression model that has been used for the total sample, but this time the transaction sample is grouped by the effect of the deal on the acquirer (positive deals and negative deals). The third group contains three regression models and analyzes the total transaction sample. Model I extends the basic model by a dummy variable for the effect on the acquirer (*Positive Deal*) and different interactions with this variable (*PD * Acquirer*

---

28 The rival characteristics that indicate likelihood of takeover are also tested for the total sample of indirect rivals, but do not have significant coefficients in line with expectations (not reported).

*CAR, PD * Acquirer Tobin's Q, PD * Acquirer Profitability, PD * Acquirer Sales Growth*). Model II applies the same extended regression, but without the rival characteristics that are linked to the Acquisition Probability Hypothesis for direct rivals and without the variable *Rival Target Relatedness* for indirect rivals. Model III differs from model I by utilizing the adjusted version of the market concentration measure. For model I, II and III of the third group, the interacting variables (*Acquirer CAR, Acquirer Tobin's Q, Acquirer Profitability, Acquirer Sales Growth*) are centered to their means to facilitate the interpretation.[29] All models of the three group include the same range of control variables.

In order to check whether the results are robust in relation to the rival selection, this study conducts the event study and multivariate regressions with a focused direct and extended indirect rival group. The direct rival set for the robustness subsection consists of 10 rivals with the closest market capitalization per 3-digit SIC code group at the 2017 calendar year-end. This leads to 3,730 event-rival observations. The extended indirect rival group includes all digital giants and Softbank Group if data is available. This leads to 2,234 event-rival observations and a varying number of rivals per event (5–7 firms). Events with more rivals, which are the more recent events, are therefore overweighed, and the results need to be interpreted carefully.

3.4 Empirical Results

3.4.1 Rival Effects on Direct and Indirect Rivals

Table 3.4.1 and table 3.4.2 present the cumulative average abnormal returns to direct (panel A) and indirect (panel B) rivals separated by digital technology giants' related and unrelated transactions, respectively. The tables also include the acquirer returns (panel C).

Direct and indirect rivals show no substantial reaction to the 231 related transactions (see table 3.4.1). All event windows are negative, but the effect is not significant and the economic impact is low. The two-week event windows for direct and indirect rivals have an insignificant abnormal return of -0.07 % and -0.01 %, respectively. In contrast, the same event win-

---

29 The coefficient of *Positive Deal*, which is the variable that interacts with the centered variables, describes the effect for an acquirer with average levels of *Acquirer CAR, Acquirer Tobin's Q, Acquirer Profitability* and *Acquirer Sales Growth*.

dow for the acquirer has an abnormal return of 0.69 % and is significant at the 5 % level.[30] These first results allow for two different explanations. On the one hand, they might be driven by an overlap of different rival reactions. This concurs with the inference by Eckbo (1983) and Chatterjee (1986) that efficiency and information effects can coexist and offset each other. On the other hand, the two rival sets might not react to digital giants' related transactions and be not influenced at all. Both explanations are analyzed in detail in the next subsections.

Table 3.4.1: *CAARs to Direct Rivals, Indirect Rivals and Acquirers for Related Transactions*

	(1) CAAR	(2) Patell-test	(3) BMP-test	(4) Sign-test	(5) Corrado-test	(6) Positive	(7) Sample
Panel A: Direct Rivals							
[-5;+5]	-0.07%	-0.73	-0.74	0.89	0.06	50%	6,930
[-2;+2]	-0.08%	-1.23	-1.19	0.20	-0.34	49%	6,930
[-1;+1]	-0.07%	-1.24	-1.20	0.89	-0.11	50%	6,930
Panel B: Indirect Rivals							
[-5;+5]	-0.01%	0.31	0.30	0.81	0.70	49%	1,155
[-2;+2]	-0.07%	-0.90	-0.90	1.46	0.17	50%	1,155
[-1;+1]	-0.03%	-0.21	-0.21	0.98	0.79	50%	1,155
Panel C: Acquirers							
[-5;+5]	0.69%	2.49 **	2.25 **	2.02 **	1.91 *	55%	231
[-2;+2]	0.17%	1.32	1.26	1.10	1.02	52%	231
[-1;+1]	0.24%	1.59	1.94 *	1.89 *	2.39 **	55%	231

Table 3.4.1 presents the abnormal share price reaction of direct rivals (panel A), indirect rivals (panel B) and acquirers (panel C) for digital technology giants' related transactions in different event windows. Column (1) displays the cumulative average abnormal return, column (2)-(5) the test statistics, column (6) the share of transactions with a positive abnormal return and column (7) the sample size per analysis. Statistical significance at 1 %, 5 % and 10 % levels is indicated with ***, ** and *, respectively.

The results for the 142 unrelated transactions show a slightly different picture (see table 3.4.2). The acquisitions lead to some significant rival effects on direct and indirect rivals. The one-week event windows have a negative CAAR of -0.17 % to direct and -0.30 % to indirect rivals, which are significant for direct rivals for the parametric tests at the 1 % level and for indirect rivals at the 5 % level, respectively.[31] The two-week and three-day event windows are also significant for the parametric tests for the direct rival set

---

30 The Corrado-test is significant at the 10 % level.
31 The Corrado-test is significant at the 5 % level and 1 % level, respectively.

and the three-day event window for indirect rivals.[32] The acquirer returns are significant in the two-week event window for the parametric tests and in the one-week event window for the Patell-test at the 10 % level. The abnormal return is -0.95 % in the [-5;+5] event window and -0.58 % in the [-2;+2] window.

Table 3.4.2: CAARs to Direct Rivals, Indirect Rivals and Acquirers for Unrelated Transactions

	(1) CAAR	(2) Patell-test	(3) BMP-test	(4) Sign-test	(5) Corrado-test	(6) Positive	(7) Sample
Panel A: Direct Rivals							
[-5;+5]	-0.10%	-1.66 *	-1.65 *	0.18	-0.50	49%	4,260
[-2;+2]	-0.17%	-3.42 ***	-3.32 ***	-1.04	-2.09 **	48%	4,260
[-1;+1]	-0.08%	-2.89 ***	-2.76 ***	-1.26	-1.44	48%	4,260
Panel B: Indirect Rivals							
[-5;+5]	-0.18%	-1.36	-1.29	0.39	-0.76	49%	710
[-2;+2]	-0.30%	-2.38 **	-2.17 **	-0.89	-2.62 ***	46%	710
[-1;+1]	-0.21%	-1.87 *	-1.79 *	-1.27	-1.93 *	46%	710
Panel C: Acquirers							
[-5;+5]	-0.95%	-1.81 *	-1.70 *	-1.13	-1.51	43%	142
[-2;+2]	-0.58%	-1.77 *	-1.58	-0.96	-1.02	44%	142
[-1;+1]	-0.25%	-0.95	-0.90	0.05	0.17	48%	142

Table 3.4.2 presents the abnormal share price reaction of direct rivals (panel A), indirect rivals (panel B) and acquirers (panel C) for digital technology giants' unrelated transactions in different event windows. Column (1) displays the cumulative average abnormal return, column (2)-(5) the test statistics, column (6) the share of transactions with a positive abnormal return and column (7) the sample size per analysis. Statistical significance at 1 %, 5 % and 10 % levels is indicated with ***, ** and *, respectively.

Other studies show different results for competitors. Gaur et al. (2013) find significant positive acquirer rival returns in the two-week event window of 0.29 % for a sample of Chinese transactions. Kohers and Kohers (2004) present a significant target rival two-day abnormal return of 1.41 % for high-technology transactions. In contrast, Jope et al. (2010) analyze transactions in the technology, media and telecommunication industry and find an insignificant negative return to acquirer rivals in the two-week event window, but a significant negative return of -0.58 % to industry-wide rivals. Akdoğu (2009) focuses on rival returns in the telecommunication industry and presents a significant positive acquirer rival return of 0.26 % for related transactions in the [-1;0] event window, while unrelated transactions lead to a significant negative return of -0.55 %. Thus, the insubstan-

---

32 The [-1;+1] event window is also significant for the Corrado-test for indirect rivals at the 10 % level.

tial effect on related transactions does not concur with other literature on the high technology industry and on rival effects. In contrast, the results for unrelated transactions might indicate the presence of negative signals and a corresponding anticipated reaction of rivals. It appears that shareholders react sensitively to negative acquirer returns to digital technology giants, and likewise expect value dilution for other companies in the market as well as for other giants, even though the economic level of the rival effects is quite low. For direct rivals, the M&A activity can transmit a negative signal to competitors in the same submarket, while for indirect rivals two main explanations seem possible. On the one hand, the indirect rivals' shareholders might fear the increasing influence on their firms' own businesses. A more diversified digital technology giant can strengthening its socio-technical ecosystem and position across submarkets (Dolata, 2018). This can affect the indirect rivals' submarkets. On the other hand, the on average value diluting unrelated transactions might be interpreted as a signal of limited growth across the digital technology industry. An alternative explanation for both rival sets is an overlap of different reactions and theories, thus supporting the Efficiency Hypothesis as well as the Signaling Hypothesis. Both effects can exist, but the magnitude might differ between the transaction types. It should be emphasized that the direct rivals can assume different roles. While the indirect rivals are only buyer-side competitors of the acquiring digital technology giant, the direct rivals can be buyer-side rivals as well as target-side rivals.

The drivers of the rival effects are analyzed in a multivariate regression setup, with the outcome presented in table 3.4.3. Column (1) contains the results for direct rivals and column (2) for indirect rivals. The analysis is conducted for the total transaction sample, related transactions and unrelated transactions. In all regressions, the influence of the cumulative abnormal return to the acquirer is striking. *Acquirer CAR* is highly significant at the 1 % significance level across the different samples, with an increase in the digital giants' abnormal return by 1 percentage point leading to a 0.1 percentage points higher rival return to direct rivals and a 0.2 percentage points increase to indirect rivals. The effect on direct rivals concurs with the study of Akdoğu (2009) who presents a similar number. The results provide support for signaling effects in terms of the Growth Probability Hypothesis as rival return is positively related to acquirer return for both deal types. The positive effect for on average value creating related transactions contradicts the expectations of the Efficiency Hypothesis. This needs to be further analyzed in the next subsections.

Table 3.4.3: Multivariate Regression Analysis of Direct Rivals and Indirect Rivals – Total and by Relatedness

	(1) Direct Rivals			(2) Indirect Rivals		
	Total	Related	Unrelated	Total	Related	Unrelated
Relatedness	0.000			-0.001		
	(-0.16)			(-0.42)		
Industry Concentration	0.000	-0.014	0.004	0.001	0.084	-0.005
	(0.00)	(-0.24)	(0.14)	(0.04)	(1.00)	(-0.15)
Acquirer CAR	0.088 ***	0.066 ***	0.114 ***	0.191 ***	0.208 ***	0.174 ***
	(6.09)	(4.00)	(4.18)	(6.48)	(5.29)	(3.83)
Acquirer Tobin's Q	-0.001	0.001	-0.002	0.000	0.001	-0.004 *
	(-1.19)	(1.55)	(-1.04)	(-0.27)	(0.81)	(-1.68)
Acquirer Profitability	0.018	-0.094 **	0.094	-0.023	0.015	-0.116
	(0.56)	(-2.42)	(1.38)	(-0.39)	(0.17)	(-1.20)
Acquirer Sales Growth	0.013 *	0.003	0.012	-0.010	-0.007	-0.014
	(1.87)	(0.29)	(0.86)	(-0.71)	(-0.36)	(-0.59)
Rival Firm Size	0.000	0.001	-0.001	-0.002	-0.001	-0.002
	(-0.38)	(0.72)	(-0.73)	(-1.12)	(-0.49)	(-1.05)
Rival Tobin's Q	0.000	0.000	0.000	-0.001 **	-0.001	-0.002 **
	(-0.77)	(-0.48)	(-0.29)	(-2.40)	(-1.25)	(-2.32)
Rival Leverage	-0.005	-0.006	-0.001			
	(-1.02)	(-1.14)	(-0.13)			
Rival Free Cash Flow	-0.010	0.002	-0.016			
	(-0.79)	(0.13)	(-0.80)			
Rival Sales Growth	0.002	-0.002	0.005			
	(0.69)	(-0.40)	(1.05)			
Rival Target Relatedness				0.003	0.001	0.006
				(1.15)	(0.30)	(1.31)
Controls						
Domestic Deal	-0.001	-0.002	0.001	0.003	0.008 **	-0.006
	(-0.40)	(-1.39)	(0.26)	(1.37)	(2.51)	(-1.56)
Public Target	-0.005	-0.009 *	0.003	-0.021 ***	-0.016 *	-0.024 **
	(-1.23)	(-1.89)	(0.39)	(-3.03)	(-1.73)	(-2.49)
High Year	0.002	-0.001	0.003	-0.003	-0.003	0.000
	(1.13)	(-0.42)	(1.18)	(-1.18)	(-0.75)	(-0.01)
Low Year	0.002	0.005 **	0.004	-0.002	-0.003	0.003
	(1.00)	(2.16)	(0.83)	(-0.49)	(-0.57)	(0.46)
Acquirer Alphabet	0.003	-0.003	0.007	0.000	0.005	0.003
	(0.97)	(-0.74)	(1.02)	(0.08)	(0.64)	(0.28)
Acquirer Free Cash Flow	0.034	0.158 ***	-0.124	-0.067	-0.085	0.076
	(0.76)	(3.16)	(-1.24)	(-0.71)	(-0.67)	(0.51)
Acquirer Leverage	0.030	0.028	0.011	-0.042	0.012	-0.059
	(1.59)	(1.38)	(0.32)	(-1.57)	(0.30)	(-1.34)
Acquirer Firm Size	0.002	-0.001	0.002	0.002	0.006	0.001
	(1.03)	(-0.32)	(0.58)	(0.70)	(1.36)	(0.18)
Acquirer Experience	0.000	0.000 **	0.000	0.000	0.000	0.000
	(0.02)	(2.56)	(-0.62)	(-1.13)	(-1.06)	(-1.54)
Constant	-0.043	-0.008	-0.026	0.018	-0.094	0.083
	(-1.20)	(-0.18)	(-0.43)	(0.32)	(-1.08)	(0.90)
Sample Size	11,190	6,930	4,260	1,865	1,155	710
Adjusted R²	0.01	0.01	0.01	0.05	0.04	0.06

Table 3.4.3 presents the impact of value drivers on the rivals' abnormal share price reaction to digital technology giants' transactions of the total sample (Total) and grouped by relatedness (Related, Unrelated). The dependent variable is the CAR to the direct rivals (1) or indirect rivals (2) over the main [-5;+5] event window. *Relatedness* is equal to 1 if the acquirer and target share the same 3-digit SIC code and 0 otherwise. *Industry Concentration* is the sales-based Herfindahl Index per 3-digit SIC code submarket. *Acquirer CAR* is defined as the CAR to the acquirer over the main two-week event window. *Rival Target Relatedness* is equal to 1 if the rival and target share the same 3-digit SIC code and 0 otherwise. *Domestic Deal* is equal to 1 if the acquirer and target are located in the same country and 0 otherwise. *Public Target* is equal

to 1 if the target is public and 0 otherwise. *High Year* is equal to 1 if the transaction is announced in 2014, 2015 or 2016 and 0 otherwise. *Low Year* is equal to 1 if the transaction is announced in 2008, 2009 or 2012 and 0 otherwise. *Acquirer Alphabet* is equal to 1 if the acquirer is Alphabet and 0 otherwise. *Acquirer Experience* is defined as number of completed acquisitions until the analyzed transaction. Please refer to the caption of table 3.3.2 for all other variables. Significance is based on robust Huber-White standard errors and t-statistics are shown in parentheses. Statistical significance at 1 %, 5 % and 10 % levels is indicated with ***, ** and *, respectively.

In contrast, no other variable is significant across both rival sets. The low variety between related and unrelated deals in the event study is supported, as *Relatedness* shows no significance and the results of the two transaction subsamples show no substantial differences for direct as well as indirect rivals. This concurs with Song and Walkling (2000) and Gaur et al. (2013) who observe an insignificant effect of relatedness for target-side and buyer-side rivals, respectively. However, a significant positive effect of relatedness can be found in other empirical studies for both rival types (e.g., Akdoğu, 2009; Kohers and Kohers, 2004). Even though relatedness has a significant positive influence on acquirers in the digital technology industry, this effect is not transmitted to competitors. In terms of the Efficiency Hypothesis, this type of competitive advantage appears to be not relevant for the direct and indirect rival sets. Only the variable *Acquirer Profitability* is significant negative for related transactions at the 5 % significance level for direct rivals, and provides some evidence for the Efficiency Hypothesis. However, *Acquirer Sales Growth* has a significant positive impact for the total sample and thus contradicts the theory.

Similarly, the results of the regressions contradict the Market Concentration Hypothesis, with the rivals experiencing no benefits from industry consolidation. For direct rivals, this study also tests rival characteristics that can indicate a more attractive target. These variables are insignificant for related as well as unrelated acquisitions, and the results provide no support for the Acquisition Probability Hypothesis. Finally, for indirect rivals the impact of *Public Target* shows an interesting effect. The acquisition of a publicly listed company has an economically and statistically strong negative effect. The indirect rival return is on average across all transactions -2.1 % lower if a digital technology giant buys a public target. This also holds true for direct rivals for related transactions, but the impact is only -0.9 %. Another variable that needs to be discussed is *Acquirer Alphabet*. The influence of Alphabet as acquirer is insignificant across the regressions, despite the large share of transactions.

In total, the results of this subsection provide some support for the Growth Probability Hypothesis for direct and indirect rivals, with Hypotheses H6 and H7 supported by the strong effect of *Acquirer CAR*. However, the results require further analysis of the implications of the acquirer return if they are to support hypothesis H1c and H2b. Some weak evidence exists for the Efficiency Hypothesis for direct rivals, but hypothesis H1a as well as H2a are neither supported nor rejected. The results do not provide any support for the Acquisition Probability Hypothesis, and hypothesis H1b as well as H5 are not supported.

3.4.2 Supplemental Analysis of Direct Rivals

The event study shows no significant impact for digital giants' related transactions and a low impact for unrelated deals on both competitor groups. This can be driven by an overlap of different effects or simply by non-existing rival effects. However, the multivariate regressions show a strong impact of acquirer return on the two rival sets and support signaling effects and imitation of the acquirer's activity as reaction of the rivals. This subsection analyzes the abnormal returns to direct rivals in more detail, and divides the transaction sample by acquirer return. Table 3.4.4 presents the results of the event study grouped by the effect on the acquirer as well as by relatedness (panel A-D), panel E tests for the difference in the two-week event window between the transaction groups. A transaction is described as positive or value creating if the acquirer experiences a positive abnormal return and as negative or value diluting if the acquirer experiences a negative abnormal return over the [-5;+5] event window.

The analysis shows significant negative reactions of direct rivals to transactions that are value diluting for the buying digital technology giant, regardless of whether the target is related to the core business of the giant or not (panel C, panel D). In contrast, the rivals only show significant positive reactions to value creating acquisitions in some event windows (panel A, panel B). The CAAR in the two-week event window is -0.32 % for negative related and -0.46 % for negative unrelated deals, while positive related deals lead to an abnormal return of 0.14 % and positive unrelated deals to an abnormal return of 0.38 %. The reaction to negative deals is significant at the 1 % level for the parametric tests and the reaction to positive deals at the 10 % level. Additionally, the Sign-test for negative unrelated transactions is significant at the 10 % level and for positive unrelated transactions at the 5 % level. Across the event windows, the reaction to value diluting as well as unrelated acquisitions is economically stronger than the reaction to value creating and related deals. Panel E shows that the difference between positive and negative deals is significant at the 1 % level for both types of transactions. The two differences between related and unrelated transactions are not significant. It provides further support for signaling effects and not for relatedness effects, even for direct rivals. The event study returns are slightly different in Gaur et al. (2013), but the magnitude is comparable. The study presents significant positive one-week event windows for value creating related and unrelated deals of 0.46 % and 0.61 %, respectively. The value diluting related transactions in the study lead to an abnormal return of -0.33 % and unrelated deals to an abnormal return of -0.31 %.

Table 3.4.4: *CAARs to Direct Rivals Grouped by Acquirer Return and by Relatedness*

	(1) CAAR	(2) Patell-test	(3) BMP-test	(4) Sign-test	(5) Corrado-test	(6) Positive	(7) Sample
Panel A: Positive Related Transactions							
[-5;+5]	0.14%	1.65 *	1.69 *	1.62	1.17	50%	3,840
[-2;+2]	0.08%	1.94 *	1.93 *	2.04 **	1.62	51%	3,840
[-1;+1]	-0.01%	0.40	0.40	1.59	0.48	50%	3,840
Panel B: Positive Unrelated Transactions							
[-5;+5]	0.38%	1.65 *	1.71 *	2.42 **	0.61	52%	1,830
[-2;+2]	0.25%	1.32	1.34	2.89 ***	0.54	52%	1,830
[-1;+1]	0.11%	0.82	0.82	1.21	0.59	50%	1,830
Panel C: Negative Related Transactions							
[-5;+5]	-0.32%	-2.93 ***	-2.90 ***	-0.47	-1.10	49%	3,090
[-2;+2]	-0.29%	-4.00 ***	-3.80 ***	-1.98 **	-2.14 **	47%	3,090
[-1;+1]	-0.15%	-2.30 **	-2.15 **	-0.43	-0.65	49%	3,090
Panel D: Negative Unrelated Transactions							
[-5;+5]	-0.46%	-3.63 ***	-3.50 ***	-1.86 *	-1.16	47%	2,430
[-2;+2]	-0.48%	-5.67 ***	-5.36 ***	-3.89 ***	-3.10 ***	45%	2,430
[-1;+1]	-0.22%	-4.55 ***	-4.20 ***	-2.71 ***	-2.33 **	46%	2,430

	(1) Δ CAAR	(2) t-test	(3) U test
Panel E: [-5;+5] Event Window - Difference (Panel / Panel)			
(A / B)	-0.24%	-1.43	-0.39
(C / D)	0.14%	0.72	1.30
(A / C)	0.46%	3.60 ***	3.29 ***
(B / D)	0.84%	3.31 ***	3.49 ***

Table 3.4.4 presents the abnormal share price reaction of direct rivals for digital technology giants' positive related transactions (panel A), positive unrelated transactions (panel B), negative related transactions (panel C), negative unrelated transactions (panel D) and the test for difference between the different panels (panel E). Column (1) displays the cumulative average abnormal return, column (2)-(5) the test statistics, column (6) the share of transactions with a positive abnormal return and column (7) the sample size per analysis. Statistical significance at 1 %, 5 % and 10 % levels is indicated with ***, ** and *, respectively.

Overall, the results are in line with the Growth Probability Hypothesis. It seems that digital technology giants' M&A activity transmits signals to direct rivals. Shareholders appear to expect these firms, which operate in the same industry as the acquirer, to mimic the competitive behavior and project similar returns. A value creating transaction supports the growth expectations while a value diluting deal sends a negative signal. The lower significance for value creating transactions might be explained with mixed effects. For positive related deals, influences of the Efficiency Hypothesis as discussed in the previous subsection can have a negative effect. For positive unrelated transactions, the potential explanation is more complex. If a digital technology giant diversifies into another industry despite value dilution, this can signal limited further growth in the main industry and transmits a negative signal to direct rivals. A positive acquisition of an unrelated company can be a sign of limited growth in the firm's own industry, but can also be the consequence of an attractive opportunity for the buyer (Gaur et al., 2013). Shareholders might expect rivals to take similar opportunities.

The drivers of the rival effects on direct competitors are further analyzed in multivariate regressions, and the results are presented in table 3.4.5. Column (1) shows the basic regression model that has been used for the total sample in table 3.4.3, but the acquisitions are grouped by the effect on the acquirer. Column (2) contains the three regressions with interaction variables on the total transaction sample. Model I contains the main regression, model II shows the regression without rival characteristics that indicate takeover probability and model III differs from model I by using the adjusted version of industry concentration. The results of the regression models concur with the previous analyses and further support the Growth Probability Hypothesis. The coefficient of the variable *Acquirer CAR* is positive significant at the 1 % level for value creating and diluting transactions by the digital giants. The negative signal is stronger than the positive, but a decrease or increase in acquirer return by 1 percentage point leads to a 0.1 percentage points lower or higher abnormal return, respectively, for the direct rival. The same is true for the two-day event window in the study by Akdoğu (2009). In the study, an increase in positive acquirer return by 1 percentage point has an impact of 0.01 percentage points, while the impact of negative acquirer return is larger with 0.03 percentage points. The effect of the model in column (1) is also observed in the three extended models with interaction variables. However, the impact of *Acquirer CAR* does not statistically differ between positive and negative signals since the coefficient of the interaction variable of acquirer return with positive deal dummy (*PD * Acquirer CAR*) is not significant across the models.

Table 3.4.5: Multivariate Regression Analysis of Direct Rivals – by Acquirer Return and with Interaction Variables

	(1) By Acquirer Return		(2) Total with Interaction Variables		
	Positive	Negative	I	II	III
Relatedness	-0.004 *	0.002	0.000	-0.001	0.000
	(-1.72)	(0.68)	(-0.26)	(-0.31)	(-0.17)
Industry Concentration	-0.078 ***	0.076 **	0.003	0.001	
	(-2.65)	(2.23)	(0.13)	(0.03)	
Industry Concentration, Adj.					0.018
					(0.37)
Positive Deal			-0.001	-0.001	-0.001
			(-0.57)	(-0.58)	(-0.56)
Acquirer CAR	0.067 ***	0.123 ***	0.122 ***	0.122 ***	0.122 ***
	(2.85)	(3.08)	(3.20)	(3.20)	(3.22)
PD * Acquirer CAR			-0.061	-0.061	-0.062
			(-1.37)	(-1.37)	(-1.37)
Acquirer Tobin's Q	0.003 ***	-0.005 ***	-0.005 ***	-0.005 ***	-0.005 ***
	(3.15)	(-3.68)	(-3.66)	(-3.67)	(-3.81)
PD * Acquirer Tobin's Q			0.006 ***	0.006 ***	0.006 ***
			(4.57)	(4.55)	(4.66)
Acquirer Profitability	-0.100 **	0.115 **	0.033	0.035	0.033
	(-2.54)	(2.29)	(0.99)	(1.03)	(1.00)
PD * Acquirer Profitability			-0.061 ***	-0.061 ***	-0.062 ***
			(-2.82)	(-2.79)	(-2.82)
Acquirer Sales Growth	-0.003	0.029 **	0.025 **	0.025 **	0.025 **
	(-0.27)	(2.21)	(2.40)	(2.42)	(2.46)
PD * Acquirer Sales Growth			-0.022 **	-0.022 **	-0.022 **
			(-2.00)	(-1.99)	(-2.00)
Rival Firm Size	-0.001	0.000	0.000	-0.001	0.000
	(-1.19)	(0.25)	(-0.56)	(-0.92)	(-0.47)
Rival Tobin's Q	-0.001	0.000	0.000	0.000	0.000
	(-0.99)	(-0.20)	(-0.74)	(-0.80)	(-0.72)
Rival Leverage	-0.013 **	0.001	-0.006		-0.005
	(-2.11)	(0.13)	(-1.04)		(-1.02)
Rival Free Cash Flow	-0.008	-0.012	-0.011		-0.010
	(-0.52)	(-0.68)	(-0.87)		(-0.85)
Rival Sales Growth	0.004	0.001	0.003		0.003
	(1.00)	(0.19)	(0.77)		(0.76)
Controls					
Domestic Deal	-0.001	0.001	0.000	0.000	0.000
	(-0.60)	(0.68)	(-0.24)	(-0.24)	(-0.26)
Public Target	0.002	-0.010 *	-0.006	-0.006	-0.006
	(0.28)	(-1.74)	(-1.39)	(-1.39)	(-1.40)
High Year	-0.001	0.002	0.002	0.002	0.002
	(-0.42)	(0.80)	(1.17)	(1.16)	(1.18)
Low Year	0.009 ***	-0.004	0.003	0.003	0.003
	(2.88)	(-1.16)	(1.24)	(1.28)	(1.21)
Acquirer Alphabet	-0.001	0.006	0.003	0.003	0.003
	(-0.30)	(1.31)	(0.91)	(0.92)	(0.89)
Acquirer Free Cash Flow	0.123 **	-0.028	0.047	0.045	0.045
	(2.26)	(-0.38)	(1.03)	(1.00)	(1.03)
Acquirer Leverage	0.041 *	0.013	0.023	0.024	0.022
	(1.75)	(0.46)	(1.24)	(1.28)	(1.24)
Acquirer Firm Size	0.004	0.000	0.002	0.002	0.002
	(1.51)	(0.10)	(0.98)	(1.05)	(1.10)
Acquirer Experience	0.000	0.000	0.000	0.000	0.000
	(0.30)	(-0.57)	(-0.74)	(-0.80)	(-0.61)
Constant	-0.047	-0.024	-0.034	-0.033	-0.039
	(-0.97)	(-0.42)	(-0.88)	(-0.86)	(-1.11)
Sample Size	5,670	5,520	11,190	11,190	11,190
Adjusted R²	0.01	0.01	0.01	0.01	0.01

Table 3.4.5 presents the impact of value drivers on the rivals' abnormal share price reaction to digital technology giants' transactions grouped by acquirer return (1), positive and negative, and of the total sample (2) with interaction variables in different regression setups (model I-

III). The dependent variable is the CAR to the direct rivals over the main [-5;+5] event window. *Industry Concentration, Adj.* is the sales-based Herfindahl Index per 3-digit SIC code submarket without the influence of the digital technology giants. *Positive Deal (PD)* is equal to 1 if the acquisition has a positive abnormal return to the acquirer and 0 otherwise. Please refer to the captions of table 3.3.2 and table 3.4.3 for all other variables. Significance is based on robust Huber-White standard errors and t-statistics are shown in parentheses. Statistical significance at 1 %, 5 % and 10 % levels is indicated with ***, ** and *, respectively.

In contrast to acquirer return, the impact of other acquirer characteristics can have a differing impact on rival effects depending on the value creation for the acquirer. In the interaction models, the variable *Acquirer Tobin's Q* has a negative coefficient and the interaction variable *PD * Acquirer Tobin's Q* a positive effect on the direct rival return. Both variables are statistically highly significant at the 1 % level. The Tobin's Q ratio of a digital giant amplifies the effect of a value creating and diluting acquisition. The regressions of column (1) show a similar effect. An increase in the Tobin's Q ratio of the digital giant by 0.1 leads to a lower abnormal rival return of -0.05 percentage points for negative deals and an increase of 0.01 – 0.03 percentage points for positive deals. Following the interpretation by Lang et al. (1991), high levels of Tobin's Q can indicate high growth opportunities for the company. Thus, positive (negative) deals in the light of further growth potential transmit stronger positive (negative) signals to competitors. The expected growth can signal higher potential for rivals to react and to conduct similar deals. This provides further support for the Growth Probability Hypothesis and imitation as anticipated reaction of rivals.

The Efficiency Hypothesis is tested by *Acquirer CAR* as well as the variables *Acquirer Profitability, Acquirer Sales Growth, Relatedness* and *Industry Concentration*. *Acquirer CAR* provides no strong indication for a competitive advantage of the buying company. If the digital giant creates value, the rivals can also benefit and if the giant dilutes value, *Acquirer CAR* leads only to a proportional decrease in rivals' abnormal returns. However, the results of *Acquirer Profitability* and *Acquirer Sales Growth* for value creating transactions are as expected by the Efficiency Hypothesis. The interaction variables with *Positive Deal* show significant negative impacts on rival return for the total sample. The effect is significant at the 1 % level for *Acquirer Profitability* and at the 5 % significance level for *Acquirer Sales Growth*. The coefficient of *Acquirer Profitability* is also significant negative for value creating transactions at the 5 % significance level. An increase in relative operating income before depreciation by 1 percentage point decreases the rival abnormal return by 0.1 percentage points. The effect of sales growth is not significant for value creating transactions, only the difference between positive and negative deals. Thus, both variables indicate that successful digital giants decrease the benefits of rivals in value creating transactions. Additionally, *Relatedness* has a significant negative effect for value creating transactions. A positive acquisition of a related target by a digital giant decreases the rival return by 0.4 percentage points. In contrast to this, the effects differ for value diluting transactions. The digital giant's previous success in terms of *Acquirer Profitability* and *Acquirer Sales Growth* has a significant positive impact on rival return. An increase in relative operating income before depreciation by 1 percentage point raises the abnormal return by 0.1 % percentage points and a similar percentage growth in sales lifts the return by 0.03 percentage points. The variable *Acquirer Sales Growth* is also significant across the interaction models at the 5 % significance level. Thus, the expected effect of the Efficiency Hypothesis is inversed for negative deals. If a more efficient giant dilutes value with an acquisition, the competitors will suffer less. This can be linked to a potential competitive disadvantage of the transaction for the acquirer, which dampens the negative signals to the rivals. This concurs with reversed network effects of online platforms as discussed by Evans (2017). The variables thus provide support for the Efficiency Hypothesis in value creating transactions and show that efficiency effects can be inversed in value diluting transactions.

Model II and III test two different versions of industry concentration. The normal *Industry Concentration* variable is negative significant at the 1 % level for value creating transactions, but positive significant at the 5 % level for value diluting transactions. Thus, higher concentrated submarkets lead to a lower abnormal rival return for positive deals and higher abnormal return for negative deals. It provides no support for the Market Concentration Hypothesis as the theory expects a positive effect for related transactions. However, the analysis grouped by relatedness in subsection 3.4.1 shows no significance, and the effect for positive deals in this analysis is contrary. The results also do not support the explanation by Kohers and Kohers (2004) that mergers and acquisitions activity in concentrated industries "may send stronger signals to industry rival firms" (p. 528) as the effect opposes the influence of acquirer value creation. The digital technology giants' transactions transmit positive or negative signals to direct competitors, with positive or negative rival effects weaker in higher concentrated submarkets. This can be driven by the effect that rivals have a less (more) favorable position in a highly concentrated industry after a positive (negative) transaction by the dominating player in the submarket.[33] The results of model III support this explanation, as the influence of market concentration is dependent on the digital giants. The regression analyzes the variable *Industry Concentration, Adj.*, which measures the effect of market concentration without the digital giants, and shows no significant influence.[34] Direct rivals benefit if a strongly dominating digital giant dilutes value, and suffer if the giant creates value. This provides support for the Efficiency Hypothesis for positive deals and an inversed effect for negative deals. Overall, the influence of efficiency effects in combination with signaling effects indicate that shareholders expect direct rivals to imitate the acquirer's behavior to a limited extent and to partially react to the signals.

While the rival reactions seem to be driven by information effects in terms of the Growth Probability Hypothesis, there is no evidence for the second Signaling Hypothesis that is discussed in the literature, the Acquisition Probability Hypothesis. This study analyzes the hypothesis by using several rival characteristics that are linked to takeover probability in previous studies (e.g., Akhigbe and Madura, 1999; Kohers and Kohers, 2004; Song and Walkling, 2000). However, the variables including *Rival Firm Size*, *Rival Tobin's Q*, *Rival Leverage*, *Rival Free Cash Flow* and *Rival Sales Growth* show no significance across the models. Only *Rival Leverage* has a significant negative effect at the 5 % level for positive deals, but the effect contradicts the expectations for this type of Signaling Hypothesis. Another perspective for leverage is presented by Chen et al. (2007). They reveal that rivals with higher leverage show lower returns as they are limited in their ability to react properly to a competitive action. Thus, there is no evidence for value cocreation as reaction and the Acquisition Probability Hypothesis, but further support for the Efficiency Hypothesis in combination with the Growth Probability Hypothesis.

To conclude, the results provide further support that direct rivals receive positive or negative signals from digital technology giants' M&A activity and shareholders expect them to react to accordingly. The acquirer and rivals experience negative abnormal returns at the same time and also positive abnormal returns at the same time; hypothesis H1c is supported. Both

---

33 This is based on the argument by Gaur et al. (2013) that related transactions can lead to a less favorable position for rivals in highly concentrated industries.

34 The multivariate regression grouped by acquirer return is also repeated with *Industry Concentration, Adj.* instead of *Industry Concentration* and shows no significance for negative deals but a weakly significant negative effect for positive deals (not reported). It supports the results of the interaction model.

returns are closely linked to each other as acquirer return has a significant positive influence on direct rivals across the different specifications. Thus, the study can support hypothesis H6. Additionally, the relation is amplified by *Acquirer Tobin's Q* as accelerator, and hypothesis H8 is partly supported. However, the observed effect of digital giants' transactions is ambiguous. Direct rivals seem to receive signals that are dampened by another effect. The results show that expected acquirer efficiency increase can have an impact on the rivals. Successful acquirers decrease the rival return for positive deals and lower the negative effect for value diluting deals, with hypothesis H3 thus partly supported. No negative abnormal return is observed for value creating deals and the value drivers have inversed effects for value diluting transactions; hypothesis H1a is not supported. This study finds no indication of target-side effects in terms of the Acquisitions Probability Hypothesis or other buyer-side effects such as the Market Concentration Hypothesis; hypothesis H1b as well as H5 are not supported. Overall, it appears that direct rival return is influenced by signaling as well as (inversed) efficiency effects.

3.4.3 Supplemental Analysis of Indirect Rivals

The results of the supplemental event study (panel A-D) and the test for difference (panel E) for indirect rivals are presented in table 3.4.6. The group of indirect rivals experience significant positive returns for value creating acquisitions by digital giants and significant negative returns for value diluting deals, regardless of relatedness. The abnormal return in the two related [-5;+5] event windows is 0.73 % and -0.92 % and significant at the 1 % significance level across the test statistics.[35] The unrelated two-week event windows have an abnormal return of 0.60 % and -0.76 % and are both significant for all test statistics at least at 10 % significance level.[36] The difference between positive related and positive unrelated transactions is not significant. The difference between negative transactions is also insignificant. However, the CAARs for value creating and value diluting transactions are significantly different at the 1 % level across both deal types and test statistics. In addition, indirect rivals have a stronger negative or positive reaction than direct rivals for all four deal types. Subsection 3.4.4 tests whether the difference is statistically significant. These results

---

35 The Sign-test for negative related transactions is significant at the 5 % level.
36 The Sign-test for negative unrelated transactions is insignificant.

provide support that the M&A activity transmits positive or negative signals to indirect rivals to which shareholders expect them to react.

Table 3.4.6: CAARs to Indirect Rivals Grouped by Acquirer Return and by Relatedness

	(1) CAAR	(2) Patell-test	(3) BMP-test	(4) Sign-test	(5) Corrado-test	(6) Positive	(7) Sample
Panel A: Positive Related Transactions							
[-5;+5]	0.73%	4.24 ***	4.35 ***	3.29 ***	3.50 ***	55%	640
[-2;+2]	0.18%	1.42	1.44	2.26 **	1.69 *	53%	640
[-1;+1]	0.06%	0.58	0.57	0.76	1.25	50%	640
Panel B: Positive Unrelated Transactions							
[-5;+5]	0.60%	2.20 **	2.06 **	1.94 *	1.98 **	53%	305
[-2;+2]	0.39%	2.40 **	2.18 **	2.28 **	1.39	54%	305
[-1;+1]	0.24%	1.88 *	1.92 *	1.02	1.24	51%	305
Panel C: Negative Related Transactions							
[-5;+5]	-0.92%	-4.27 ***	-4.20 ***	-2.46 **	-2.93 ***	43%	515
[-2;+2]	-0.39%	-2.93 ***	-2.94 ***	-0.34	-1.65 *	47%	515
[-1;+1]	-0.12%	-0.96	-0.97	0.63	-0.27	50%	515
Panel D: Negative Unrelated Transactions							
[-5;+5]	-0.76%	-3.70 ***	-3.62 ***	-1.17	-2.56 **	45%	405
[-2;+2]	-0.82%	-5.23 ***	-4.93 ***	-3.16 ***	-4.36 ***	40%	405
[-1;+1]	-0.55%	-4.11 ***	-3.84 ***	-2.56 **	-3.40 ***	42%	405

	(1) Δ CAAR	(2) t-test	(3) U test
Panel E: [-5;+5] Event Window - Difference (Panel / Panel)			
(A / B)	0.13%	0.39	0.59
(C / D)	-0.16%	-0.47	-0.80
(A / C)	1.65%	5.66 ***	5.78 ***
(B / D)	1.36%	3.62 ***	3.37 ***

Table 3.4.6 presents the abnormal share price reaction of indirect rivals for digital technology giants' positive related transactions (panel A), positive unrelated transactions (panel B), negative related transactions (panel C), negative unrelated transactions (panel D) and the test for difference between the different panels (panel E). Column (1) displays the cumulative average abnormal return, column (2)-(5) the test statistics, column (6) the share of transactions with a positive abnormal return and column (7) the sample size per analysis. Statistical significance at 1 %, 5 % and 10 % levels is indicated with ***, ** and *, respectively.

The results of the multivariate regressions for indirect rivals are shown in table 3.4.7. The regressions of column (1) and (2) are close to the models for direct rivals. The only difference is regarding the analyzed rival characteristics, as in table 3.4.3. The driver analysis provides further support for the Growth Probability Hypothesis. *Acquirer CAR* has a significant positive impact across all models. The economic effect for value diluting deals is similar to that of the direct rivals, while for value creating deals an increase in *Acquirer CAR* by 1 percentage point leads to an increase in rival abnormal return by 0.2 percentage points, which is significant at the 1 % level. In the other regression models, the coefficient is significant at the 5 % level. However, the difference between both deal types is not statistically significant with regard to the interaction variable (*PD * Acquirer CAR*). In line with the results for direct rivals, *Acquirer Tobin's Q* shows an amplifying effect on the results of indirect rivals. *Acquirer Tobin's Q* and the interaction variable (*PD * Acquirer Tobin's Q*) are significant in all three extended regression models. However, the effect is less significant for indirect rivals; *Acquirer Tobin's Q* is significant at the 10 % level and the interaction variable at the 5 % level across the models while the variable is not significant in the divided transaction sample.[37] For value diluting acquisitions, an increase in the digital giant's Tobin's Q ratio by 0.1 leads to a lower abnormal rival return of -0.04 percentage points and for value creating transactions to a higher return of 0.01 – 0.02 percentage points. Thus, acquirer growth potential also fosters information signals and indicates opportunities to react for indirect rivals. In addition, the rival growth potential with regard to *Rival Tobin's Q* accelerates the negative impact for value diluting deals. The significant negative influence of *Rival Tobin's Q* on the abnormal return to indirect rivals supports the transmission of a warning signal and the Growth Probability Hypothesis. An increase in *Rival Tobin's Q* by 0.1 points leads to a decrease in the rival return by -0.02 percentage points. This concurs with the argumentation by Kohers and Kohers (2004). They suppose that high growth opportunities can drive higher valuation uncertainty, so that transactions in industries with high Tobin's Q can be expected to have a higher information effect. The effect for value creating transactions is insignificant.

The reaction of indirect rivals to value creating acquisitions is less ambiguous than the reaction of direct rivals. On the one hand, the value creating transactions by digital technology giants have a positive influence on the indirect rival. The significant effect of *Acquirer CAR* and *Acquirer Tobin's Q* supports the Signaling Hypothesis and imitation of the competitive action as response. On the other hand, the magnitude of the cumulative average abnormal rival return for value creating transactions is lower than for value diluting transactions. Further factors might limit the reaction of indirect rivals, and the influence offset some parts of the positive signaling effects and strengthen the effect for value diluting transactions. This effect could be the outcome of a stronger competitive advantage for the acquirer. The variable *Rival Target Relatedness* is a dummy variable to test if rival and target share the same submarket and can indicate a missed opportunity for

---

37 *Acquirer Tobin's Q* is significant at the 5 % level for model II, which excludes the variable *Rival Target Relatedness*.

Table 3.4.7: Multivariate Regression Analysis of Indirect Rivals – by Acquirer Return and with Interaction Variables

	(1) By Acquirer Return		(2) Total with Interaction Variables		
	Positive	Negative	I	II	III
Relatedness	0.002	-0.004	-0.001	0.000	-0.002
	(0.46)	(-0.90)	(-0.24)	(-0.05)	(-0.75)
Industry Concentration	-0.009	0.036	0.001	0.006	
	(-0.21)	(0.83)	(0.04)	(0.23)	
Industry Concentration, Adj.					-0.062
					(-1.14)
Positive Deal			0.003	0.003	0.003
			(0.92)	(0.87)	(0.90)
Acquirer CAR	0.187 ***	0.145 **	0.146 **	0.148 **	0.147 **
	(3.27)	(2.25)	(2.31)	(2.34)	(2.32)
PD * Acquirer CAR			0.040	0.039	0.040
			(0.47)	(0.46)	(0.46)
Acquirer Tobin's Q	0.002	-0.003	-0.004 *	-0.004 **	-0.004 *
	(1.20)	(-1.36)	(-1.90)	(-1.97)	(-1.84)
PD * Acquirer Tobin's Q			0.006 **	0.006 **	0.005 **
			(2.54)	(2.55)	(2.45)
Acquirer Profitability	-0.088	0.048	-0.041	-0.038	-0.056
	(-1.11)	(0.51)	(-0.64)	(-0.60)	(-0.97)
PD * Acquirer Profitability			0.018	0.018	0.022
			(0.45)	(0.45)	(0.57)
Acquirer Sales Growth	-0.034 *	0.022	0.007	0.008	0.003
	(-1.87)	(0.93)	(0.41)	(0.47)	(0.15)
PD * Acquirer Sales Growth			-0.032 *	-0.032 *	-0.031 *
			(-1.75)	(-1.74)	(-1.73)
Rival Firm Size	0.000	-0.003	-0.002	-0.001	-0.002
	(-0.02)	(-1.49)	(-1.17)	(-1.00)	(-1.24)
Rival Tobin's Q	0.000	-0.002 ***	-0.001 **	-0.001 **	-0.001 **
	(-0.27)	(-2.92)	(-2.26)	(-2.03)	(-2.22)
Rival Target Relatedness	-0.002	0.007 *	0.003		0.003
	(-0.47)	(1.87)	(1.17)		(1.29)
Controls					
Domestic Deal	0.004	0.004	0.003	0.003	0.003
	(1.31)	(0.88)	(1.31)	(1.35)	(1.35)
Public Target	0.009	-0.033 ***	-0.019 ***	-0.019 ***	-0.019 ***
	(1.06)	(-3.87)	(-2.86)	(-2.93)	(-2.87)
High Year	-0.006	-0.004	-0.003	-0.003	-0.003
	(-1.47)	(-0.97)	(-1.18)	(-1.09)	(-1.31)
Low Year	0.010 *	-0.014 **	-0.001	-0.001	0.000
	(1.65)	(-2.40)	(-0.19)	(-0.17)	(0.04)
Acquirer Alphabet	-0.001	0.006	0.003	0.003	0.003
	(-0.30)	(1.31)	(0.91)	(0.92)	(0.89)
Acquirer Free Cash Flow	-0.042	-0.065	-0.056	-0.056	-0.039
	(-0.34)	(-0.45)	(-0.59)	(-0.59)	(-0.43)
Acquirer Leverage	-0.079 **	-0.006	-0.039	-0.038	-0.038
	(-2.13)	(-0.14)	(-1.43)	(-1.39)	(-1.39)
Acquirer Firm Size	0.006	-0.002	0.002	0.002	0.002
	(1.60)	(-0.57)	(0.85)	(0.86)	(0.71)
Acquirer Experience	0.000	0.000	0.000	0.000	0.000 *
	(-1.24)	(0.13)	(-1.37)	(-1.41)	(-1.68)
Constant	-0.085	0.109	0.000	-0.006	0.012
	(-1.12)	(1.34)	(-0.01)	(-0.11)	(0.22)
Sample Size	945	920	1,865	1,865	1,865
Adjusted R^2	0.02	0.04	0.05	0.05	0.05

Table 3.4.7 presents the impact of value drivers on the rivals' abnormal share price reaction to digital technology giants' transactions grouped by acquirer return (1), positive and negative, and of the total sample (2) with interaction variables in different regression setups (model I-III). The dependent variable is the CAR to the indirect rivals over the main [-5;+5] event window. *Industry Concentration, Adj.* is the sales-based Herfindahl Index per 3-digit SIC code sub-

market without the influence of the digital technology giants. *Positive Deal (PD)* is equal to 1 if the acquisition has a positive abnormal return to the acquirer and 0 otherwise. Please refer to the captions of table 3.3.2 and table 3.4.3 for all other variables. Significance is based on robust Huber-White standard errors and t-statistics are shown in parentheses. Statistical significance at 1 %, 5 % and 10 % levels is indicated with ***, ** and *, respectively.

the rival. The variable shows a significant positive effect of 0.7 % for negative transactions. Thus, if a digital technology giant dilutes value by buying a target that is close to the competitor, the rival effects are less negative. This can indicate an inversed efficiency effect for value diluting transactions. However, the variable is insignificant for positive transactions and provides no evidence of efficiency effects for these deals. In line with this, the variables *Relatedness* and *Acquirer Profitability* show no significant effect for both deal types. Only *Acquirer Sales Growth* is significant negative for value creating transactions at the 10 % level. An increase in the growth rate of net sales by 1 percentage point lowers the rival return by -0.03 percentage points. Similarly, the interaction variable *PD * Acquirer Sales Growth* is significant negative at the 10 % level. Successful digital giants in terms of past sales growth decrease the positive rival effects of value creating deals. However, no other support exists for the Efficiency Hypothesis for indirect rivals.

Finally, the impact of two control variables further supports the Growth Probability Hypothesis. The variable *Low Year* is positive significant at the 10 % level for positive deals and negative significant at the 5 % level for negative deals. Thus, low transaction activity of digital giants increases the indirect rival abnormal return by 1 percentage point for value creating transactions, and decreases it by 1.4 percentage points for value diluting transactions. In a year with a lower number of transactions, the rivals' shareholders have less reference events to evaluate digital technology companies and put more emphasize on the few remaining transactions by digital giants. The variable is also positive significant for the group of direct rivals, but only for value creating deals. The variable Public Target has a strong negative impact for negative transactions and no effect for positive deals. The value diluting acquisition of a public company by a digital giant leads to a significant -3.3 percentage points lower abnormal return to indirect rivals and -1 percentage point lower return to direct rivals. Public companies are better covered, and a value diluting acquisition of such a target can send a strong information signal to competitors. It can accelerate negative rival effects, thus supporting the Signaling Hypothesis.

In total, the results support the Growth Probability Hypothesis. Indirect rivals evidently receive signals from digital giants' transactions, with their shareholders expecting them to react to these signals. The indirect rivals experience highly significant positive abnormal returns for digital giants' value creating deals and negative returns for value diluting transactions, regardless of relatedness; hypothesis H2b is supported. A strong relation between acquirer return and rival return can be observed in both deal types and provide further support for signaling effects. Thus, hypothesis H7 is supported. Some of the other information variables amplify signaling effects and hypothesis H9 is partly supported. In contrast to this, there is only low evidence for the potential impact of a competitive advantage in terms of *Acquirer Sales Growth*, and only for value creating deals; hypothesis H4 is not supported. Finally, value creating deals lead to positive rival effects and the multivariate regression results provide no substantial support for the Efficiency Hypothesis in value diluting deals. Therefore, hypothesis H2a is not supported. It appears that indirect rivals' returns are only influenced by signals and that shareholders expect these rivals to imitate the acquirer's competitive move and thus experience similar effects.

3.4.4 Comparison of Direct and Indirect Rival Effects

The previous subsections indicate that direct and indirect rivals react to digital technology giants' M&A activity. It seems that digital giants as main players in the industry transmit signals to competitors and shareholders expect the rivals to imitate the competitive action. The anticipated reaction and the induced rival effects are dependent on the digital giants' own value creation or dilution. Figure 3.4.1 shows the reaction of both rival sets to positive and negative transactions over the two-week event window. Indirect rivals react more strongly than direct rivals to all transaction types. This can be driven by a weaker anticipated reaction and the influence of efficiency increase as a counteracting effect on direct competitors. The study finds no evidence for impact of collusion or acquisition probability on both rival sets.

Figure 3.4.1: CAARs to Direct and Indirect Rivals for Digital Giants' Positive and Negative Transactions

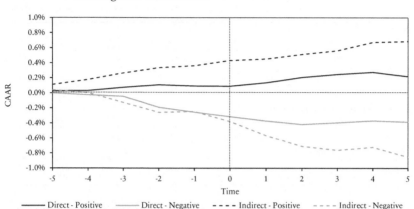

Figure 3.4.1 presents the abnormal share price reaction of direct and indirect rivals for digital technology giants' value creating and value diluting transactions over the two-week main event window.

Table 3.4.8 shows the rival returns for positive (panel A) and negative transactions (panel B) for direct rivals as well as for positive (panel C) and negative transactions (panel D) for indirect rivals. The test for the difference between positive and negative deals by both rival groups is also included (panel E). The reaction to both transaction types of digital giants is statistically different between both rival groups. The difference between both groups is -0.47 % for positive and 0.47 % for negative deals. The difference for value creating deals is significant at the 5 % level for the two-sided t-test and at the 1 % level for the Mann-Whitney U test. The significance for value diluting deals is slightly lower at the 10 % and 5 % levels, respectively. The reaction of indirect rivals thus is significantly more positive or negative for both types of transactions. This can be linked to a stronger impact of efficiency increase on direct rivals for positive transactions and an inversed effect for negative deals. Shareholders might anticipate a weaker reaction and a disadvantage (advantage) for direct rivals from a stronger (weaker) digital giant.

Table 3.4.8: CAARs to Direct and Indirect Rivals Grouped by Acquirer Return

	(1) CAAR	(2) Patell-test	(3) BMP-test	(4) Sign-test	(5) Corrado-test	(6) Positive	(7) Sample
Panel A: Direct Rivals - Positive Transactions							
[-5;+5]	0.22%	2.30 **	2.36 **	2.71 ***	1.38	51%	5,670
[-2;+2]	0.13%	2.35 **	2.35 **	3.32 ***	1.72 *	51%	5,670
[-1;+1]	0.03%	0.79	0.79	1.99 **	0.77	50%	5,670
Panel B: Direct Rivals - Negative Transactions							
[-5;+5]	-0.38%	-4.60 ***	-4.50 ***	-1.59	-1.61	48%	5,520
[-2;+2]	-0.37%	-6.76 ***	-6.40 ***	-4.06 ***	-3.66 ***	46%	5,520
[-1;+1]	-0.18%	-4.74 ***	-4.41 ***	-2.12 **	-2.01 **	48%	5,520
Panel C: Indirect Rivals - Positive Transactions							
[-5;+5]	0.69%	4.74 ***	4.71 ***	3.81 ***	3.75 ***	54%	945
[-2;+2]	0.25%	2.53 **	2.47 **	3.16 ***	2.03 **	53%	945
[-1;+1]	0.11%	1.55	1.55	1.20	1.61	50%	945
Panel D: Indirect Rivals - Negative Transactions							
[-5;+5]	-0.85%	-5.65 ***	-5.55 ***	-2.61 ***	-3.76 ***	44%	920
[-2;+2]	-0.58%	-5.66 ***	-5.51 ***	-2.35 **	-4.00 ***	44%	920
[-1;+1]	-0.31%	-3.45 ***	-3.35 ***	-1.23	-2.38 **	46%	920

	(1) Δ CAAR	(2) t-test	(3) U test
Panel E: [-5;+5] Event Window - Difference (Direct Rivals / Indirect Rivals)			
Positive	-0.47%	-2.33 **	-3.00 ***
Negative	0.47%	1.87 *	2.57 **

Table 3.4.8 presents the abnormal share price reaction of direct and indirect rivals for digital technology giants' positive transactions (panel A, C) and negative transactions (panel B, D) and the test for difference between both rival groups (panel E). Column (1) displays the cumulative average abnormal return, column (2)-(5) the test statistics, column (6) the share of transactions with a positive abnormal return and column (7) the sample size per analysis. Statistical significance at 1 %, 5 % and 10 % levels is indicated with ***, ** and *, respectively.

3.4.5 Robustness Analysis

The event study and multivariate regressions are repeated with focused direct and extended indirect rival sets in order to validate whether the results are driven by the rival selection approach. The results are presented in table 3.4.9 and table 3.4.10.

Table 3.4.9 shows the event windows grouped by direct rivals (panel A and B) and indirect rivals (panel C and D) and acquirer return (positive or negative). The event study presents comparable rival effects on direct and indirect competitors across the deal types. The abnormal returns show a slightly lower significance across the event windows for direct rivals which can be linked to the smaller number of observations. The significance is similar for indirect rivals. The results strengthen the validity of the previous event study analysis.

Table 3.4.9: Robustness Analysis with Alternative Samples – CAARs

	(1) CAAR	(2) Patell-test	(3) BMP-test	(4) Sign-test	(5) Corrado-test	(6) Positive	(7) Sample
Panel A: Direct Rivals - Positive Transactions							
[-5;+5]	0.21%	1.35	1.35	1.67 *	1.81 *	51%	1,890
[-2;+2]	0.11%	1.39	1.39	2.82 ***	1.52	52%	1,890
[-1;+1]	0.02%	0.51	0.51	1.58	1.02	51%	1,890
Panel B: Direct Rivals - Negative Transactions							
[-5;+5]	-0.48%	-3.38 ***	-3.22 ***	-2.07 **	-2.14 **	46%	1,840
[-2;+2]	-0.32%	-4.20 ***	-3.90 ***	-2.91 ***	-3.20 ***	45%	1,840
[-1;+1]	-0.14%	-2.73 ***	-2.51 **	-1.97 **	-1.66 *	47%	1,840
Panel C: Indirect Rivals - Positive Transactions							
[-5;+5]	0.77%	5.74 ***	5.66 ***	4.55 ***	4.08 ***	55%	1,140
[-2;+2]	0.27%	3.12 ***	3.04 ***	3.72 ***	2.30 **	54%	1,140
[-1;+1]	0.10%	1.61	1.61	1.59	1.57	50%	1,140
Panel D: Indirect Rivals - Negative Transactions							
[-5;+5]	-0.81%	-5.75 ***	-5.64 ***	-2.67 ***	-3.95 ***	44%	1,094
[-2;+2]	-0.50%	-5.30 ***	-4.98 ***	-2.31 **	-3.80 ***	45%	1,094
[-1;+1]	-0.28%	-3.40 ***	-3.23 ***	-1.52	-2.41 **	46%	1,094

Table 3.4.9 presents the abnormal share price reaction of direct and indirect rivals for digital technology giants' positive transactions (panel A, C) and negative transactions (panel B, D). The robustness analysis applies for direct rivals a focused sample that consists of 10 rivals with the closest market capitalization per 3-digit SIC code group and for indirect rivals an extended sample that includes all digital giants and Softbank Group if data is available. Column (1) displays the cumulative average abnormal return, column (2)-(5) the test statistics, column (6) the share of transactions with a positive abnormal return and column (7) the sample size per analysis. Statistical significance at 1 %, 5 % and 10 % levels is indicated with ***, ** and *, respectively.

Table 3.4.10 contains the multivariate regression models with the robustness rival sets. The study repeats the main regression model as in table 3.4.3 and the regressions grouped by positive and negative transactions by digital giants as in table 3.4.5 (direct rivals) and table 3.4.7 (indirect rivals). Column I shows the results for the direct rivals and column II for the indirect rivals. Overall, the results for direct rivals are comparable between the robustness and main rival set. Across both transaction types, the *Acquirer CAR* has a higher economic impact for the robustness rival set, but lower statistical significance. Additionally, the *Industry Concentration* is less significant for value diluting deals and has no significance for positive deals. For positive deals, *Relatedness* and *Rival Leverage* are not significant and *Acquirer Tobin's Q* is less significant. However, the economic impact of *Acquirer Profitability* is higher. For negative deals, the variables *Acquirer Profitability* and *Acquirer Sales Growth* are not significant in the robustness analysis, but the economic impact is similar.

Table 3.4.10: Robustness Analysis with Alternative Samples – Multivariate Regression Analysis

	(1) Direct Rivals			(2) Indirect Rivals		
	Total	Positive	Negative	Total	Positive	Negative
Relatedness	0.002	0.001	0.003	-0.001	0.003	-0.004
	(0.85)	(0.18)	(0.75)	(-0.40)	(0.62)	(-0.98)
Industry Concentration	0.025	-0.059	0.107 *	0.002	0.006	0.023
	(0.73)	(-1.26)	(1.95)	(0.09)	(0.16)	(0.57)
Acquirer CAR	0.112 ***	0.106 **	0.140 **	0.198 ***	0.180 ***	0.181 ***
	(4.36)	(2.38)	(2.09)	(6.73)	(2.99)	(2.91)
Acquirer Tobin's Q	-0.001	0.003 *	-0.006 ***	0.000	0.001	-0.002
	(-0.92)	(1.89)	(-2.67)	(-0.35)	(0.60)	(-0.97)
Acquirer Profitability	0.000	-0.150 **	0.120	-0.020	-0.063	0.033
	(0.01)	(-2.24)	(1.41)	(-0.36)	(-0.86)	(0.36)
Acquirer Sales Growth	0.003	-0.019	0.027	-0.004	-0.022	0.023
	(0.25)	(-1.21)	(1.22)	(-0.27)	(-1.09)	(0.97)
Rival Firm Size	0.001	-0.001	0.002	-0.002	0.000	-0.003
	(0.89)	(-0.39)	(1.44)	(-1.17)	(-0.11)	(-1.50)
Rival Tobin's Q	-0.001	-0.001	-0.001	-0.001 **	0.000	-0.002 ***
	(-0.87)	(-0.63)	(-0.57)	(-2.34)	(0.02)	(-3.12)
Rival Leverage	-0.010	-0.008	-0.011			
	(-0.92)	(-0.59)	(-0.68)			
Rival Free Cash Flow	-0.022	-0.021	-0.020			
	(-1.20)	(-1.06)	(-0.74)			
Rival Sales Growth	0.006	0.004	0.006			
	(1.27)	(0.75)	(0.95)			
Rival Target Relatedness				0.004 *	0.001	0.008 **
				(1.92)	(0.17)	(2.28)
Controls						
Domestic Deal	0.001	0.000	0.004	0.004 *	0.006 **	0.003
	(0.64)	(0.16)	(1.08)	(1.76)	(1.97)	(0.67)
Public Target	-0.009	0.001	-0.016 *	-0.016 **	0.013	-0.030 ***
	(-1.37)	(0.08)	(-1.78)	(-2.49)	(1.57)	(-3.74)
High Year	0.002	-0.004	0.004	-0.002	-0.003	-0.003
	(0.59)	(-1.00)	(1.07)	(-0.75)	(-0.82)	(-0.85)
Low Year	0.005	0.009 *	0.002	-0.003	0.009	-0.014 **
	(1.38)	(1.77)	(0.37)	(-0.63)	(1.41)	(-2.54)
Acquirer Alphabet	0.002	-0.009	0.010	-0.001	-0.006	0.002
	(0.30)	(-1.37)	(1.31)	(-0.15)	(-0.83)	(0.26)
Acquirer Free Cash Flow	0.023	0.132	-0.039	-0.045	-0.038	-0.031
	(0.30)	(1.42)	(-0.30)	(-0.50)	(-0.32)	(-0.22)
Acquirer Leverage	0.021	0.009	0.026	-0.033	-0.070 **	0.003
	(0.76)	(0.24)	(0.62)	(-1.29)	(-2.01)	(0.07)
Acquirer Firm Size	0.002	0.005	-0.001	0.003	0.009 **	-0.003
	(0.72)	(1.27)	(-0.12)	(1.17)	(2.19)	(-0.78)
Acquirer Experience	0.000	0.000	0.000	0.000	0.000 *	0.000
	(-0.91)	(-0.31)	(-0.99)	(-1.21)	(-1.76)	(0.40)
Constant	-0.060	-0.066	-0.038	-0.011	-0.140 *	0.119
	(-1.06)	(-0.85)	(-0.42)	(-0.21)	(-1.76)	(1.53)
Sample Size	3,730	1,890	1,840	2,234	1,140	1,094
Adjusted R²	0.01	0.00	0.02	0.04	0.01	0.04

Table 3.4.10 presents the impact of value drivers on the rivals' abnormal share price reaction to digital technology giants' transactions of the total sample (total) and grouped by acquirer return (positive, negative). The dependent variable is the CAR to the direct rivals (1) or indirect rivals (2) over the main [-5;+5] event window. The robustness analysis applies for direct rivals a focused sample that consists of 10 rivals with the closest market capitalization per 3-digit SIC code group and for indirect rivals an extended sample that includes all digital giants and Softbank Group if data is available. Please refer to the captions of table 3.3.2 and table 3.4.3 for the variables. Significance is based on robust Huber-White standard errors and t-

statistics are shown in parentheses. Statistical significance at 1 %, 5 % and 10 % levels is indicated with ***, ** and *, respectively.

The extended indirect rival set presents results similar to those of the main rival set. There are some differences for value creating transactions by digital technology giants. The variable *Acquirer Sales Growth* that might indicate a slight impact of increased efficiency in the main analysis shows no significant reaction in this robustness regression. This emphasizes the low relevance of the Efficiency Hypothesis for indirect rivals and provides further support that the theory can be disregarded for these rivals. For value diluting transactions, the results present slightly higher significance of *Acquirer CAR* and *Rival Target Relatedness* as well as an increased economic impact.

To conclude, the results concur with the previous subsections and validate that the research methodology is robust relative to alternative specifications. For direct rivals, the results also indicate mixed effects. For indirect rivals, it supports the inference that the Efficiency Hypothesis is not relevant, but the Growth Probability Hypothesis is relevant.

3.5 Discussion

This contribution investigates how competitive actions in terms of M&A activity influence the industry and analyzes rival effects of digital technology giants' transactions. Three immediate anticipated reactions and responding rival stories are therefore examined, 373 deals between 2008 and 2017 selected and two distinct rival sets defined. The event study and multivariate regression models are based on 11,190 event-rival observations for direct rivals and 1,865 event-rival observations for indirect rivals. The results show a significant positive effect for value creating transactions and a significant negative effect for value diluting transactions by digital technology giants on both rival sets. These signaling effects are significantly stronger for indirect rivals, while direct rivals are also influenced by variables that can be linked to efficiency increases. The study finds no evidence for an impact of collusion.

The results present three key insights on digital technology giants' rival effects. First, the study sheds light on the implications of platform boundary expansion and competitive dynamics in the digital technology industry. In general, the digital giants' M&A activity has neither a positive nor a negative effect on rivals, but transmits positive or negative signals depending on the acquirer value creation. The external investment does not necessarily lead to increased market power or efficiency for the acquirer but reduces uncertainty in the industry and acts as guidance for the reaction of rivals. The value effect is driven by acquirer and deal characteristics while the attributes of the specific rivals are less important. Research needs to focus not only on the negative externalities of competitive actions but must also shed further light on positive attention spillover and signaling effects. Platform boundary expansion can increase the value for platform owners and users, but also for other firms across platform ecosystems. In practice, antitrust actions and general restrictions on M&A activity can foster information asymmetry in the market and decrease value for all actors and responders. Thus, competition authorities should incorporate the positive effect of signaling and carefully consider the implications on other firms in the platform ecosystems and across platforms. Managers in the digital technology industry need to closely monitor external investments and modifications of platform boundaries by digital giants and evaluate the influence on their own business while planning potential competitive reactions.

Second, the varying results for direct and indirect rivals emphasize the importance of understanding the implications of competitive actions for different responders in a market. On the one hand, rival sets need to be defined carefully and targeted for a specific purpose. This study focuses on less covered buyer-side rivals. However, results for buyer-side rivals are not necessarily relevant for target-side rivals and vice versa. On the other hand, the digital giants transmit signals across submarkets to other giants. Strong rival effects despite different core businesses show that traditional market definition is not applicable in the digital technology industry. Digital giants compete not only in product or service rivalry, but also for customer attention, new opportunities and capabilities across markets and platforms. Network effects also drive this type of competition; however, "winner-take-all" outcomes do not exist in platform rivalry and the rivals compete on a level playing field in this competitive context. It highlights the need for researchers and regulators to differentiate between different rival groups and adapt market definitions to changing competitive dynamics and boundary expansion of platforms. For example, efficiency increase shows no direct impact on the indirect rival set, while classifying competitors to different rival groups poses another challenge. In practice, managers and owners need to observe the full competitive landscape and frequently challenge their own market definition and the presumed competitive context.

Third, the study discusses different potential rival reactions and finds evidence for an overlap of two effects for direct rivals. Digital technology giants dominate the competition in their own submarkets. Platform expansion by external investments seems to strengthen the digital giants' competitive advantages and counteract signaling effects on direct rivals. Efficiency increase can have a negative effect for value creating transactions but also an inversed positive effect for value diluting transactions, which can be linked to reversed network effects. Thus, direct rivals benefit (suffer) less from a stronger giant that conducts a positive (negative) acquisition. In contrast, the value creation potential of relatedness is not passed positively or negatively to direct or indirect rivals. Research needs not only to analyze different types of competitive actions but also the broad range of potential reactions of rivals. Usually, the main competitive reaction can be identified over longer time periods, but a mix of various reactions and rival effects are common at first. The proper measurement and segregation of different reactions and effects is key to future research. In practice, antitrust regulators should incorporate the influence of efficiency increases in the assessment of M&A activity in the digital technology industry, but carefully trade off the competitive advantage against the information power of a transaction. Digital giants should emphasize the positive signaling effects on the industry in antitrust investigations, while industry rivals need to focus attention on both effects.

The research has some limitations. First, the study analyzes the response of rivals by measuring the rival return for digital technology giants' transactions. Usually, the competitors do not directly react during the event period so that the share price can only reflect the behavior that is immediately anticipated by shareholders. However, the anticipated and realized response can vary and lead to different rival value effects. Future research should therefore investigate the long-term reaction and identify other proxies to measure the response of rivals. Second, the transaction and rival samples might have a selection bias, and limited data on digital giants' transactions reduces the range of analyzed variables. Information is gathered from different sources to ensure a strong database and derive a large deal sample. However, data on non-disclosed transactions and analysis of non-listed rivals would further strengthen the validity of the results. The study shows that further research is required. The high relevance of the Growth Probability Hypothesis in the digital technology industry, which is less covered in literature than other hypotheses, emphasizes that further work in this vein is worthwhile. In addition, the dynamic environment of the digital technology industry with evolving platform boundaries and frequently changing rivals, suggests the need for further research on digital technology giants and competitive dynamics. Future studies should discuss the market definition in dynamic competitive contexts and the impact on other research in this field of study.

4 Dotcom Giants vs. Digital Giants: Two Groups of Leading Digital Technology Players from Different Periods

4.1 Introduction

The dotcom boom of the late 1990s represented the first rise of the digital technology industry and ended with a crash in the beginning of the 2000s. It was not only reflected in rapidly growing share prices but also in increasing news coverage and media hype of internet stocks (Bhattacharya et al., 2009; Shiller, 2015). A group of leading digital technology-focused companies, the dotcom giants (Cisco, IBM, Intel, Microsoft, Nokia and Oracle), grew strongly and became part of the largest companies worldwide. A new phase of technology companies' dominance was expected, and even dotcom company name changes created firm value (Cooper et al., 2001). However, only two years after Microsoft had become the largest company worldwide in 1998, the dotcom bubble burst and the value of technology firms plummeted.[38] Research indicates that the forming of a bubble and overpricing was not obvious at that time, and markets had issues with estimating the true value of firms in a new industry with new market dynamics (e.g., Battalio and Schultz, 2006). Shortly after the burst, Howcroft (2001) expected large media conglomerates to dominate the industry in the future. However, both groups, the dotcom giants and global media companies, were overtaken by a different cohort of companies, most of which had been newly founded during the dotcom boom and were already creating value at that time (Cusumano et al., 2019; Hendershott, 2004).

A decade and a few years later, the seven digital technology giants dominate the list of the largest publicly traded companies worldwide. At the same time, a new group of digital-focused start-ups is emerging and competing with the digital giants in several submarkets, for example Spotify in the music streaming market. Additionally, companies such as the office-sharing start-up WeWork are positioning themselves as digital technology-focused firms to increase firm valuation (Govindarajan and Srivastava,

---

38 Market capitalization data is based on the Datastream database. See Griffin et al. (2011) for an analysis of trading patterns of different market participants during the development and burst of the dotcom bubble.

2019). Markets took a more critical view of WeWork, with investors revaluing the company one month after it had filed for initial public offering, leading to a value dilution of $40 billion and a deferral of the IPO (Laughlin, 2019). Some observers already argue that similarities exist between both digital technology booms, that of the late 1990s and that of the late 2010s (e.g., Driebusch and Farrell, 2018; Mackintosh, 2019; Ryan, 2019). These developments raise the question, "What can digital technology giants learn from dotcom giants, and do capital markets exaggerate digital technology giants' value creation?"

The group of dotcom giants consists of the six largest companies in the digital technology industry during the dotcom boom. In the last two decades, the digital technology industry has experienced significant changes, including a shift from product to platform business, rise of new competitors and rapid technological transition (e.g., Chambers, 2015; Cusumano et al., 2019; Evans and Schmalensee, 2016). The dotcom giants have decreased in relevance in the industry while new digital technology giants have moved into the spotlight. On the one hand, the digital giants have achieved a distinct financial strength and taken up a unique position in the industry (Dolata, 2018). In addition, these firms create value in mergers and acquisitions and transmit signals to rivals. On the other hand, the dotcom giants have undergone a transition process in face of the change, with varying impact on shareholder value. The group can be divided into growing dotcom giants (Cisco, Intel, Oracle) and shrinking dotcom giants (IBM, Nokia), while Microsoft occupies a special position as the only dotcom giant company that is also part of the group of digital technology giants. The specific situation of the dotcom giants has an impact on the shareholders' perspective on M&A activity (e.g., Chambers, 2015; Graebner et al., 2010). The digital technology industry strengthens larger players, and relatedness can have a positive effect due to complementarities and network effects (e.g., Crémer et al., 2019; Furman et al., 2019). In contrast, the industry transition can favor diversifying transactions to establish operations in new submarkets and integrate businesses across platforms (e.g., Bower, 2001; Rhéaume and Bhabra, 2008). The influence of liquidity can also have opposing effects on companies in the industry. On the one hand, high levels of available financial resources decrease control by capital markets and can lead to corporate governance issues (e.g., Jensen, 1986; Lang et al., 1991). On the other hand, they increase financial flexibility and can enable necessary investments (e.g., Chen et al., 2018; Denis and Sibilkov, 2010).

This study investigates the effects of dotcom giants' M&A activity by analyzing 365 transactions by the firms between 2008 and 2017. In addition, the study compares these acquisitions with the M&A activity of digital technology giants and analyzes rival effects of dotcom giants on digital technology giants and vice versa. The results indicate no relatedness effect for dotcom giants unlike for digital technology giants, but show that unrelated acquisitions lead to opposing effects. Growing dotcom giants experience negative abnormal returns and shrinking dotcom giants positive returns. Overall, the return differs between the two giant groups across both deal types, with shareholders expecting higher value creation in transactions by shrinking dotcom giants. Furthermore, liquidity has a positive effect for these firms, while the effect is insignificant for growing dotcom giants. Rival effects between dotcom giants and digital technology giants are ambiguous, and no main anticipated reaction can be identified. It exist some evidence for signaling effects and some evidence for efficiency increase effects.

The study makes three main contributions to the literature. First, it analyzes the effect of dotcom giants' M&A activity after the dotcom boom. While previous studies focus on transaction samples with specific acquirer characteristics (e.g., Moeller et al., 2004), target characteristics (e.g., Ransbotham and Mitra, 2010) or deal characteristics (e.g., Flanagan and O'Shaughnessy, 2003) at the time of the transaction, this study analyzes the transaction sample of dotcom giants after they have passed the dominant position in the industry. It analyzes the differing reactions of two subgroups, growing and shrinking dotcom giants, as well as the special role of Microsoft. The transformation process can drive the positive reaction of shrinking dotcom giants and the positive influence of liquidity on acquisitions by these firms. Prior literature emphasizes that economies of scale and "winner-take-all" outcomes foster the dominant position of large players (e.g., McIntyre and Chintakananda, 2014). However, analyzing the group of dotcom giants highlights that dominant companies are subject to several influences, and that the composition of a leading group can change (e.g., Evans and Schmalensee, 2002; Spulber and Yoo, 2015). Second, this research compares the M&A activity of dotcom giants with acquisitions by digital technology giants and shows that digital giants' effect on shareholder value is special, even in the digital technology industry. The market dynamics in the industry in terms of high economies of scale and scope and strong network effects indicate a positive effect of transactions, especially of related deals, on the shareholder value of acquirers (e.g., Furman et al., 2019; Gao and Iyer, 2006). However, the study shows that the significant positive effect of related deals, which is identified in the previous chapter, cannot be generalized. It emphasizes the unique role of digital technology giants which can be driven by the market dominance and strong platform ecosystems. Third, the group of digital technology giants has a dominant position in the digital technology industry in terms of their distinct financial strength including high levels of M&A activity and significant financial liquidity (Dolata, 2018). Literature discusses different structures of competitive dynamics (e.g., Akdoğu, 2009; Gaur et al., 2013), and the study in the preceding chapter shows significant signaling effects of digital technology giants on rivals. However, this study finds only weak rival effects between dotcom giants and digital technology giants. The increasing spread between both giant groups in terms of relative market valuation and media coverage can lower the linkage between both groups' value creation. Shareholders seem to separate the previous from the current giant group.

The remainder of this chapter is organized as follows. Section 4.2 reviews the group of dotcom giants and their M&A activity. Section 4.3 describes the data sample and the research methodology. Section 4.4 discusses the empirical results. The final section summarizes the findings and derives implications for future research.

4.2 Literature Review and Research Hypotheses

During the end of the 1990s and beginning of the 2000s, technology companies across the world experienced unprecedented growth, with their shares accounting for large parts of the trading volumes in the markets (Ofek and Richardson, 2003). In March 2000, the dotcom bubble burst and share prices of technology companies plummeted. In the aftermath, many young online companies without sustainable business models left the market (e.g., etoys, pets.com), while the market capitalization of most technology companies significantly decreased and subsequently recovered. Research suggests different explanations for the development of the bubble, including short-sale restrictions (Ofek and Richardson, 2003), investor irrationality (Cooper et al., 2001; Shiller, 2015), inexperience with new industry (Battalio and Schultz, 2006), professional investors not acting as a correcting force (Brunnenmeier and Nagel, 2004; Griffin et al., 2011) and other undetermined drivers (Bhattacharya et al., 2009).

4.2.1 The Group of Dotcom Giants

The dotcom boom was accompanied by the rise of a variety of large digital technology-focused companies. These dotcom giants became part of the largest publicly listed companies worldwide, with Microsoft even reaching the leading position in 1998.[39] This thesis defines dotcom giants as the largest digital technology-focused companies in terms of the market capitalization as of December 31, 2000 (see table 4.2.1). This date is slightly behind the peak of the dotcom boom, but the digital technology companies were in the spotlight of shareholders' attention and the media similar to that of the digital technology giants at the end of the 2010s. Three restriction apply. First, telecommunication providers are excluded from the group as these companies are subject to different influences, especially from a regulatory perspective (e.g., Akdoğu, 2009). Second, the focus is only on surviving firms to enable a comparison of the M&A activity with transactions by digital technology giants in the same time period. Third, this study applies a market capitalization threshold. The definition only includes companies with a market capitalization above $100 billion, because of the large difference in firm size between the dotcom giants above the threshold and the next largest player (difference of $60 billion). In total, the group of dotcom giants consists of six companies that operate in different and changing submarkets. The group contains the two vendors of enterprise software and hardware, IBM and Oracle, Microsoft as a vendor of consumer and business software and hardware, the two communication and network-focused companies, Cisco and Nokia, and Intel as a manufacturer of semiconductor chips. To some extent, these companies operate platform businesses which were part of their success story during the dotcom boom (Gawer and Cusumano, 2002, 2014).

The dotcom giants dominated the digital technology industry during the dotcom boom but experienced a decrease in market capitalization after the burst of the bubble, similar to the rest of the market. They have subsequently recovered, but the business development differs between the companies. An analysis of the value growth of the dotcom giants based on the market capitalization between the years 2008 and 2017, the same period for which the previous chapters analyze digital giants' M&A activity, reveals two main groups (see table 4.2.2). First, the growing dotcom giants that are increasing shareholder value (Cisco, Intel, Oracle) and second, the shrinking dotcom giants that are decreasing shareholder value (IBM,

---

39 Market capitalization data is based on the Datastream database.

Table 4.2.1: Largest Publicly Traded Companies Worldwide by Market Capitalization in 2000

Rank	Company	Founded	Headquarters	Market Capitalization
1	General Electric Co.	1889 *	United States	475,003
2	Exxon Mobil Corp.	1870 *	United States	302,211
3	Pfizer Inc.	1849	United States	290,216
4	Citigroup Inc.	1812 *	United States	275,673
5	**Cisco Systems Inc.**	**1984**	**United States**	**268,662**
6	Walmart Inc.	1945 *	United States	237,274
7	Vodafone Group PLC	1982 *	Great Britain	236,831
8	**Microsoft Corp.**	**1975**	**United States**	**231,290**
9	American International Group Inc.	1919 *	United States	228,227
10	Merck & Co Inc.	1891 *	United States	215,908
11	Royal Dutch Shell PLC	1890 *	Netherlands	212,920
12	**Nokia Oyj**	**1865 ***	**Finland**	**209,357**
13	**Intel Corp.**	**1968**	**United States**	**202,321**
14	BP PLC	1909 *	Great Britain	181,777
15	GlaxoSmithKline PLC	1873 *	Great Britain	177,627
16	NTT Docomo Inc.	1991	Japan	165,190
17	**Oracle Corp.**	**1977 ***	**United States**	**162,676**
18	AT&T Inc.	1885 *	United States	162,321
19	Coca-Cola Co.	1892	United States	151,112
20	**International Business Machines Corp.**	**1889 ***	**United States**	**150,241**

Table 4.2.1 presents the market capitalization per company of the largest publicly traded companies worldwide. Dotcom giants are marked bold. Market capitalization is measured in $ million as of December 31, 2000. * indicates that the predecessor was founded at this date.

Nokia). In addition, Microsoft has a special role since the firm is not only part of the group of dotcom giants but also part of the group of digital technology giants, and thus needs to be analyzed separately. The spread in value growth between both groups of dotcom giants might be driven by the developments in the digital technology industry and differing reactions between the companies in the years after the dotcom boom. The industry is facing significant changes. The prevalent business model is moving from product to platform, and the emergence of multi-sided platforms that are embedded in strong platform ecosystems is shifting the industry structure (Cusumano et al., 2019; Evans and Schmalensee, 2016). In addition, new digital-enabled companies including the digital technology giants are entering the markets and emerging from the dotcom bubble in a stronger position (Cusumano et al., 2019; Hendershott, 2004). Finally, the technological transformation with the shift to the cloud, mobility and the internet of things is challenging the dotcom giants and necessitating significant investments (Chambers, 2015; Metz, 2015).

Table 4.2.2: Market Capitalization and News Coverage of Dotcom Giants in 2007 and 2017

Company	Group	2007 Market Capitalization	2007 News Coverage	2017 Market Capitalization	2017 News Coverage
Cisco	Growing Dotcom Giant	164,232	223	189,341	68
IBM	Shrinking Dotcom Giant	149,744	269	142,035	105
Intel	Growing Dotcom Giant	155,881	419	216,029	192
Microsoft	Microsoft	333,054	1,022	659,906	461
Nokia	Shrinking Dotcom Giant	152,721	285	27,304	27
Oracle	Growing Dotcom Giant	115,984	186	195,720	89

Table 4.2.2 presents the market capitalization and news coverage per dotcom giant. Market capitalization is measured in $ million as of December 31, 2007 and December 31, 2017. News coverage is measured in number of articles that have been published in the printed version of Wall Street Journal and mention the company in the respective year.

4.2.2 Mergers and Acquisitions and Dotcom Giants

Literature describes three main market dynamics that influence the digital technology industry as discussed in the previous chapters. First, strong economies of scale and scope that favor larger companies and M&A activity in the market (e.g., Furman et al., 2019; Mchawrab, 2016). Second, strong network effects and complementarities that accelerate "winner-take-all" outcomes and strengthen the value of related acquisitions (e.g., Crémer et al., 2019; Gao and Iyer, 2006). Both dynamics decrease competition. Third, low market entry barriers due to direct user access and low switching costs that increase competition and limit the dominant position. In this context, unrelated acquisitions bear a higher inherent risk and opportunity costs (e.g., van Gorp and Batura, 2015; Wilcox et al., 2001). The three market dynamics have influence on both types of rivalry in the digital technology industry. The product and service rivalry experiences sequential "winner-take-all" outcomes with regard to Schumpeterian competition that a leading firm is replaced by a following dominant player, while "winner-take-all" outcomes do not exist in platform rivalry (Evans and Schmalensee, 2002; Haucap and Heimeshoff, 2014; Spulber and Yoo, 2015).

In addition, the market environment can affect mergers and acquisitions by dotcom giants similar to transactions by digital technology giants. However, the change in the digital technology industry seems to influence the group of dotcom giants more strongly than the emerging firms, despite the ability of the platform leaders to set the direction of innovation in the markets (Gawer and Cusumano, 2002). The "innovator's dilemma" is the term used to describe when a firm's success makes it more reluctant to adapt to change, with platform leadership hampering the evolution of a platform (Gawer and Cusumano, 2014). The dotcom firms as platform leaders in their submarkets face the challenge of a changing business environment, with a shift in the business model, new competitors and technological change. It forces the dotcom giants into a transition process. On the one hand, in face of technological change, companies can continue with current technology in a niche as a rational strategic decision (Adner and Snow, 2010). On the other hand, they can drive the change internally through research and development or externally through acquisitions (Chambers, 2015). Firms use M&A to add strategic resources, defy the competition and enable strategical renewal (Graebner et al., 2010). Platforms in the digital technology industry are not stable but evolve over time and create innovation through the recombination of digital and physical resources (Staykova and Damsgaard, 2017; Yoo et al., 2012; Yoo et al., 2010). This recombination activity in terms of mergers and acquisitions can create value for users and owners of the platform (Brousseau and Penard, 2007; Henfridsson et al., 2018; Sirmon et al., 2007).

4.2.3 Relatedness Effects and Dotcom Giants

Companies in the digital technology industry use acquisitions not only to strengthen the core business but also to integrate new business segments across platforms (van Gorp and Batura, 2015). They can acquire targets that are related to the core business or conduct unrelated transactions to diversify the business.

In the course of this, a distinction needs to be made between the two main groups, the growing and the shrinking dotcom giants. Growing dotcom giants succeeded in transforming their own business and in increasing shareholder value. They might benefit from complementarities and network effects in related transactions (Gao and Iyer, 2006). Bundles of products and services and the integration of operations and technologies can create value (Amit and Zott, 2001). The strong network effects favor "winner-take-all" outcomes and strengthen the dominant player (McIntyre and Chintakananda, 2014; van Gorp and Batura, 2015). However, the successful domination of a market is not guaranteed and depends on a distinct strategic position of a platform towards users and other entities (Cennamo and Santalo, 2013). Thus, shareholders might be appreciative if a successful dotcom giant follows a distinct strategy and further foster its core business by related transactions.

This effect can differ with shrinking giants. The success in a platform business depends not only on network effects and distinct strategy but also on entry barriers, including differentiation opportunities for competitors and the level of switching costs (Cusumano et al., 2019). Additionally, the dominance of the dotcom giants in their submarkets and focus on related transactions to increase user size might not directly reinforce network effects. The structure and conduct of a network also influences the user value of a network and, by extension, the owner value (Afuah, 2013). Shareholders might therefore critically value further investments into value diluting operations in a challenging business environment if a shrinking dotcom giant acquirer has no distinct strategy and focuses solely on expected network effects through an improved market position.

This study expects growing dotcom giants to create value in related transactions. Shrinking dotcom giants appear to benefit less in this type of deals. The study expects a significant difference in the value creation for both groups of dotcom giants.

Hypothesis 1. *Related transactions by growing dotcom giants result in positive abnormal returns to the acquirer. The abnormal return for related transactions by growing dotcom giants is different to the abnormal return for related transactions by shrinking dotcom giants.*

In unrelated transactions, companies are unable to profit from network effects and a dominant market position. However, the competition in the digital technology industry has increased in the last decade, and technological and market change are forcing dotcom giants to diversify their businesses and to enhance their platform ecosystems. The innovator's dilemma might decelerate the required process here and contribute to the decreasing value of shrinking dotcom giants (Gawer and Cusumano, 2014). For example in the late 2000s, Nokia was reluctant to adapt its mobile operating system Symbian, and the low level of complementarities decreased the attractiveness of the platform (Cusumano et al., 2019; Evans and Schmalensee, 2016). Similarly, IBM's products face strong challenges from changing technological requirements (Metz, 2015). In this situation, M&A can be an alternative to internal research and development and a strategy to establish operations in new submarkets in the digital technology industry (Bower, 2001). Shareholders might expect value creation in unrelated transactions by shrinking dotcom giants due to new business opportunities also strengthening the firm's own ecosystem and acting as a hedging strategy against technological uncertainty (Dolata, 2018; Rhéaume and Bhabra, 2008). In contrast, shareholders of growing dotcom giants are more likely to have no positive expectations of a business shift but instead critically value the higher uncertainty of unrelated deals and take opportunity costs into account (Wilcox et al., 2001).

This study thus expects that shrinking dotcom giants create value in unrelated transactions, while growing dotcom giants, similar to digital technology giants, experience a negative share price reaction.

Hypothesis 2. *Unrelated transactions by shrinking dotcom giants result in positive abnormal returns to the acquirer. The abnormal return for unrelated transactions by shrinking dotcom giants is different to the abnormal return for unrelated transactions by growing dotcom giants and to the abnormal return for unrelated transactions by digital technology giants.*

4.2.4 Liquidity Effects and Dotcom Giants

The previous chapters discuss financial strength as a distinct characteristic of the group of digital technology giants, as expressed in the form of high levels of liquidity. The results show free cash flow to have a significant negative influence on the abnormal return to the digital technology giants in related as well as unrelated acquisitions. This effect can evidence agency conflicts between management and owner and indicate managerial self-interest based on the free cash flow theory by Jensen (1986, 1988). It has been empirically tested in several studies (e.g., Lang et al., 1991; Schlingemann, 2004). The liquidity of the dotcom giants differs from digital technology giants, and the level of free cash flow varies within the group. The descriptive statistics for the different acquirer groups in table 4.3.2 show an average relative free cash flow of 11 % for shrinking dotcom giants, 13 % for growing dotcom giants and 13–14 % for digital technology giants. Thus, the liquidity of growing dotcom giants is close to the one of digital giants, but shrinking dotcom giants experience lower levels of free cash flow.

The relative level of liquidity can have an impact on the extent of corporate governance issues, and this study expects a similar effect of free cash flow for growing dotcom giants as for digital technology giants.

Hypothesis 3. *Free cash flow has a negative influence on the abnormal returns to growing dotcom giants.*

The transformation phase after the dotcom boom and higher required investments by shrinking dotcom giants can lower the level of liquidity and form the gap in relative free cash flow. However, the decreasing financial flexibility leads to stronger corporate control by capital markets. It can decrease the potential of transactions that are not in the interest of shareholders but are motived by managerial self-interest or other considerations. The negative effect of free cash flow can thus be less relevant for shrinking giants. In contrast with the agency costs of free cash flow as discussed by Jensen (1986, 1988), increasing levels of liquidity and cash saving can also have positive effects. Literature discusses precautionary motives of cash saving that reduce financial risk and act as investment buffer for periods of financial constraint (e.g., Bates et al., 2009; Denis and Sibilkov, 2010). Chen et al. (2018) analyze the effect of negative external shocks on financially constrained firms with regard to the impact of the dotcom bubble burst in 2000 and the global financial crisis in 2008. They argue that shareholders value the pre-saved cash as it allows these firms to conduct acquisitions and exploit investment opportunities during challenging phases. Taking this a step further, shrinking dotcom giants might experience increasing costs of external financing and be able to benefit from higher levels of free cash flow and cash savings. In line with this, a large share of investments in the digital technology industry is intangible. Debt financing is more challenging for this type of asset than for tangible assets since intangible capital cannot be used as collateral. Thus, higher liquidity can be seen as a competitive advantage (Furman et al., 2019).

Summing up, this study expects that free cash flow has a positive effect on the mergers and acquisitions by shrinking dotcom giants.

Hypothesis 4. *Free cash flow has a positive influence on the abnormal returns to shrinking dotcom giants.*

4.2.5 Rival Effects between Dotcom Giants and Digital Giants

M&A activity has a direct influence on acquirers and targets but also on competitors in the industry (Binder, 1998). Literature describes several possible rival reactions and rival effects theories, including Market Concentration Hypothesis (e.g., Eckbo, 1983), Efficiency Hypothesis (e.g., Akdoğu, 2009), Acquisition Probability Hypothesis (e.g., Song and Walkling, 2000) and Growth Probability Hypothesis (e.g., Gaur et al., 2013), as discussed in the previous study. The previous chapter shows strong signaling effects of digital technology giants' transactions within the group of digital giants and on other firms in the industry. Shareholders seem to expect rivals to react and mimic the competitive action of digital technology giants. The Growth Probability Hypothesis assumes that an acquisition of one player in the industry can transmit growth signals but also growth warnings to other companies in the market (Gaur et al., 2013). In line with this, the Future Acquirer Anticipation Hypothesis expects rivals to conduct future M&A and this reaction to be already anticipated at the time of the first acquisition (Cai et al., 2011). While the digital technology giants have had an outstanding position in the global economy in recent years, the dotcom giants had a strong position in the digital technology industry during the dotcom boom. Since these years, however, the firm value and financial strength of the dotcom giants has decreased in relative terms, and the group has passed the prominent position on to the group of digital technology giants. While the aggregated market capitalization of dotcom giants increased from 2007 to 2017 by 4 %, digital technology giants' value increased by 502 %.[40] In addition, news coverage on dotcom giants strongly decreased while increasing in the same period for digital giants (see table 4.2.2 and table 4.2.3). In total, it can be assumed that the decreased relevance of dotcom giants and increased size difference can lead to diminishing signaling effects of dotcom giants' M&A activity. The study expects no observable influence of the transactions on digital technology giants' value creation.

In contrast, digital technology giants have become the largest publicly traded companies in the world and have been dominating the digital technology industry in recent years. They are characterized by their distinct financial strength, large number of transactions and high level of financial flexibility (Dolata, 2018). The strong position increases the relevance of these firms for rivals in the industry. Dotcom giants' shareholders might monitor the value creation for digital giants closely and imitate the competitive moves accordingly. Additionally, some of the dotcom giants have been included in the direct and indirect rival sets of the previous chapter (IBM, Microsoft, Oracle) which are noting significant signaling effects.

---

40 Dotcom giants' value does not include Microsoft, while digital technology giants' value does not include Alibaba, Facebook and Microsoft.

Table 4.2.3: Market Capitalization and News Coverage of Digital Technology Giants in 2007 and 2017

		2007		2017	
Company	Group	Market Capitalization	News Coverage	Market Capitalization	News Coverage
Alibaba	Digital Technology Giant	n/a	32	441,620	256
Alphabet	Digital Technology Giant	215,958	996	729,457	1,294
Amazon	Digital Technology Giant	38,462	357	563,535	1,197
Apple	Digital Technology Giant	173,427	963	868,879	1,198
Facebook	Digital Technology Giant	n/a	201	512,757	1,230
Microsoft	Digital Technology Giant	333,054	1,022	659,906	461
Tencent	Digital Technology Giant	13,545	9	493,340	184

Table 4.2.3 presents the market capitalization and news coverage per digital technology giant. Market capitalization is measured in $ million as of December 31, 2007 and December 31, 2017. News coverage is measured in number of articles that have been published in the printed version of Wall Street Journal and mention the company in the respective year.

This study therefore expects the M&A activity of digital giants to transmit positive or negative signals to the dotcom giants, and these firms to react accordingly, as observed with direct and indirect rivals in the previous chapter.

Hypothesis 5. *Value creating transactions by digital technology giants result in positive abnormal returns and value diluting transactions in negative abnormal returns to dotcom giants.*

4.3 Data and Research Methodology

4.3.1 Data Sample and Rival Selection

This study analyzes transactions completed by one of the dotcom giants (Cisco Systems Inc., International Business Machines Corp., Intel Corp., Microsoft Corp., Nokia Oyj., Oracle Corp.) and announced between January 1, 2008 and December 31, 2017. The M&A data for growing and shrinking dotcom giants is gathered from the Securities Data Company database and a first sample that has been cleaned for double or wrong entries contains 450 transactions. Several selection criteria are applied to determine the final transaction sample:

1. The transaction is a merger or acquisition and the acquirer or acquirer ultimate parent company is a growing or shrinking dotcom giant.
2. The transaction is successfully completed and leads to a change in majority holding in the target company.

3. All necessary information (e.g., share price data, financial data) is available to analyze the transaction.
4. The transaction is the only relevant transaction by a growing or shrinking dotcom giant on the announcement date and there is no significant confounding event (e.g., announcement of first dividend, earnings surprise) of the acquirer in the two-week event window.

The selection criteria lead to 269 transactions by the dotcom giants excluding Microsoft. The M&A data from the first study is used for Microsoft, the only dotcom giant that is also part of the group of digital technology giants, and also for the other digital giants. All deals with overlapping event dates across the group are eliminated from the digital technology giants' sample. In total, the final dotcom giants' sample includes 365 transactions by the group including Microsoft. Table 4.3.1 presents an overview of the deal distribution across the six acquirers and years. The sample is relatively evenly distributed across the firms, with a peak for Microsoft with 96 deals and a low for Nokia with 22 deals. The growing dotcom giant subsample includes 174 transactions and the shrinking group includes 95 transactions.

Table 4.3.1: Distribution of Deals by Acquirer and Year

	Number of Deals by		Growing DCG			Shrinking DCG		DCG & DTG
	Total	in %	Cisco	Intel	Oracle	IBM	Nokia	Microsoft
2008	46	13%	5	3	9	9	2	18
2009	28	8%	5	3	5	4	4	7
2010	37	10%	4	6	8	11	5	3
2011	32	9%	5	10	6	6	0	5
2012	38	10%	8	4	11	8	1	6
2013	41	11%	9	10	5	10	0	7
2014	29	8%	5	5	3	4	3	9
2015	39	11%	5	4	1	8	2	19
2016	49	13%	6	9	8	11	4	11
2017	26	7%	8	1	3	2	1	11
Total	365	100%	60	55	59	73	22	96

Table 4.3.1 presents the number of transactions per acquirer and year. The acquirers are grouped into growing dotcom giants (growing DCG), shrinking dotcom giants (shrinking DCG) and dotcom giants and digital technology giants (DCG & DTG).

Following the approach of the studies in the previous chapters, the announcement date is set at the first date at which a deal is confirmed (officially or unofficially), and if an announcement date falls on a weekend it moves to the next trading date. In addition to the SDC database, the study gathers stock and benchmark data (Datastream Total Return Index) from the Datastream database and company financials from the Worldscope database. In line with the previous chapter, the dotcom giants' rival set consists only of digital technology giants with available share price data for the full time period including Microsoft. The digital technology giants' rival set contains all dotcom giants including Microsoft.

4.3.2 Definition of Variables

Several acquirer, target, deal and rival characteristics are applied as independent variables in the multivariate regression models of this study. The list of variables in the main analysis of dotcom giants' transactions includes *Growing Dotcom Giant, Relatedness, Free Cash Flow, Firm Size, Acquirer Experience, Tobin's Q, Sales Growth.* Additionally, in the rival effects analyses this study applies *Positive Deal, Acquirer CAR, Acquirer Leverage, Acquirer Profitability* and *Rival Target Relatedness* as independent variables. All variables are defined in accordance with the previous two studies to enable comparison of results, and are only briefly described in this chapter.

Growing Dotcom Giant is a dummy variable that indicates if the acquirer is a dotcom giant that has increased shareholder value on the basis of the market capitalization between January 1, 2008 and December 31, 2017. *Relatedness* is a dummy variable that compares the primary 3-digit SIC code of acquirer and target. This study applies two different measures to determine *Free Cash Flow* in accordance with the first study. The first proxy (*Free Cash Flow 1*) starts from the operating income and is based on Lehn and Poulsen (1989) as presented in formula (4.3.1):

$$FCF_1 = OPI + DEP - TAX - INT - DIV,　\qquad (4.3.1)$$

where *OPI* represents the operating income, *DEP* the depreciation and amortization, *TAX* the total income tax minus change in deferred taxes, *INT* the gross interest expenses on debt and *DIV* the sum of dividends paid on preferred and common stocks. The other proxy (*Free Cash Flow 2*) starts from the operating cash flow and is calculated based on Brealey et al. (2017) as presented in formula (4.3.2):

$$FCF_2 = CFO - CAP,　\qquad (4.3.2)$$

where *CFO* represents the operating cash flow and *CAP* the capital expenditures. Both proxies are normalized by the book value of total assets. *Firm Size* is defined as the natural logarithm of the total equity market capitalization. *Acquirer Experience* is calculated as the number of all completed acquisitions by the acquirer that are listed in the SDC database until the analyzed transaction. The study uses for *Tobin's Q* a proxy suggested by Chung and Pruitt (1994) as presented in formula (4.3.3):

$$Tobin's\ Q = \frac{MVE + PRS + (CLI - CAS) + LTD}{TAS}, \qquad (4.3.3)$$

where *MVE* represents the market value of equity, *PRS* the liquidating value of preferred stock, *CLI* the current liabilities, *CLA* the current assets, *LTD* the long-term debt and *TAS* the total assets.[41] The variable *Sales Growth* represents the geometric average of the net sales growth of the last two fiscal years prior to the event.

In addition, the rival effects analyses include the dummy variable *Positive Deal* that indicates if the two-week cumulative abnormal return to the acquirer is positive, and the variable *Acquirer CAR* that equals the two-week cumulative abnormal return to the acquirer. *Leverage* equals the long-term debt and *Acquirer Profitability* equals the operating income before depreciation and amortization. Both variables are scaled to the book value of total assets. *Rival Target Relatedness* is a dummy variable that indicates if rival and target share the same 3-digit SIC code. Financial figures are measured at the fiscal year prior to the acquisition announcement, unless stated differently.

Finally, the main and rival effects regression models include several control variables. *Domestic Deal* indicates if the acquirer and target are located in the same country, *US Target* if the target is located in the United States and *Public Target* if the target is a public company. The rival effects analysis of transactions by digital technology giants also includes the dummy variables *High Year* and *Low Year*, which indicate the three years (2014, 2015, 2016) with the highest and the three years (2008, 2009, 2012) with the lowest number of deals per company across the digital technology giant sample. *Acquirer Alphabet* indicates if the buyer is Alphabet. *Rival Microsoft* indicates if the rival is Microsoft. Table 4.3.2 presents the descriptive statistics of the dotcom giant data sample grouped by growing giants, shrinking giants and Microsoft, as well as the statistics of the reduced digital technology giants' sample (without Microsoft).

---

41 Negative values for Tobin's Q are set at 0.

4.3.3 Research Methodology

The study analyzes the M&A activity of dotcom giants and Microsoft isolated (main analysis) and in relation to digital technology giants (rival effects analysis). The analyses are conducted separately for the three acquirer subsamples – the growing dotcom giants, the shrinking dotcom giants and Microsoft. The standard event study methodology as described in detail in the previous chapters and different multivariate regression models as described below are used.

The event study setup is similar for both analyses. The market model is utilized as return generating model, and realized returns are computed as log returns. The S&P 500 index is used as benchmark for companies located in the US and the MSCI ACWI index for all other companies. The length of the estimation window is set at 145 trading days [-150;-6], and the event windows include two weeks [-5;+5], one week [-2;+2] and three days [-1;+1]. The cumulative average abnormal returns of the different subsamples are analyzed using the Patell's Z-test (1976), the standardized cross-sectional test by Boehmer et al. (1991), the Rank-test by Corrado (1989) and Corrado and Zivney (1992), and the generalized Sign-test by Cowan (1992). The subsamples are tested for difference using the two-sided t-test for independent samples and the Mann-Whitney U test (1947).

Table 4.3.2: Characteristics of Transactions and Acquirers by Dotcom Giants and Digital Technology Giants

	Mean				Median				Standard Deviation			
	Grow. DCG	Shri. DCG	Micro-soft	Digital Giants	Grow. DCG	Shri. DCG	Micro-soft	Digital Giants	Grow. DCG	Shri. DCG	Micro-soft	Digital Giants
CAR	-0.4	0.6	-0.6	0.2	-0.3	0.6	-0.5	0.4	3.1	4.0	3.4	5.2
Relatedness	40	68	86	56	0	100	100	100	49	47	34	50
FCF 1	13	11	13	13	15	11	12	14	4	4	4	4
FCF 2	13	11	19	14	12	13	17	14	3	5	5	6
Firm Size	131	142	311	280	130	157	288	209	30	61	73	173
Acq. Exp.	127	218	169	79	119	250	168	61	42	91	25	53
Tobin's Q	1.6	1.5	2.3	3.6	1.5	1.6	1.8	3.2	0.6	0.4	0.9	1.5
Sales Grow.	8	-2	8	29	7	-2	9	26	9	13	5	15

Table 4.3.2 presents the mean, median and standard deviation of the cumulative abnormal return as well as *Relatedness, Free Cash Flow 1, Free Cash Flow 2, Firm Size, Acquirer Experience, Tobin's Q,* and *Sales Growth* of growing dotcom giants, shrinking dotcom giants, Microsoft and digital technology giants. *CAR* equals the cumulative abnormal return over the [-5;+5] event window. *Relatedness* is equal to 1 if the acquirer and target share the same 3-digit SIC code and 0 otherwise. *Free Cash Flow 1* is calculated as operating income before depreciation and amortization minus income tax minus interest expenses minus dividends, deflated by book value of total assets. *Free Cash Flow 2* is calculated as operating cash flow minus capital expenditures, deflated by book value of total assets. *Firm Size* is the natural logarithm of total

equity market capitalization and presented in $ billion without the natural logarithm transformation. *Acquirer Experience* is defined as number of completed acquisitions until the analyzed transaction. *Tobin's Q* is calculated as market value of equity plus liquidating value of preferred stock plus difference of current liabilities minus current assets plus long-term debt, deflated by book value of total assets. *Sales Growth* is defined as the geometric average of net sales growth of the last two years. *CAR, Relatedness, Free Cash Flow 1, Free Cash Flow 2* and *Sales Growth* are shown in percentage.

The main analysis includes three multivariate regression models (I, II and III). The models are based on an OLS-regression with time-fixed effects as supported by the Durbin-Wu-Hausman test and joint F-test on year dummies, and are separately analyzed for both *Free Cash Flow* measures (column 1 for *Free Cash Flow 1* and column 2 for *Free Cash Flow 2*). The dependent variable is the two-week cumulative abnormal return to the acquirer. Robust Huber-White standard errors are used as recommended by Petersen (2009) due to the fact that the comparison with time-cluster and firm-cluster standard errors shows no large difference. Model I shows the analysis with the independent variables and control variables as described in subsection 4.3.2, with model II additionally including two interaction variables (*Growing Dotcom Giant * Relatedness, Growing Dotcom Giant * Free Cash Flow*). In model II, *Relatedness* and *Free Cash Flow* are centered to their means in order to facilitate the interpretation of *Growing Dotcom Giant*. Model III replicates the setup of model I for transactions conducted by Microsoft.

The rival effects analysis is divided into two parts and analyzes the interactions between the two giant groups and the special role of Microsoft which is related to both groups. The first part analyzes the effect of dotcom giants' transactions (excluding Microsoft's deals) on the value of digital technology giants, the second part the effect of digital technology giants' transactions (excluding Microsoft's deals) on the value of dotcom giants. Microsoft is included in both rival sets. The two parts are analyzed using three OLS-regressions. The rival effects analysis of dotcom giants' transactions applies time-fixed effects in accordance with the main analysis subsection, while the rival effects analysis of digital giant's transactions applies no fixed effects in accordance with the previous chapter. The dependent variable for each sample is the CAR to the individual rivals. Robust Huber-White standard errors are applied. The first model (1) includes the independent variables as described in subsection 4.3.2 and the interactions of *Positive Deal* with different variables (*PD * Relatedness, PD * Acquirer CAR, PD * Acquirer Tobin's Q, PD * Acquirer Profitability, PD * Acquirer Sales Growth*). The second model (2) excludes *Positive Deal* and the interaction variables, and is grouped by the acquirer return (positive or negative) into two regressions. The interacting variables (*Relatedness, Acquirer CAR, Acquirer Tobin's Q, Acquirer Profitability, Acquirer Sales Growth*) in model I are centered to their means to facilitate interpretation. The rival effects regressions include the control variables of the main model and additionally *Acquirer Free Cash Flow, Acquirer Leverage, Acquirer Firm Size, Acquirer Experience* and *Rival Microsoft*. The analysis of the dotcom giant's transactions also includes the dummy *Acquirer Growing Dotcom Giant*, and the analysis of the digital giant's transactions the dummies *Acquirer Alphabet, High Year* and *Low Year*. All regressions of the rival effects analysis use the first free cash flow measure for the variable *Acquirer Free Cash Flow*.

4.4 Empirical Results

4.4.1 Value Creation in Dotcom Giants' Transactions

The share price reactions of the two dotcom giant groups and Microsoft grouped by related and unrelated transactions are presented in table 4.4.1. Panel A-B shows the abnormal returns to growing dotcom giants, panel C-D to shrinking dotcom giants and panel E-F to Microsoft. The table also contains the test for difference between the acquirer groups in panel G.

Growing dotcom giants experience negative abnormal returns across both transaction types and all event windows. Only the three-day event window for related transactions shows a small positive, but insignificant cumulative average abnormal return. The other event windows for related transactions by growing dotcom giants are also insignificant. In contrast, the group shows significant negative CAARs for unrelated transactions. The one-week event window has a negative return of -0.53 %, which is significant at the 5 % (BMP-test, Corrado-test) and 10 % (Patell-test, Sign-test) level. The [-1;+1] window has a slightly negative return of -0.23 % that is significant at the 5 % level for the sign test and at the 10 % level for the BMP-test. Microsoft as acquirer shows a related picture as the growing dotcom giants. Related transactions have insignificant and negative event windows, while unrelated acquisitions lead to some significant negative results. The [-1;+1] event window has a negative CAAR of -1.24 % that is significant at the 10 % level for the Patell-test. The abnormal return in the two-week event window is -1.41 % and significant at the 10 % level for the Sign-test. The group of shrinking dotcom giants has also economically and statistically insignificant returns for related transactions. However, the

Table 4.4.1: *CAARs to Growing Dotcom Giants, Shrinking Dotcom Giants and Microsoft Grouped by Relatedness*

	(1) CAAR	(2) Patell-test	(3) BMP-test	(4) Sign-test	(5) Corrado-test	(6) Positive	(7) Sample
Panel A: Growing Dotcom Giants - Related Transactions							
[-5;+5]	-0.17%	-0.41	-0.49	0.48	-0.72	53%	70
[-2;+2]	-0.11%	-0.52	-0.60	-0.96	-0.95	44%	70
[-1;+1]	0.12%	0.31	0.35	0.24	0.31	51%	70
Panel B: Growing Dotcom Giants - Unrelated Transactions							
[-5;+5]	-0.52%	-1.29	-1.61	-0.75	-1.38	46%	104
[-2;+2]	-0.53%	-1.87 *	-2.54 **	-1.73 *	-2.46 **	41%	104
[-1;+1]	-0.23%	-1.09	-1.65 *	-2.32 **	-1.41	38%	104
Panel C: Shrinking Dotcom Giants - Related Transactions							
[-5;+5]	0.19%	0.50	0.51	0.92	-0.02	57%	65
[-2;+2]	0.01%	0.39	0.39	-0.32	-0.20	49%	65
[-1;+1]	-0.03%	0.20	0.19	-0.32	-0.32	49%	65
Panel D: Shrinking Dotcom Giants - Unrelated Transactions							
[-5;+5]	1.45%	1.43	1.89 *	1.25	1.10	63%	30
[-2;+2]	1.68%	2.05 **	2.58 ***	1.25	2.22 **	63%	30
[-1;+1]	0.80%	1.37	2.07 **	1.98 **	1.59	70%	30
Panel E: Microsoft - Related Transactions							
[-5;+5]	-0.42%	-1.08	-1.19	-1.53	-0.57	40%	83
[-2;+2]	-0.25%	-1.25	-1.27	-1.31	-0.92	41%	83
[-1;+1]	-0.07%	-0.27	-0.35	-0.21	-0.28	47%	83
Panel F: Microsoft - Unrelated Transactions							
[-5;+5]	-1.41%	-1.07	-0.98	-1.89 *	-1.33	23%	13
[-2;+2]	-0.75%	-0.92	-0.81	-0.22	-0.55	46%	13
[-1;+1]	-1.24%	-1.80 *	-1.63	-1.33	-1.61	31%	13

	(1) Δ CAAR	(2) t-test	(3) U test
Panel G: [-5;+5] Event Window - Difference (Panel / Panel)			
(A / C)	-0.36%	-0.66	-0.45
(A / E)	0.24%	0.47	0.77
(C / E)	0.61%	1.12	1.22
(B / D)	-1.97%	-2.59 **	-2.20 **
(B / F)	0.89%	0.91	1.52
(D / F)	2.86%	1.74 *	2.04 **

Table 4.4.1 presents the abnormal share price reaction of growing dotcom giants, shrinking dotcom giants and Microsoft for related transactions (panel A, C, E) and unrelated transactions (panel B, D, F) and the test for difference between the panels (panel G). Column (1) displays the cumulative average abnormal return, column (2)-(5) the test statistics, column (6) the share of transactions with a positive abnormal return and column (7) the sample size per analysis. Statistical significance at 1 %, 5 % and 10 % levels is indicated with ***, ** and *, respectively.

firms experience significant positive abnormal returns for diversifying acquisitions. The [-2;+2] event window has a positive return of 1.68 % and is significant at the 5 % significance level.[42] The three-day event window has a positive CAAR of 0.80 % that is significant at the 5 % level for the BMP-test and Sign-test.

---

42 The BMP-test is significant at the 1 % level and the sign test is insignificant.

The test for difference provides further evidence that the results for related transactions do not vary across the three acquirer groups. However, the tests for unrelated deals show a significant different share price reaction of shrinking dotcom giants on the one side and growing dotcom giants and Microsoft on the other. The parametric and non-parametric tests show that the [-5;+5] event windows for both comparisons are significantly different at the 5 % significance level.[43]

Table 4.4.2: CAARs to Digital Technology Giants Grouped by Relatedness

	(1) CAAR	(2) Patell-test	(3) BMP-test	(4) Sign-test	(5) Corrado-test	(6) Positive	(7) Sample
Panel A: Digital Technology Giants - Related Transactions							
[-5;+5]	1.10%	3.40 ***	2.87 ***	3.42 ***	2.71 ***	63%	163
[-2;+2]	0.32%	2.18 **	1.99 **	2.48 **	1.96 *	59%	163
[-1;+1]	0.38%	2.03 **	2.47 **	2.48 **	3.06 ***	59%	163
Panel B: Digital Technology Giants - Unrelated Transactions							
[-5;+5]	-0.91%	-1.59	-1.50	-0.66	-1.12	45%	130
[-2;+2]	-0.58%	-1.64 *	-1.47	-1.01	-0.96	43%	130
[-1;+1]	-0.15%	-0.48	-0.46	0.40	0.63	49%	130

	(1) Δ CAAR	(2) t-test	(3) U test
Panel C: [-5;+5] Event Window - Difference (Panel / Panel)			
(A / 4.1 A)	1.27%	1.96 *	1.75 *
(A / 4.1 C)	0.91%	1.34	1.11
(A / 4.1 E)	1.51%	2.49 **	2.41 **
(B / 4.1 B)	-0.38%	-0.67	-0.59
(B / 4.1 D)	-2.35%	-2.26 **	-2.11 **
(B / 4.1 F)	0.51%	0.34	0.89

Table 4.4.2 presents the abnormal share price reaction of digital technology giants for related transactions (panel A) and unrelated transactions (panel B) and the test for difference between the two panels and respective panels of table 4.4.1 (panel C). Column (1) displays the cumulative average abnormal return, column (2)-(5) the test statistics, column (6) the share of transactions with a positive abnormal return and column (7) the sample size per analysis. Statistical significance at 1 %, 5 % and 10 % levels is indicated with ***, ** and *, respectively.

Table 4.4.2 shows the cumulative average abnormal returns for digital technology giants' transactions (without Microsoft) and the test for difference between the share price reaction of growing dotcom giants, shrinking dotcom giants or Microsoft on the one side and digital technology giants on the other. Panel A shows the abnormal returns for related deals, panel B for unrelated deals and panel C the test for difference. The results support the previous observations. The share price reaction of shrinking dotcom giants to unrelated deals is also significantly different at the 5 % level

---

43 The t-test between shrinking dotcom giants and Microsoft is only significant at the 10 % level.

across both test statistics which further highlights a different perspective of shareholders on unrelated acquisitions by shrinking dotcom giants. Interestingly, the reactions of growing dotcom giants and Microsoft on the one side and digital technology giants on the other are statistically different for related transactions at the 10 % level and 5 % level, respectively. Despite the insignificant results for related transactions in table 4.4.1, the effect for digital technology giants significantly differs and emphasizes the special role of relatedness for the digital technology giants.

Overall, the results of the event study show an interesting pattern. The three analyzed acquirer groups experience no significant share price reaction to related transactions but some significant differences between the groups and digital technology giants exist. The shareholders appear not to expect a positive effect of relatedness in terms of network effects or complementarities for the different acquirer groups of dotcom giants. In contrast, the results for unrelated acquisitions significantly vary between shrinking dotcom giants and the other acquirers. This provides two insights on transactions by dotcom giants and digital technology giants. First, the study finds negative abnormal returns to growing dotcom giants and Microsoft. These companies have successfully operated in a changing industry environment in the recent decade and increased firm value. Shareholders seem to appreciate the continuation of the current operations through the focus on related transactions. They appears not to expect any abnormal, positive or negative, value change but anticipate value preservation from these deals. In contrast, diversifying acquisitions might lead to negative abnormal returns because successful companies have a higher hurdle rate of return for new investments. Alternatively, shareholders might critically monitor unrelated deals as they expect value dilution from reshaping the business focus in general. Second, the study observes positive abnormal returns to shrinking dotcom giants. They have faced decreasing firm value in recent years due to the changing industry environment. Therefore, positive abnormal returns might be easier to reach with a lower hurdle rate of return for acquisitions by unsuccessful firms. Alternatively, shareholders might appreciate diversifying transactions as they generally expect positive effects for these acquirers. In total, the event study shows insignificant returns for related transactions by the three acquirer groups and provides no evidence to support hypothesis H1. In contrast, the results present a positive return for unrelated deals by shrinking dotcom giants. The return is significant different to the returns to growing dotcom giants, Microsoft and digital technology giants; hypothesis H2 is supported.

4.4.2 Value Drivers in Dotcom Giants' Transactions

The event study shows significant different results for unrelated acquisitions by shrinking dotcom giants on the one side and by growing dotcom giants and Microsoft on the other, but insignificant results for related deals. This study analyzes the value drivers of M&A activity with three multivariate regression models and two free cash flow measures. Table 4.4.3 presents the results of the regressions. Model I and model II show the main regression model and interaction model for the dotcom giants, and model III shows the main regression for Microsoft. Column (1) contains the results of the regressions with the variable *Free Cash Flow 1*, and column (2) the results with *Free Cash Flow 2*.

The results for growing and shrinking dotcom giants are consistent across regression model I and II and both free cash flow measures. The dummy variable *Growing Giants* is significant negative at the 5 % level in the models with *Free Cash Flow 1* and at the 1 % level in the models with *Free Cash Flow 2*. On average across all transactions, a growing dotcom giant experiences a -1.7 – -3.0 % lower abnormal return than a shrinking dotcom giant. *Relatedness* has a negative but not significant effect on the abnormal return. The inclusion of the interaction variable *Growing Dotcom Giant * Relatedness* in model II does not change the results. Even though *Relatedness* has a positive influence for growing dotcom giants, the effect is not significant. Thus, the observed positive effect of shrinking giants' unrelated transactions in the event study is not limited to diversifying actions, but exists across both deal types. The shareholders seem to appreciate the M&A activity of these firms more than the transactions by growing dotcom giants. Alternatively, the lower abnormal return to successfully growing dotcom giants might be driven by managerial hubris (e.g., Morck et al., 1990). Interestingly, Microsoft as the only company that is part of both the group of dotcom giants and the group of digital technology giants, also experiences no significant effect of *Relatedness*. This is different to the results of the total group of digital technology giants in chapter 2.

Table 4.4.3: Multivariate Regression Analysis of Dotcom Giants' Transactions

	Model I		Model II		Model III	
	(1)	(2)	(1)	(2)	(1)	(2)
Growing DCG	-0.017 **	-0.022 ***	-0.017 **	-0.030 ***		
	(-2.14)	(-2.66)	(-1.98)	(-3.19)		
Relatedness	-0.001	-0.002	-0.009	-0.007	0.007	0.009
	(-0.24)	(-0.35)	(-1.00)	(-0.71)	(0.61)	(0.76)
Growing DCG * Rel.			0.012	0.011		
			(1.06)	(0.95)		
Free Cash Flow	0.135 *	0.216 **	0.253 **	0.463 ***	-0.185	0.153
	(1.66)	(2.04)	(2.03)	(3.23)	(-0.63)	(0.48)
Growing DCG * FCF			-0.167	-0.464 ***		
			(-1.11)	(-2.61)		
Firm Size	-0.023 **	-0.026 ***	-0.023 **	-0.041 ***	-0.051	-0.039
	(-2.33)	(-2.64)	(-2.39)	(-3.56)	(-0.69)	(-0.52)
Acquirer Experience	0.000	0.000	0.000	0.000	0.003 **	0.003 **
	(1.10)	(0.33)	(0.95)	(0.28)	(2.22)	(2.19)
Tobin's Q	0.001	0.002	0.001	0.007	0.062 **	0.062 **
	(0.18)	(0.24)	(0.13)	(0.93)	(2.51)	(2.47)
Sales Growth	0.103 ***	0.089 ***	0.094 ***	0.075 **	-0.105	-0.191
	(3.25)	(2.77)	(2.86)	(2.29)	(-0.59)	(-1.25)
Controls						
Domestic Deal	-0.010	-0.005	-0.010	-0.004	-0.003	-0.003
	(-0.81)	(-0.43)	(-0.81)	(-0.29)	(-0.38)	(-0.39)
Public Target	-0.001	0.000	-0.001	0.000	0.007	0.006
	(-0.10)	(-0.01)	(-0.09)	(0.00)	(0.31)	(0.29)
US Target	0.018	0.012	0.017	0.011	0.000	0.000
	(1.50)	(1.04)	(1.43)	(0.97)	(0.00)	(0.00)
Time-fixed Effects	Yes	Yes	Yes	Yes	Yes	Yes
Constant	0.380 **	0.448 ***	0.417 **	0.750 ***	0.403	0.124
	(2.31)	(2.65)	(2.48)	(3.67)	(0.31)	(0.09)
Sample Size	269	269	269	269	96	96
Adjusted R²	0.08	0.08	0.08	0.10	0.00	0.00

Table 4.4.3 presents the impact of value drivers on the abnormal share price reaction of growing and shrinking dotcom giants' transactions (model I-II) and Microsoft's transactions (model III). The dependent variable is the CAR over the main [-5;+5] event window. Column (1) displays the results calculated with *Free Cash Flow 1* for *Free Cash Flow* and both interaction variables and column (2) with *Free Cash Flow 2*. *Growing DCG* is equal to 1 if the acquirer is a dotcom giant that has increased shareholder value on basis of market capitalization between January 1, 2008 and December 31, 2017 and 0 otherwise. *Relatedness* is equal to 1 if the acquirer and target share the same 3-digit SIC code and 0 otherwise. *Free Cash Flow 1* is calculated as operating income before depreciation and amortization minus income tax minus interest expenses minus dividends, deflated by book value of total assets. *Free Cash Flow 2* is calculated as operating cash flow minus capital expenditures, deflated by book value of total assets. *Firm Size* is the natural logarithm of total equity market capitalization. *Acquirer Experience* is defined as number of completed acquisitions until the analyzed transaction. *Tobin's Q* is calculated as market value of equity plus liquidating value of preferred stock plus difference of current liabilities minus current assets plus long-term debt, deflated by book value of total assets. *Sales Growth* is defined as the geometric average of net sales growth of the last two years. *Domestic Deal* is equal to 1 if the acquirer and target are located in the same country and 0 otherwise. *Public Target* is equal to 1 if the target is public and 0 otherwise. *US Target* is equal to 1 if the target is located in the United States and 0 otherwise. Time-fixed effects are included in all specifications. Significance is based on robust Huber-White standard errors and t-

statistics are shown in parentheses. Statistical significance at 1 %, 5 % and 10 % levels is indicated with ***, ** and *, respectively.

In contrast, the effect of free cash flow is significant across growing and
shrinking dotcom giants for *Free Cash Flow 1* and *Free Cash Flow 2* at the
10 % and 5 % level in model I, respectively. A growth of relative free cash
flow by 1 percentage point increases the cumulative abnormal return by
0.1 – 0.2 percentage points. Thus, transactions with higher available liquidity yield higher abnormal returns. This effect differs for shrinking dotcom
giants on the one side and growing dotcom giants and Microsoft on the
other. In the interaction model (model II), the influence of free cash flow
is even higher with an increase of 0.3 – 0.5 percentage points significant at
the 1 % level and 5 % level for *Free Cash Flow 2* and *Free Cash Flow 1*, respectively. This can be traced back to a lower effect for growing dotcom
giants. The variable *Growing Dotcom Giant * Free Cash Flow* is significant
negative at the 1 % level for *Free Cash Flow 2* and negative, but insignificant for *Free Cash Flow 1*. The combination of both free cash flow variables
leads to an economically insignificant effect of relative free cash flow for
growing giants. In model III, the effect of free cash flow is insignificant for
acquisitions by Microsoft. The positive impact of free cash flow on shrinking dotcom giants can be driven by lower costs of internal financing and
higher financial flexibility. It can enable the firms to pursue a transformation process. In contrast, the insignificant effect of free cash flow on growing dotcom giants and Microsoft can be the outcome of two overlapping
effects. On the one hand, lower financing costs as described above can
have a positive impact on transactions. On the other hand, free cash flow
can lower the control by capital markets. Management can focus on self-
interest motives for acquisitions instead of increasing shareholder value,
leading to lower returns.

Some other variables show interesting effects for dotcom giants and Microsoft. First, across all models *Firm Size* has a significant negative influence and *Sales Growth* a significant positive influence on dotcom giants.
Thus, larger firms experience lower abnormal returns, with an increase in
the net sales growth rate by 1 percentage point raising the cumulative abnormal return by 0.1 percentage points. The firm size effect provides support for potential corporate governance issues, similar to the negative effect of free cash flow. It can indicate managerial hubris (e.g., Moeller et al.,
2004; Roll, 1986). However, the sales growth effect contradicts the hubris
theory because it shows that successful managers with regard to higher net
sales experience higher abnormal returns. Second, *Acquirer Experience* and

151

Tobin's Q have a significant positive influence on Microsoft. It seems that the company benefits from learning effects of previous transactions as each successfully completed deal increases the abnormal return for future transactions (e.g., Haleblian and Finkelstein, 1999). Additionally, shareholders reward acquisitions if Microsoft has increased growth potential in terms of higher Tobin's Q. This can be also interpreted as reward for successful management, similar to the sales growth effect (e.g., Lang et al., 1989).

In total, the results of the multivariate regressions are different to the analysis of digital technology giants in chapter 2 and vary between the groups of shrinking dotcom giants, growing dotcom giants and Microsoft. The regressions provide three insights into the value drivers of dotcom giants' and digital technology giants' mergers and acquisitions. First, relatedness has no significant effect on the abnormal return for transactions by dotcom giants. These firms, whether growing or shrinking dotcom giants appear not to benefit from complementarities and network effects, and even Microsoft shows an insignificant impact. This is contrary to the observed effect for the digital technology giants as a group. It seems that relatedness does not in general have a positive influence on transactions by all platform businesses and that other factors can influence the relatedness effect, for example the platform ecosystems (Cusumano et al., 2019; Parker and van Alstyne, 2008). It provides further evidence against a relatedness effect for growing dotcom giants and against hypothesis H1. Second, the significant different reaction to unrelated transactions between growing and shrinking dotcom giants can be attributed to an overall more positive abnormal return to shrinking dotcom giants. Shareholders of these firms seem to reward any kind of M&A activity as part of a potential transition process. The declining value of shrinking giants can decrease the hurdle rate of return for future transactions and support the positive effect. Another potential inference can be that managerial hubris of successful growing dotcom giants lowers the overall abnormal return. The influence of firm size supports this, but the influences of sales growth and Tobin's Q oppose it. Further investigation is needed to better understand the effect. The results partially contradict hypothesis H2. Even though a difference in returns for unrelated deals can be observed, the regressions provide evidence that this is not driven by relatedness but rather by an overall shrinking giant effect. Nevertheless, this concurs with the argumentation that shareholders expect a positive influence from unrelated M&A activity of shrinking dotcom giants. Third, the influence of free cash flow differs between the different acquirer groups. The previous study shows that the available level of liquidity has a significant negative influence on transactions by digital technology giants, possibly indicative of corporate governance issues. This is not the case for dotcom giants. Acquisitions by shrinking dotcom giants benefit from higher levels of free cash flow, while growing dotcom giants and Microsoft experience no significant influence. The positive effect can be evidence of an advantage due to lower costs of internal capital, with shareholders possibly appreciating the financial flexibility. The insignificant effect on transactions by the other firms can be driven by an overlap of both influences. The shrinking dotcom giants have a lower average level of free cash flow than growing giants and digital technology giants do. It suggests that the relative level of liquidity can also have an influence on transactions in the digital technology industry.

To conclude, the results of the multivariate regressions support hypothesis H4 that free cash flow has a positive influence on shrinking dotcom giants. However, hypothesis H3 is not supported as the combined effect on growing dotcom giants is insignificant in the interaction model. The significant negative effect of *Growing Dotcom Giant * Free Cash Flow* in column (2) of model II provides some evidence for a negative influence of free cash flow on growing dotcom giants.

4.4.3 Rival Effects Analysis

This study analyzes rival effects between dotcom giants and digital technology giants from two perspectives. Table 4.4.4 and table 4.4.5 show the effects of dotcom giants' transactions on digital technology giants' abnormal returns, while table 4.4.6 and table 4.4.7 show the effect of digital technology giants' transactions on dotcom giants' abnormal returns. Both analyses contain an event study (table 4.4.4 and table 4.4.6) grouped by positive transactions (panel A) and negative transactions (panel B) and a test for difference (panel C) as well as two multivariate regression models (table 4.4.5 and table 4.4.7). Model I is an interaction model and model II a non-interaction model which is grouped by transactions that create value for the acquirer (positive deals) and transactions that dilute value for the acquirer (negative deals). The analyses deliver ambiguous results.

The rival effects event study on the M&A activity of dotcom giants in table 4.4.4 shows negative effects across most event windows, but only one window per transaction type is significant. The three-day event window for related transactions shows a negative return of -0.35 % that is significant at the 1 % level for the parametric tests, and the two-week event window for unrelated deals has a CAAR of -0.54 % that is significant at the 1 % level

(Patell-test) and 5 % level (BMP-test and Corrado-test). The negative cumulative average abnormal return increases with the length of the event window for value diluting deals while decreasing for value creating deals. The test for difference shows that the two [-5;+5] event windows differ significantly, and that value creating deals lead to significantly more positive rival effects.

Table 4.4.4: *CAARs to Digital Technology Giants as Rivals Grouped by Acquirer Return*

	(1) CAAR	(2) Patell-test	(3) BMP-test	(4) Sign-test	(5) Corrado-test	(6) Positive	(7) Sample
Panel A: Positive Transactions							
[-5;+5]	0.00%	-0.06	-0.06	0.89	-0.49	50%	705
[-2;+2]	-0.27%	-1.55	-1.53	-0.46	-1.07	48%	705
[-1;+1]	-0.35%	-2.72 ***	-2.82 ***	-1.59	-1.49	45%	705
Panel B: Negative Transactions							
[-5;+5]	-0.54%	-2.58 ***	-2.36 **	-0.49	-2.06 **	47%	640
[-2;+2]	-0.11%	-1.13	-1.01	-0.49	-1.28	47%	640
[-1;+1]	0.09%	0.54	0.52	1.49	0.39	51%	640

	(1) Δ CAAR	(2) t-test	(3) U test
Panel C: [-5;+5] Event Window - Difference (Panel / Panel)			
(A / B)	0.54%	1.83 *	1.98 **

Table 4.4.4 presents the abnormal share price reaction of digital technology giants as rivals for value creating transactions (panel A) and value diluting transactions (panel B) by dotcom giants and the test for difference between the two panels (panel C). Column (1) displays the cumulative average abnormal return, column (2)-(5) the test statistics, column (6) the share of transactions with a positive abnormal return and column (7) the sample size per analysis. Statistical significance at 1 %, 5 % and 10 % levels is indicated with ***, ** and *, respectively.

The multivariate regressions in table 4.4.5 present two interesting observations. First, the variable *Positive Deal* has a positive effect that is significant at the 5 % level. It supports the observation of the test for difference and indicates that a transaction that creates value for a dotcom giant acquirer increases the return to a digital technology giant rival by 0.9 percentage points. In contrast, *Acquirer CAR*, which is the abnormal return to the acquirer in the two-week the event window, has a negative influence on the rival return for positive transactions which is significant at the 5 % level. A growth of *Acquirer CAR* by 1 percentage point decreases the CAR to the rival by -0.2 percentage points. Thus, a value creating transaction by a dotcom giant has a positive influence on digital giants, but if the abnormal return to the acquirer is above 4.4 %, other things equal, the effect is offset.

Table 4.4.5: Multivariate Regression Analysis of Digital Technology Giants as Rivals – Total and by Acquirer Return

	(1) Total	(2) By Acquirer Return	
		Positive	Negative
Positive Deal	0.009 **		
	(2.01)		
Relatedness	0.009	0.003	0.005
	(1.49)	(0.55)	(0.76)
PD * Relatedness	-0.010		
	(-1.38)		
Acquirer CAR	0.045	-0.206 **	-0.059
	(0.43)	(-1.98)	(-0.48)
PD * Acquirer CAR	-0.191		
	(-1.29)		
Acquirer Tobin's Q	-0.002	0.013	0.002
	(-0.27)	(1.38)	(0.19)
PD * Acquirer Tobin's Q	0.018 **		
	(1.96)		
Acquirer Profitability	-0.009	-0.019	0.095
	(-0.13)	(-0.23)	(0.77)
PD * Acquirer Profitability	-0.050		
	(-0.69)		
Acquirer Sales Growth	-0.056 *	-0.014	-0.083 *
	(-1.69)	(-0.39)	(-1.90)
PD * Acquirer Sales Growth	0.045		
	(1.33)		
Rival Firm Size	-0.003	-0.004	-0.002
	(-0.97)	(-0.92)	(-0.40)
Rival Tobin's Q	-0.001	-0.001	0.000
	(-0.48)	(-0.56)	(-0.07)
Rival Target Relatedness	-0.002	-0.002	-0.001
	(-0.69)	(-0.60)	(-0.23)
Controls			
Domestic Deal	-0.010	-0.004	-0.017
	(-1.39)	(-0.36)	(-1.23)
Public Target	0.008	0.011	0.007
	(1.60)	(1.44)	(0.94)
US Target	0.011	0.006	0.015
	(1.61)	(0.58)	(1.13)
Acquirer Free Cash Flow	0.012	0.043	-0.167
	(0.15)	(0.33)	(-1.10)
Acquirer Leverage	-0.010	-0.037	0.042
	(-0.28)	(-0.77)	(0.69)
Acquirer Firm Size	0.006	0.000	0.010
	(0.73)	(-0.02)	(0.69)
Acquirer Experience	0.000	0.000	0.000
	(0.18)	(-0.22)	(0.70)
Acquirer Growing Dotcom Giant	0.004	0.003	0.016
	(0.69)	(0.35)	(1.53)
Rival Microsoft	-0.001	0.000	-0.002
	(-0.27)	(-0.08)	(-0.41)
Time-fixed Effects	Yes	Yes	Yes
Constant	-0.087	0.052	-0.224
	(-0.53)	(0.25)	(-0.85)
Sample Size	1,345	705	640
Adjusted R²	0.02	0.02	0.02

Table 4.4.5 presents the impact of value drivers on the rivals' abnormal share price reaction to dotcom giants' transactions of the total sample (1) and grouped by acquirer return (2), positive and negative. The dependent variable is the CAR to the digital technology giants over the main [-5;+5] event window. *Positive Deal (PD)* is equal to 1 if the acquisition has a positive abnormal return to the acquirer and 0 otherwise. *Acquirer CAR* is defined as the CAR to the acquirer over the main two-week event window. *Acquirer Profitability* equals operating in-

come before depreciation and amortization, deflated by book value of total assets. *Rival Target Relatedness* is equal to 1 if the rival and target share the same 3-digit SIC code and 0 otherwise. *Acquirer Free Cash Flow* is *Free Cash Flow 1*. *Acquirer Leverage* equals long-term debt, deflated by book value of total assets. *Rival Microsoft* is equal to 1 if the rival is Microsoft and 0 otherwise. Please refer to the caption of table 4.4.3 for all other variables. Time-fixed effects are included in all specifications. Significance is based on robust Huber-White standard errors and t-statistics are shown in parentheses. Statistical significance at 1 %, 5 % and 10 % levels is indicated with ***, ** and *, respectively.

Second, *Acquirer Sales Growth* has a significant negative influence on rival return for all transactions which is driven by negative deals, and *Acquirer Tobin's Q* has a significant higher effect for positive than for negative deals. Overall, the results are ambiguous. Some results can support signaling effects (*Positive Deal, Acquirer Tobin's Q*), but others can indicate efficiency increase effects (*Acquirer CAR, Acquirer Sales Growth*).[44] A further analysis of the drivers is required.

The previous study shows that the group of digital technology giants has signaling power to other digital giants and to direct rivals in the industry. Table 4.4.6 provides the event study on the influence of digital technology giants' transactions on the rival return to dotcom giants. The results show insignificant effects for negative transactions, but a significant negative return of -0.13 % for positive deals over the three-day event window. The effect is significant at the 5 % level for the parametric test statistics and at the 10 % level for the Sign-test. The event study results provide no evidence for signaling effects of digital technology giants' transactions on dotcom giants, but instead indicate some effects of efficiency increase. Alternatively, a potential overlap of different influences can lead to the missing signaling power on dotcom giants, which is analyzed in the multivariate regressions.

---

44 See chapter 3 for a detailed discussion on the theoretical implications of the effects.

Table 4.4.6: CAARs to Dotcom Giants as Rivals Grouped by Acquirer Return

	(1) CAAR	(2) Patell-test	(3) BMP-test	(4) Sign-test	(5) Corrado-test	(6) Positive	(7) Sample
Panel A: Positive Transactions							
[-5;+5]	0.04%	-0.45	-0.40	-0.62	-0.42	49%	960
[-2;+2]	-0.03%	-0.72	-0.66	-0.30	-0.65	49%	960
[-1;+1]	-0.13%	-2.24 **	-2.09 **	-1.79 *	-1.51	47%	960
Panel B: Negative Transactions							
[-5;+5]	-0.05%	-0.03	-0.03	-0.79	0.12	48%	798
[-2;+2]	-0.12%	-0.96	-0.92	-1.64	-1.29	47%	798
[-1;+1]	0.07%	0.73	0.68	0.70	0.78	51%	798

	(1) Δ CAAR	(2) t-test	(3) U test
Panel C: [-5;+5] Event Window - Difference (Panel / Panel)			
(A / B)	0.09%	0.39	0.10

Table 4.4.6 presents the abnormal share price reaction of dotcom giants as rivals for value creating transactions (panel A) and value diluting transactions (panel B) by digital technology giants and the test for difference between the two panels (panel C). Column (1) displays the cumulative average abnormal return, column (2)-(5) the test statistics, column (6) the share of transactions with a positive abnormal return and column (7) the sample size per analysis. Statistical significance at 1 %, 5 % and 10 % levels is indicated with ***, ** and *, respectively.

The results of the regressions in table 4.4.7 provide only weak indication of overlapping effects. Even though some variables support signaling effects (*Acquirer Tobin's Q, Rival Tobin's Q, Rival Firm Size, Lower Year*) and other variables support efficiency increase effects (*Acquirer Profitability, Acquirer Sales Growth*), the low significance of the variables in combination with the low adjusted R^2 of the regressions limit the explanatory power of the results.[45] However, the significant positive effect of *Rival Microsoft* for value creating deals and the negative effect for value diluting deals provide further support for signaling effects among the group of digital technology giants as discussed in the previous chapter. In total, the results do not indicate that digital giants transmit signals to dotcom giants and provide no evidence to support hypothesis H5. Further analysis of the drivers is thus needed to better understand the relations.

---

45 In general, the adjusted R^2 of multivariate regressions in a rival effects study is low.

Table 4.4.7: Multivariate Regression Analysis of Dotcom Giants as Rivals – Total and by Acquirer Return

	(1) Total	(2) By Acquirer Return	
		Positive	Negative
Positive Deal	0.000		
	(0.05)		
Relatedness	-0.005	0.003	-0.006
	(-1.25)	(0.61)	(-1.08)
PD * Relatedness	0.006		
	(1.17)		
Acquirer CAR	0.012	0.002	0.010
	(0.22)	(0.03)	(0.17)
PD * Acquirer CAR	-0.003		
	(-0.04)		
Acquirer Tobin's Q	0.001	0.003 *	-0.001
	(0.27)	(1.94)	(-0.28)
PD * Acquirer Tobin's Q	0.001		
	(0.54)		
Acquirer Profitability	0.102 *	0.046	0.105
	(1.78)	(0.67)	(1.23)
PD * Acquirer Profitability	-0.086 *		
	(-1.81)		
Acquirer Sales Growth	-0.020	-0.041 **	-0.010
	(-0.93)	(-2.10)	(-0.42)
PD * Acquirer Sales Growth	-0.008		
	(-0.35)		
Rival Firm Size	0.005	0.000	0.013 **
	(1.61)	(-0.11)	(2.30)
Rival Tobin's Q	-0.008 **	-0.005	-0.012 **
	(-2.03)	(-0.87)	(-2.04)
Rival Target Relatedness	0.000	-0.003	0.004
	(-0.06)	(-0.89)	(0.90)
Controls			
Domestic Deal	0.015 ***	0.013 **	0.032 ***
	(2.96)	(2.23)	(2.58)
Public Target	-0.003	-0.014 *	0.009
	(-0.34)	(-1.80)	(0.60)
US Target	-0.015 ***	-0.012 **	-0.033 ***
	(-2.94)	(-2.05)	(-2.72)
High Year	0.000	-0.003	0.002
	(-0.10)	(-0.87)	(0.52)
Low Year	0.012 **	0.021 **	0.000
	(1.98)	(2.39)	(-0.03)
Acquirer Free Cash Flow	-0.105	-0.217 *	0.036
	(-1.06)	(-1.72)	(0.22)
Acquirer Leverage	-0.014	-0.026	0.004
	(-0.49)	(-0.64)	(0.11)
Acquirer Firm Size	0.000	0.003	-0.009 *
	(-0.04)	(0.60)	(-1.79)
Acquirer Experience	0.000	0.000	0.000
	(-0.58)	(-0.81)	(1.22)
Acquirer Alphabet	0.007	0.008	-0.003
	(1.11)	(1.04)	(-0.29)
Rival Microsoft	0.001	0.010 **	-0.011 **
	(0.19)	(2.27)	(-2.12)
Constant	-0.075	-0.015	-0.062
	(-0.95)	(-0.13)	(-0.55)
Sample Size	1,758	960	798
Adjusted R^2	0.01	0.01	0.01

Table 4.4.7 presents the impact of value drivers on the rivals' abnormal share price reaction to digital technology giants' transactions of the total sample (1) and grouped by acquirer return (2), positive and negative. The dependent variable is the CAR to the dotcom giants over the main [-5;+5] event window. *High Year* is equal to 1 if the transaction is announced in 2014,

2015 or 2016 and 0 otherwise. *Low Year* is equal to 1 if the transaction is announced in 2008, 2009 or 2012 and 0 otherwise. *Acquirer Alphabet* is equal to 1 if the acquirer is Alphabet and 0 otherwise. Please refer to the caption of table 4.4.3 and table 4.4.5 for all other variables. Significance is based on robust Huber-White standard errors and t-statistics are shown in parentheses. Statistical significance at 1 %, 5 % and 10 % levels is indicated with ***, ** and *, respectively.

4.5 Discussion

This contribution investigates the value effects of dotcom giants' M&A activity and compares them with the effects of digital technology giants' transactions. The study therefore determines two groups of dotcom giants, growing and shrinking dotcom giants, and analyzes 365 transactions that have been conducted by these firms between 2008 and 2017. Related transactions lead to insignificant results for all subsamples, while unrelated deals have varying impact. Growing dotcom giants and Microsoft (the firm is separately analyzed since it is the only firm that is part of the group of dotcom giants and the group of digital technology giants) experience significant negative results, while shrinking dotcom giants experience significant positive results. In general, relatedness has no significant impact on dotcom giants, but shrinking dotcom giants experience significantly higher returns across deal types than growing dotcom giants, and free cash flow has a positive influence on shrinking dotcom giants. The results of the rival effects analysis between dotcom giants and digital technology giants are ambiguous.

In total, this study provides two primary insights. First, the contribution sheds light on the M&A value creation for dotcom giants and shows shareholders to react differently to acquisitions. The group of dotcom giants faces a changing environment and decreasing relevance in the industry. They are undergoing a transition process and can utilize M&A to transform their business. Shareholders appreciate diversifying actions of shrinking dotcom giants and seem to expect value creation through a shift in the business focus. In contrast, growing giants are in general unable to benefit from related as well as unrelated transactions. Shareholders might view a business change critically and want to maintain the current business focus while preserving value, despite the decreasing relative position in the market. This concurs with a positive effect of free cash flow on shrinking giants and an insignificant effect on growing giants. High levels of liquidity increase the financial flexibility and can support the transition process. Literature on the digital technology industry focuses largely on economics of scale and scope, network effects and "winner-take-all"-outcomes. However, the market is also characterized by low entry barriers. The path of dotcom giants in the last two decades as well as the M&A value creation show that the leading position of a large player in the market can change and that size does not guarantee long-term dominance or positive relatedness effects. Research needs to better understand the industry environment when discussing the digital technology industry and concentrate on long-term studies to analyze the market dynamics, including market dominance and composition of players. In practice, management cannot expect "winner-take-all" outcomes to last over a long period and should not overestimate a size advantage. Additionally, the best reaction to industry change can differ between firms, and focusing on M&A activity is not in every case a viable approach to increase shareholder value. Owners need to constantly monitor the developments in the industry and regularly reassess the own expectations on the future developments.

Second, this research highlights the distinct position of digital technology giants in the industry. Shareholders expect neither value creation nor value dilution in transactions that are related to the core business of growing or shrinking dotcom giants. In contrast, they expect a significant increase in shareholder value from related acquisitions by digital technology giants. Even though firms can utilize network effects and complementarities in related transactions and thus decrease competition in the digital technology industry, dotcom giants are unable to benefit from this. It seems that the digital technology giants occupy a special role in the industry, have stronger platform ecosystems, or an unidentified factor negatively influences dotcom giants' transactions. The signals that digital giants transmit to industry rivals and to other digital giants but not to dotcom giants supports this conjecture. Research needs to analyze the digital technology industry on a granular level and be mindful of the special role of digital technology giants. Management of competitors should focus attention on the group of digital giants and less on the dotcom giants in order to observe signals. Although the latter has conducted some prominent transactions in recent years (e.g., Intel's acquisition of Altera), shareholders and managers should monitor the M&A activity of digital giants closely and react to it.

This research has some limitations. First, the study defines dotcom giants as the largest digital technology-focused companies in the world at the end of 2000. The decisions for a specific reference date as well as market capitalization threshold are arguable. Similarly, the definition of growing and shrinking dotcom giants also depends on applied reference dates.

However, the group of dotcom giants consists of the same companies if year-end 1999 (a date before the peak of the dotcom boom) is taken as the reference date and a large size difference exists between the defined group of dotcom giants and the next largest digital technology-focused firm. Second, the rival effects analysis in this study is limited to the cross-effects between both giant groups. The effect of dotcom giants' M&A activity on other industry rivals can differ from the effect on digital giants. Yet there is no evidence for this. Overall, this study indicates that further research is required. The role of company-specific and management-specific factors in the success of acquisitions needs to be further investigated. This study explains several M&A value creation drivers of dotcom giants and puts the activity of dotcom giants in relation to acquisitions by digital technology giants. However, it remains unclear as to why some companies continue to be successful (e.g., Microsoft) and others not (e.g., Nokia), and why some companies grow rapidly (e.g., Tencent). Transactions can contribute to the success (e.g., Facebook's acquisition of Instagram) but can also dilute the value of acquirer and target (e.g., News Corp acquisition of Myspace). The M&A value creation and success might be connected to the strong personalities leading the digital technology giants (e.g., Alibaba's Jack Ma, Amazon's Jeff Bezos, Facebook's Mark Zuckerberg) and their great faith in the company's business model and strategy. Future work should analyze the management teams and the different M&A strategies in order to shed further light on the M&A value creation drivers in the digital technology industry.

5 Overall Conclusion and Contribution

5.1 Summary of Results

This dissertation investigates the mergers and acquisitions activity of digital technology giants. It analyzes the effect on the value of acquirers and rivals. In addition, the effect of digital technology giants' transactions is compared with the effect of dotcom giants' transactions.

The thesis therefore answers three main research questions. The *first research question* (chapter 2) discusses the effect of mergers and acquisitions on the value creation for digital technology giants. The M&A activity of digital technology giants neither creates nor dilutes value on average but differs on a granular level. On the one hand, related transactions can reshape platform boundaries and are part of the digital giants' growth story. The acquisitions can profit from reinforcing network effects, complementarities and decreasing competition. On the other hand, diversifying deals seem to bear high opportunity costs and dilute value. Digital giants can use unrelated transactions to seek attractive new markets when facing competition, but are unable to profit from favorable market conditions with this type of transaction. In addition, the distinct financial strength of digital technology giants can dilute value across both deal types. The thesis reveals that free cash flow has a significantly negative effect on the value creation for digital giants. The level of available financial resources decreases corporate control by capital markets and can drive managerial self-interest. Thus, the market environment of the digital technology industry and the financial strength of the digital giants can influence the acquirers' value creation.

The *second research question* (chapter 3) examines the reaction of competitors to digital giants' mergers and acquisitions. The thesis shows that platform boundary expansion in terms of related transactions has no value impact on digital giants' rivals, and that unrelated transactions lead to a slightly negative reaction. However, industry rivals and other giants react significantly positively to acquisitions that create value for the acquirer and significantly negatively to acquisitions that dilute value for the acquirer. It seems that shareholders expect rivals to replicate the transaction behavior of digital giants, and that transactions reduce uncertainty and transmit positive or negative signals to competitors. Signaling effects are stronger for other digital giants than for direct industry rivals, despite different core businesses. It supports the conjecture that digital technology diminishes industry and product boundaries and that traditional market definition is not applicable in this industry. The digital giants compete across markets and platforms for new opportunities, capabilities and customer attention. Industry rivals seem to experience two overlapping effects as they can be additionally influenced by the efficiency increase of the buying giant. A value creating acquisition can strengthen the competitive position of the acquirer in the submarket, but the effect is inversed for value diluting acquisitions.

The *third research question* (chapter 4) investigates the value effects of digital technology giants' mergers and acquisitions in comparison with dotcom giants' transactions. The dissertation emphasizes the special role of digital giants with relatedness effect and signaling power to the industry. The results show that related transactions by dotcom giants neither create nor dilute value for the acquirer, and that dotcom giants cannot benefit from the market environment in the same way as the digital giants. The reaction to unrelated transactions differs between dotcom giants that have increased value in the last decade and those that have decreased value. Growing giants dilute value in diversifying transactions, while shrinking giants create value. It seems that owners of growing giants want to preserve business value and view unrelated M&A activity critically. In contrast, owners of shrinking giants appear to appreciate shifts in business focus and expect future growth. The positive influence of liquidity in terms of free cash flow indicates that owners can benefit from higher financial flexibility in a transition process and thus support this conjecture. The M&A activity of growing and shrinking dotcom giants seems to be more strongly affected by the change in the industry and characterized by transition, while digital technology giants' expansion of platform boundaries can benefit from the market environment and assume a signaling role in the industry.

Overall, this dissertation provides a comprehensive study of mergers and acquisitions by digital technology giants and analyzes the value creation from three perspectives. First, the thesis examines the value creation for digital giants as acquirers. Second, it investigates the rival reactions to digital giants' transactions and the value effects of these competitive moves. Third, it compares the M&A value creation for digital giants as acquirers with the value creation for dotcom giants as acquirers. The results support that the group of digital technology giants is influenced by the market environment and financial strength, transmits signals to rivals and experiences unique effects in comparison with other firms in the industry. These findings emphasize the special role of digital technology giants, and provide implications for several groups and open avenues for future research.

5.2 Implications for Research and Practice

The results of this dissertation are relevant for researchers and practitioners and draw several implications for both groups.

For *researchers*, the thesis advances the knowledge on M&A value creation. It is the first detailed study on value creation in mergers and acquisitions in the digital technology industry. The thesis discusses user and owner value and shows the linkage between both concepts. An owner expects some level of profitability when operating a platform, thus making sustainable user value dependent on potential owner value. As user value is difficult to measure, research can utilize owner value in terms of shareholder value as an early indicator for expected user value. In addition, the effect on shareholder value varies between deal types and acquirer groups, and the results highlight that transactions in the digital technology industry need to be analyzed on a granular level. The findings of this dissertation indicate that three factors – market environment, company-specific characteristics and management teams – drive the value creation for companies in this industry. First, research needs to incorporate the influence of the industry environment in terms of network effects and complementarities, which is different between acquirers. Second, the company-specific characteristics in terms of financial strength can have a strong influence on the value effects. Research needs to distinguish between the positive and the negative effects of liquidity. On the one hand, it can offer financial flexibility to the acquirer and enable required investments without access to external financing. On the other hand, the financial strength decreases corporate control by capital markets and can create corporate governance issues. Third, the management team interacts with the company-specific factor. Research needs to regard management as an agent that acts for the owners, but that might also pursue own interests besides user and owner value. Studies need to consider managerial self-interest and managerial hubris as potential drivers of M&A activity even when dealing with successful digital technology giants.

Furthermore, the findings of this thesis add to the rival effects and competitive dynamics literature. They emphasize that researchers need to carefully study competitive actions of firms in the digital technology industry and distinguish between different groups of rivals and different competitive moves and reactions. First, the digital technology giants face rivals in various competitive contexts. They experience standard market competition but also compete for customer attention, opportunities and capabilities across platforms and submarkets. The observations on competitive dynamics in one context cannot be directly applied to other situations here. For example, the return reaction of buyer-side rivals is different to the return reaction of target-side rivals, with the value drivers varying. Thus, the analyzed rival groups need to be thoroughly defined and selected for the specific purpose. Second, the groups of rivals can differ in their response, but each group also has a range of possible reactions. The results of the thesis indicate that shareholders anticipate different responses of rivals to competitive actions with regard to mergers and acquisitions by digital technology giants. Studies should not focus on one potential reaction but analyze different rival stories. In a short-term window different reactions might overlap, but over a long-term horizon a main competitive reaction can usually be identified. While critically scrutinizing digital technology giants' M&A activity, the dissertation also puts emphasis on the positive externalities of the transactions. Researchers need to incorporate the potential positive attention spillover and signaling effects of acquisitions. In total, they need to adapt market definition and rival groups to changing competitive dynamics and properly measure and segregate competitive actions and reactions.

For *practitioners*, the dissertation has several implications for managers, firm owners and regulators in the digital technology industry. Managers of digital technology giants should focus the M&A activity on related transactions to increase value creation. There might be rational motives for diversification, but leadership needs to critically challenge the potential influence of hubris and other biases. Management of firms in the industry, regardless of position in terms of market dominance or firm size, can monitor digital technology giants' acquisitions in order to learn about the situation of the industry and receive signals. They can react according to the value creation in digital giants' transactions, change their own plans and adapt M&A efforts. In antitrust litigation and discussion with regulators, digital giants should emphasize the positive signaling effects of acquisitions on the industry, while management of industry rivals needs to monitor the effect on the competitive situation and the potential competitive advantage for the acquirer. Overall, management of digital technology firms needs to regularly update its own market definition and expected competitive context as the competitive landscape is rapidly changing. The market dynamics in terms of economies of scale and scope, "winner-take-all" outcomes and other factors can change and put even large firms under pressure. For managers, the best reaction to this change in competition and technology transition can differ between firms, and M&A cannot increase or preserve value for every firm.

This thesis analyzes the value effect of mergers and acquisitions on owners of digital technology giants. The results emphasize that owners need to critically monitor the M&A activity initiated by management, and question unrelated transactions. The group of owners needs to incorporate potential corporate governance issues and be sensitive to the potential influence of managerial self-interest and hubris. A protective measure is to increase capital markets control and increase the level of debt or reduce available financial resources. Owners can reduce the liquidity by share buyback and dividend programs. In addition, they should demand a high level of transparency on M&A activity, at least subsequent to the completion of deals. Moreover, the group of owners, similar to management of firms, needs to observe the digital technology industry across submarkets and regularly update the market definition. Additionally, owners need to question whether the competitive dynamics and the risk and return profile are aligned with their own expectations and requirements. Market dynamics can be changed by certain industry developments and technological transition, thus quickly changing the competitive position of firms in the digital technology industry, even the position of previously leading players. Owners therefore need to constantly keep track of the activity in the industry and their own firm.

Finally, the thesis is also relevant for regulators and antitrust investigators. The results indicate that the M&A activity of digital technology giants has positive and negative influences on the value creation for the acquirer and the rivals. Thus, officials need to trade-off between the positive influence of transactions in terms of information power and signaling effects and the negative influence in terms of increased efficiency and competitive advantage for the acquirer. While general restrictions on M&A activity can strengthen smaller players in the industry, it can also foster information asymmetry and decrease value creation for all firms in the industry. The results indicate that the potential of efficiency increase is limited and that the dominant position of previously leading firms can erode, as similarly happened with the dotcom giants, whereas strong signaling effects can be observed across submarkets of the digital technology industry.

5.3 Avenues for Future Research

The dissertation presents interesting avenues for future research. First, the connection between user value and owner value requires further analysis from different perspectives. This thesis treats shareholder value and owner value equally and links them to user value. However, other factors besides share price exist that can influence owner value, including other stakeholders, interests and objectives. Moreover, acquisitions can increase value for users by way of additional features, new regions or other benefits, but transactions also exist that can lead to decreasing user value. For example, Microsoft acquired Wunderlist in 2015, aiming to integrate it into another application. While not all functions have been transferred, Microsoft nonetheless announced to quit Wunderlist in 2020 (Wunderlist, 2019). Future work should find different ways to measure owner value and user value and put it in relation to shareholder value and M&A activity. Similarly, the long-term effect of transactions requires further investigations and should be compared with the short-term effect that is presented in this thesis.

Second, the dissertation shows that digital technology giants might be prone to corporate governance issues. Research needs to separate the interests of owners and management and further analyze potential agency conflicts. As digital platforms become mature businesses and founders exit the management boards, managements' interest can deviate from owners' interest. Management can be influenced by hubris or guided by self-interest and owners need to ensure control mechanisms and transparency. Further research on M&A strategy and acquisition motives in the digital technology industry is required. The composition of management teams and the influence of other stakeholders can shed light on further M&A value creation and dilution drivers.

Finally, competitive dynamics in the digital technology industry appear a promising field for further study. The thesis indicates a strong influence of digital technology giants' M&A activity on other firms in the industry but no effects between dotcom giants and digital giants. Future studies should further investigate the drivers of signaling effects and continue to dismantle the competitive structure in the industry. This thesis links digital platforms to digital businesses and to digital technology giants as platform owners. However, some digital giants operate several platforms that are in competition with each other (e.g., Facebook with Instagram, WhatsApp and Facebook), and other giants operate platforms in different competitive contexts (e.g., Amazon with Marketplace in competition with

AliExpress and Amazon Web Services in competition with Microsoft Azure and Google Cloud Platform). In a next step, research needs to analyze competitive dynamics on a more granular level and separately compare the effect of boundary expansion on the value of the different platforms. In this context, definition of submarkets in the digital technology industry and shift of boundaries appear interesting topics for further studies.

References

Acquisti, A., Friedman, A., Telang, R., 2006. Is There a Cost to Privacy Breaches? An Event Study, in: Proceedings of the 27th International Conference on Information Systems (ICIS), Milwaukee, Wisconsin.

Adner, R., Snow, D., 2010. Old technology responses to new technology threats: Demand heterogeneity and technology retreats. Industrial and Corporate Change 19, 1655–1675.

Afuah, A., 2013. Are network effects really all about size?: The role of structure and conduct. Strategic Management Journal 34, 257–273.

Agrawal, A., Walkling, R.A., 1994. Executive Careers and Compensation Surrounding Takeover Bids. The Journal of Finance 49, 985–1014.

Akdoğu, E., 2009. Gaining a competitive edge through acquisitions: Evidence from the telecommunications industry. Journal of Corporate Finance 15, 99–112.

Akdoğu, E., 2011. Value-Maximizing Managers, Value-Increasing Mergers, and Overbidding. The Journal of Financial and Quantitative Analysis 46, 83–110.

Akhigbe, A., Madura, J., 1999. The Industry Effects Regarding the Probability of Takeovers. The Financial Review 34, 1–17.

Amit, R., Zott, C., 2001. Value creation in E-business. Strategic Management Journal 22, 493–520.

Andrade, G., Mitchell, M., Stafford, E., 2001. New Evidence and Perspectives on Mergers. Journal of Economic Perspectives 15, 103–120.

Barney, J., 1991. Firm Resources and Sustained Competitive Advantage. Journal of Management 17, 99–120.

Bates, T.W., Kahle, K.M., Stulz, R.M., 2009. Why Do U.S. Firms Hold So Much More Cash than They Used To? The Journal of Finance 64, 1985–2021.

Battalio, R., Schultz, P., 2006. Options and the Bubble. The Journal of Finance 61, 2071–2102.

Bauer, F., Matzler, K., 2014. Antecedents of M&A success: The role of strategic complementarity, cultural fit, and degree and speed of integration. Strategic Management Journal 35, 269–291.

Benson, D., Ziedonis, R.H., 2010. Corporate venture capital and the returns to acquiring portfolio companies. Journal of Financial Economics 98, 478–499.

Berger, P.D., Eechambadi, N., George, M., Lehmann, D.R., Rizley, R., Venkatesan, R., 2006. From Customer Lifetime Value to Shareholder Value. Journal of Service Research 9, 156–167.

Bharadwaj, A., El Sawy, O.A., Pavlou, P.A., Venkatraman, N., 2013. Digital Business Strategy: Toward a Next Generation of Insights. MIS Quarterly 37, 471–482.

Bhattacharya, U., Galpin, N., Ray, R., Yu, X., 2009. The Role of the Media in the Internet IPO Bubble. The Journal of Financial and Quantitative Analysis 44, 657–682.

Binder, J., 1998. The Event Study Methodology Since 1969. Review of Quantitative Finance and Accounting 11, 111–137.

Bittlingmayer, G., Hazlett, T.W., 2000. DOS Kapital: Has antitrust action against Microsoft created value in the computer industry? Journal of Financial Economics 55, 329–359.

Boehmer, E., Masumeci, J., Poulsen, A.B., 1991. Event-study methodology under conditions of event-induced variance. Journal of Financial Economics 30, 253–272.

Bower, J.L., 2001. Not All M&As Are Alike - and That Matters. Harvard Business Review 79, 92–101.

Brealey, R.A., Myers, S.C., Marcus, A.J., 2017. Fundamentals of Corporate Finance. McGraw-Hill, New York.

Brousseau, E., Penard, T., 2007. The Economics of Digital Business Models: A Framework for Analyzing the Economics of Platforms. Review of Network Economics 6, 81–114.

Brown, S.J., Warner, J.B., 1980. Measuring security price performance. Journal of Financial Economics 8, 205–258.

Brown, S.J., Warner, J.B., 1985. Using daily stock returns: The case of event studies. Journal of Financial Economics 14, 3–31.

Bruner, R.F., 2002. Does M&A pay?: A survey of evidence for the decision-maker. Journal of Applied Finance 12, 48–68.

Brunnenmeier, M.K., Nagel, S., 2004. Hedge Funds and the Technology Bubble. The Journal of Finance 59, 2013–2040.

Cai, J., Song, M.H., Walkling, R.A., 2011. Anticipation, Acquisitions, and Bidder Returns: Industry Shocks and the Transfer of Information across Rivals. Review of Financial Studies 24, 2242–2285.

Campbell, C.J., Cowan, A.R., Salotti, V., 2010. Multi-country event-study methods. Journal of Banking & Finance 34, 3078–3090.

Campbell, C.J., Wesley, C.E., 1993. Measuring security price performance using daily NASDAQ returns. Journal of Financial Economics 33, 73–92.

Campbell, J.Y., Lo, A.W., MacKinlay, A.C., 1997. The Econometrics of Financial Markets. Princeton University Press, Princeton.

Capron, L., Dussauge, P., Mitchell, W., 1998. Resource redeployment following horizontal acquisitions in Europe and North America, 1988-1992. Strategic Management Journal 19, 631–661.

Cennamo, C., Santalo, J., 2013. Platform competition: Strategic trade-offs in platform markets. Strategic Management Journal 34, 1331–1350.

Chambers, J., 2015. Cisco's CEO on Staying Ahead of Technology Shifts. Harvard Business Review 93, 35–38.

Chang, S., 1998. Takeovers of Privately Held Targets, Methods of Payment, and Bidder Returns. The Journal of Finance 53, 773–784.

Chari, A., Ouimet, P.P., Tesar, L.L., 2010. The Value of Control in Emerging Markets. Review of Financial Studies 23, 1741–1770.

Chatterjee, S., 1986. Types of synergy and economic value: The impact of acquisitions on merging and rival firms. Strategic Management Journal 7, 119–139.

Chen, H.-C., Chou, R.K., Lu, C.-L., 2018. Saving for a rainy day: Evidence from the 2000 dot-com crash and the 2008 credit crisis. Journal of Corporate Finance 48, 680–699.

Chen, P.-Y., Hitt, L.M., 2002. Measuring Switching Costs and the Determinants of Customer Retention in Internet-Enabled Businesses: A Study of the Online Brokerage Industry. Information Systems Research 13, 255–274.

Chen, S.-S., Ho, L.-C., Shih, Y.-C., 2007. Intra-Industry Effects of Corporate Capital Investment Announcements. Financial Management 36, 1–21.

Chi, J., Sun, Q., Young, M., 2011. Performance and characteristics of acquiring firms in the Chinese stock markets. Emerging Markets Review 12, 152–170.

Chung, K.H., Pruitt, S.W., 1994. A Simple Approximation of Tobin's q. Financial Management 23, 70–74.

Clemons, E.K., Madhani, N., 2010. Regulation of Digital Businesses with Natural Monopolies or Third-Party Payment Business Models: Antitrust Lessons from the Analysis of Google. Journal of Management Information Systems 27, 43–80.

Clougherty, J.A., Duso, T., 2009. The Impact of Horizontal Mergers on Rivals: Gains to Being Left Outside a Merger. Journal of Management Studies 46, 1365–1395.

Clougherty, J.A., Duso, T., 2011. Using rival effects to identify synergies and improve merger typologies. Strategic Organization 9, 310–335.

Conger, K., 2018. Google Removes 'Don't Be Evil' Clause From Its Code of Conduct. Gizmodo. https://gizmodo.com/google-removes-nearly-all-mentions-of-dont-be-evil-from-1826153393. Accessed January 10, 2020.

Constantinides, P., Henfridsson, O., Parker, G.G., 2018. Introduction—Platforms and Infrastructures in the Digital Age. Information Systems Research 29, 381–400.

Cooper, M.J., Dimitrov, O., Rau, P.R., 2001. A Rose.com by Any Other Name. The Journal of Finance 56, 2371–2388.

Corrado, C.J., 1989. A nonparametric test for abnormal security-price performance in event studies. Journal of Financial Economics 23, 385–395.

Corrado, C.J., 2011. Event studies: A methodology review. Accounting & Finance 51, 207–234.

Corrado, C.J., Truong, C., 2008. Conducting event studies with Asia-Pacific security market data. Pacific-Basin Finance Journal 16, 493–521.

Corrado, C.J., Zivney, T.L., 1992. The Specification and Power of the Sign Test in Event Study Hypothesis Tests Using Daily Stock Returns. The Journal of Financial and Quantitative Analysis 27, 465–478.

Cowan, A.R., 1992. Nonparametric event study tests. Review of Quantitative Finance and Accounting 2, 343–358.

Crémer, J., Montjoye, Y.-A., Schweitzer, H., 2019. Competition Policy for the digital era: Final report. Publications Office of the European Union, Luxembourg.

Croci, E., Petmezas, D., Vagenas-Nanos, E., 2010. Managerial overconfidence in high and low valuation markets and gains to acquisitions. International Review of Financial Analysis 19, 368–378.

Cusumano, M.A., 2017. Is Google's Alphabet a Good Bet? Communications of the ACM 60, 22–25.

Cusumano, M.A., Gawer, A., Yoffie, D.B., 2019. The Business of Platforms: Strategy in the Age of Digital Competition, Innovation, and Power. HarperCollins Publishers, New York.

Damodaran, A., 2018. The Dark Side of Valuation: Valuing Young, Distressed, and Complex Businesses. Pearson Education, Upper Saddle River.

Danbolt, J., Maciver, G., 2012. Cross-Border versus Domestic Acquisitions and the Impact on Shareholder Wealth. Journal of Business Finance & Accounting 39, 1028–1067.

Dehning, Richardson, Zmud, 2003. The Value Relevance of Announcements of Transformational Information Technology Investments. MIS Quarterly 27, 637–656.

Denis, D.J., Sibilkov, V., 2010. Financial Constraints, Investment, and the Value of Cash Holdings. Review of Financial Studies 23, 247–269.

Devos, E., Kadapakkam, P.-R., Krishnamurthy, S., 2009. How Do Mergers Create Value?: A Comparison of Taxes, Market Power, and Efficiency Improvements as Explanations for Synergies. Review of Financial Studies 22, 1179–1211.

Dolata, U., 2018. Internet Companies: Market Concentration, Competition and Power, in: Dolata, U., Schrape, J.-F. (Eds.), Collectivity and Power on the Internet: A Sociological Perspective. Springer International Publishing, Cham, pp. 85–108.

Dolata, U., 2019. Privatization, curation, commodification. Österreichische Zeitschrift für Soziologie 44, 181–197.

Dos Santos, B.L., Peffers, K., Mauer, D.C., 1993. The Impact of Information Technology Investment Announcements on the Market Value of the Firm. Information Systems Research 4, 1–23.

Driebusch, C., Farrell, M., 2018. No Profit, No Problem In Hot IPO Market. Wall Street Journal. October 2.

Eckbo, B.E., 1983. Horizontal mergers, collusion, and stockholder wealth. Journal of Financial Economics 11, 241–273.

Eckbo, B.E., 1985. Mergers and the Market Concentration Doctrine: Evidence from the Capital Market. The Journal of Business 58, 325–349.

Eisenmann, T., Parker, G., van Alstyne, M.W., 2006. Strategies for two-sided markets. Harvard Business Review 84, 92–101.

Evans, D.S., 2013. Attention Rivalry Among Online Platforms. Journal of Competition Law and Economics 9, 313–357.

Evans, D.S., 2017. Why the Dynamics of Competition for Online Platforms Leads to Sleepless Nights But Not Sleepy Monopolies. Working Paper, 1–37.

Evans, D.S., Schmalensee, R., 2002. Some Economic Aspects of Antitrust Analysis in Dynamically Competitive Industries. Innovation Policy and the Economy 2, 1–49.

Evans, D.S., Schmalensee, R., 2015. The Antitrust Analysis of Multisided Platform Businesses, in: Blair, R.D., Sokol, D.D. (Eds.), The Oxford Handbook of International Antitrust Economics, Volume 1. Oxford University Press, Oxford, pp. 404–448.

Evans, D.S., Schmalensee, R., 2016. Matchmakers: The New Economics of multisided Platforms. Harvard Business Review Press, Boston.

Fama, E.F., 1970. Efficient Capital Markets: A Review of Theory and Empirical Work. The Journal of Finance 25, 383–417.

Fama, E.F., French, K.R., 1992. The Cross-Section of Expected Stock Returns. The Journal of Finance 47, 427–465.

Fama, E.F., French, K.R., 1993. Common risk factors in the returns on stocks and bonds. Journal of Financial Economics 33, 3–56.

Farrell, J., Saloner, G., 1985. Standardization, Compatibility, and Innovation. The RAND Journal of Economics 16, 70–83.

Fee, C.E., Thomas, S., 2004. Sources of gains in horizontal mergers: Evidence from customer, supplier, and rival firms. Journal of Financial Economics 74, 423–460.

Ferrier, W.J., 2001. Navigating the Competitive Landscape: The Drivers and Consequences of Competitive Aggressiveness. Academy of Management Journal 44, 858–877.

Ferrier, W.J., Holsapple, C.W., Sabherwal, R., 2010. Editorial Commentary —Digital Systems and Competition. Information Systems Research 21, 413–422.

Flanagan, D.J., O'Shaughnessy, K.C., 2003. Core-related acquisitions, multiple bidders and tender offer premiums. Journal of Business Research 56, 573–585.

Foerderer, J., Kude, T., Mithas, S., Heinzl, A., 2018. Does Platform Owner's Entry Crowd Out Innovation?: Evidence from Google Photos. Information Systems Research 29, 444–460.

Fuller, K., Netter, J., Stegemoller, M., 2002. What Do Returns to Acquiring Firms Tell Us?: Evidence from Firms That Make Many Acquisitions. The Journal of Finance 57, 1763–1793.

Furman, J., Coyle, D., Fletcher, A., McAuley, D., Marsden, P., 2019. Unlocking digital competition: Report of the Digital Competition Expert Panel. HM Treasury, London.

Gallaugher, J.M., Wang, Y.-M., 2002. Understanding Network Effects in Software Markets: Evidence from Web Server Pricing. MIS Quarterly 26, 303–327.

Gao, L.S., Iyer, B., 2006. Analyzing Complementarities Using Software Stacks for Software Industry Acquisitions. Journal of Management Information Systems 23, 119–147.

Gaspar, J.-M., Massa, M., Matos, P., 2005. Shareholder investment horizons and the market for corporate control. Journal of Financial Economics 76, 135–165.

Gaur, A.S., Malhotra, S., Zhu, P., 2013. Acquisition announcements and stock market valuations of acquiring firms' rivals: A test of the growth probability hypothesis in China. Strategic Management Journal 34, 215–232.

Gawer, A., Cusumano, M.A., 2002. Platform Leadership: How Intel, Microsoft, and Cisco Drive Industry Innovation. Harvard Business Review Press, Boston.

Gawer, A., Cusumano, M.A., 2014. Industry Platforms and Ecosystem Innovation. Journal of Product Innovation Management 31, 417–433.

Ghazawneh, A., Mansour, O., 2015. Value Creation in Digital Application Marketplaces: A Developer's Perspective, in: Proceedings of the 36th International Conference on Information Systems (ICIS), Fort Worth, Texas.

Gnyawali, D.R., Fan, W., Penner, J., 2010. Competitive Actions and Dynamics in the Digital Age: An Empirical Investigation of Social Networking Firms. Information Systems Research 21, 594–613.

Govindarajan, V., Srivastava, A., 2019. No, WeWork Isn't a Tech Company. Here's Why That Matters. Harvard Business Review. https://hbr.org/2019/08/no-wewor k-isnt-a-tech-company-heres-why-that-matters. Accessed January 10, 2020.

Graebner, M.E., Eisenhardt, K.M., Roundy, P.T., 2010. Success and Failure in Technology Acquisitions: Lessons for Buyers and Sellers. Academy of Management Perspectives 24, 73–92.

Griffin, J.M., Harris, J.H., Shu, T.A.O., Topaloglu, S., 2011. Who Drove and Burst the Tech Bubble? The Journal of Finance 66, 1251–1290.

Gupta, S., Lehmann, D.R., Stuart, J.A., 2004. Valuing Customers. Journal of Marketing Research 41, 7–18.

Haleblian, J., Devers, C.E., McNamara, G., Carpenter, M.A., Davison, R.B., 2009. Taking Stock of What We Know About Mergers and Acquisitions: A Review and Research Agenda. Journal of Management 35, 469–502.

Haleblian, J., Finkelstein, S., 1999. The Influence of Organizational Acquisition Experience on Acquisition Performance: A Behavioral Learning Perspective. Administrative Science Quarterly 44, 29–56.

Harford, J., 1999. Corporate Cash Reserves and Acquisitions. The Journal of Finance 54, 1969–1997.

Haucap, J., Heimeshoff, U., 2014. Google, Facebook, Amazon, eBay: Is the Internet driving competition or market monopolization? International Economics and Economic Policy 11, 49–61.

Hayward, M.L.A., 2002. When do firms learn from their acquisition experience?: Evidence from 1990 to 1995. Strategic Management Journal 23, 21–39.

Hendershott, R.J., 2004. Net value: Wealth creation (and destruction) during the internet boom. Journal of Corporate Finance 10, 281–299.

Henfridsson, O., Nandhakumar, J., Scarbrough, H., Panourgias, N., 2018. Recombination in the open-ended value landscape of digital innovation. Information and Organization 28, 89–100.

Herzog, B., 2018. Valuation of Digital Platforms: Experimental Evidence for Google and Facebook. International Journal of Financial Studies 6, 87.

Hou, K., Robinson, D.T., 2006. Industry Concentration and Average Stock Returns. The Journal of Finance 61, 1927–1956.

Howcroft, D., 2001. After the Goldrush: Deconstructing the Myths of the dot.com Market. Journal of Information Technology 16, 195–204.

Jensen, M.C., 1986. Agency Costs of Free Cash Flow, Corporate Finance, and Takeovers. The American Economic Review 76, 323–329.

Jensen, M.C., 1988. Takeovers: Their Causes and Consequences. Journal of Economic Perspectives 2, 21–48.

Jope, F., Schiereck, D., Zeidler, F., 2010. Value generation of mergers and acquisitions in the technology, media. Journal of Telecommunications Management 2, 369–386.

Katz, M.L., Shapiro, C., 1985. Network Externalities, Competition, and Compatibility. The American Economic Review 75, 424–440.

Kim, E.H., Singal, V., 1993. Mergers and Market Power: Evidence from the Airline Industry. The American Economic Review 83, 549–569.

Kim, K., Gopal, A., Hoberg, G., 2016. Does Product Market Competition Drive CVC Investment?: Evidence from the U.S. IT Industry. Information Systems Research 27, 259–281.

King, D.R., Dalton, D.R., Daily, C.M., Covin, J.G., 2004. Meta-analyses of post-acquisition performance: Indications of unidentified moderators. Strategic Management Journal 25, 187–200.

Kohers, N., Kohers, T., 2000. The Value Creation Potential of High-Tech Mergers. Financial Analysts Journal 56, 40–50.

Kohers, N., Kohers, T., 2004. Information sensitivity of high tech industries: Evidence from merger announcements. Applied Financial Economics 14, 525–536.

Kohli, R., Grover, V., 2008. Business Value of IT: An Essay on Expanding Research Directions to Keep up with the Times. Journal of the Association for Information Systems 9, 23–39.

Kolari, J.W., Pynnönen, S., 2010. Event Study Testing with Cross-sectional Correlation of Abnormal Returns. Review of Financial Studies 23, 3996–4025.

Kothari, S.P., Warner, J.B., 2007. Econometrics of Event Studies, in: Eckbo, B.E. (Ed.), Handbook of Corporate Finance. Empirical Corporate Finance. Elsevier, North-Holland, pp. 3–36.

Kuchinke, B.A., Vidal, M., 2016. Exclusionary strategies and the rise of winner-takes-it-all markets on the Internet. Telecommunications Policy 40, 582–592.

Kujala, S., Väänänen, K., 2009. Value of information systems and products: Understanding the users' perspective and values. Journal of Information Technology Theory and Application 9, 23–39.

Laamanen, T., Brauer, M., Junna, O., 2014. Performance of acquirers of divested assets: Evidence from the U.S. software industry. Strategic Management Journal 35, 914–925.

Lamoreaux, N.R., 2019. The Problem of Bigness: From Standard Oil to Google. Journal of Economic Perspectives 33, 94–117.

Lang, L., Stulz, R., Walkling, R.A., 1989. Managerial performance, Tobin's Q, and the gains from successful tender offers. Journal of Financial Economics 24, 137–154.

Lang, L.H.P., Stulz, R.M., Walkling, R.A., 1991. A test of the free cash flow hypothesis. Journal of Financial Economics 29, 315–335.

Laughlin, L.S., 2019. Life Goes On After WeWork: As spectacular as the unicorn's value collapse is, its impact will remain. Wall Street Journal. October 23.

Lee, S.-Y.T., 2000. Bundling strategy in base-supplemental goods markets: The case of Microsoft. European Journal of Information Systems 9, 217–225.

Lehn, K., Poulsen, A., 1989. Free Cash Flow and Stockholder Gains in Going Private Transactions. The Journal of Finance 44, 771–787.

Lerner, J., Sorensen, M., Strömberg, P., 2011. Private Equity and Long-Run Investment: The Case of Innovation. The Journal of Finance 66, 445–477.

Li, S., Shang, J., Slaughter, S.A., 2010. Why Do Software Firms Fail?: Capabilities, Competitive Actions, and Firm Survival in the Software Industry from 1995 to 2007. Information Systems Research 21, 631–654.

Lubatkin, M., 1983. Mergers and the Performance of the Acquiring Firm. Academy of Management Review 8, 218–225.

Lubatkin, M., 1987. Merger strategies and stockholder value. Strategic Management Journal 8, 39–53.

MacKinlay, A.C., 1997. Event Studies in Economics and Finance. Journal of Economic Literature 35, 13–39.

Mackintosh, J., 2019. Streetwise: WeWork Teaches a Valuable Lesson. Wall Street Journal. October 30.

Malmendier, U., Tate, G., 2005. CEO Overconfidence and Corporate Investment. The Journal of Finance 60, 2661–2700.

Malmendier, U., Tate, G., 2008. Who makes acquisitions?: CEO overconfidence and the market's reaction. Journal of Financial Economics 89, 20–43.

Mann, H.B., Whitney, D.R., 1947. On a Test of Whether one of Two Random Variables is Stochastically Larger than the Other. The Annals of Mathematical Statistics 18, 50–60.

Marks, J.M., Musumeci, J., 2017. Misspecification in event studies. Journal of Corporate Finance 45, 333–341.

Martin, J.D., Sayrak, A., 2003. Corporate diversification and shareholder value: A survey of recent literature. Journal of Corporate Finance 9, 37–57.

Martynova, M., Renneboog, L., 2008. A century of corporate takeovers: What have we learned and where do we stand? Journal of Banking & Finance 32, 2148–2177.

Mattioli, D., 2017. Fear of Tech Giants Fuels Deal Boom: Amazon, Facebook, Google and Netflix prod slower-growing companies into takeovers. Wall Street Journal. November 21.

McCarthy, D.M., Fader, P.S., Hardie, B.G.S., 2017. Valuing Subscription-Based Businesses Using Publicly Disclosed Customer Data. Journal of Marketing 81, 17–35.

Mchawrab, S., 2016. M&A in the high tech industry: Value and valuation. Strategic Direction 32, 12–14.

McIntyre, D.P., Chintakananda, A., 2014. Competing in network markets: Can the winner take all? Business Horizons 57, 117–125.

McIntyre, D.P., Srinivasan, A., 2017. Networks, platforms, and strategy: Emerging views and next steps. Strategic Management Journal 38, 141–160.

Mcnamara, G.M., Haleblian, J., Dykes, B.J., 2008. The Performance Implications of Participating in an Acquisition Wave: Early Mover Advantages, Bandwagon Effects, and The Moderating Influence of Industry Characteristics and Acquirer Tactics. Academy of Management Journal 51, 113–130.

McWilliams, A., Siegel, D., 1997. Event studies in management research: Theoretical and empirical issues. Academy of Management Journal 40, 626–657.

Metz, C., 2015. Dell. EMC. HP. Cisco. These Tech Giants Are the Walking Dead. Wired. https://www.wired.com/2015/10/meet-walking-dead-hp-cisco-dell-emc-ibm-oracle. Accessed January 10, 2020.

Mickle, T., 2017. Apple's Mountain of Cash Is Set to Top $250 Billion. Wall Street Journal. May 1.

Mims, C., 2017. Analysis: Tech Companies Spread Their Tentacles. Wall Street Journal. June 17.

Moeller, S.B., Schlingemann, F.P., Stulz, R.M., 2004. Firm size and the gains from acquisitions. Journal of Financial Economics 73, 201–228.

Molnar, J., 2007. Pre-Emptive Horizontal Mergers: Theory and Evidence. Working Paper, 1–35.

Montgomery, C.A., 1982. The Measurement of Firm Diversification: Some New Empirical Evidence. Academy of Management Journal 25, 299–307.

Morck, R., Shleifer, A., Vishny, R.W., 1990. Do Managerial Objectives Drive Bad Acquisitions? The Journal of Finance 45, 31–48.

N.A., 2019. Decade in Review: A Special Report - What Was News, 2010-19. Wall Street Journal. December 18.

Ofek, E., Richardson, M., 2003. DotCom Mania: The Rise and Fall of Internet Stock Prices. The Journal of Finance 58, 1113–1137.

Oh, W., Kim, J., 2001. The Effects of Firm Characteristics on Investor Reaction to IT Investment Announcements, in: Proceedings of the 22nd International Conference on Information Systems (ICIS), New Orleans, Louisiana.

Pan, Y., Huang, P., Gopal, A., 2019. Storm Clouds on the Horizon?: New Entry Threats and R&D Investments in the U.S. IT Industry. Information Systems Research 30, 540–562.

Park, N.K., 2004. A guide to using event study methods in multi-country settings. Strategic Management Journal 25, 655–668.

Parker, G., van Alstyne, M., 2008. Managing Platform Ecosystems, in: Proceedings of the 29th International Conference on Information Systems (ICIS), Paris, France.

Patell, J.M., 1976. Corporate Forecasts of Earnings Per Share and Stock Price Behavior: Empirical Test. Journal of Accounting Research 14, 246–276.

Petersen, M.A., 2009. Estimating Standard Errors in Finance Panel Data Sets: Comparing Approaches. Review of Financial Studies 22, 435–480.

Raice, S., Ante, S.E., Glazer, E., 2012. In Facebook Deal, Board Was All But Out of Picture. Wall Street Journal. April 18.

Ransbotham, S., Mitra, S., 2010. Target Age and the Acquisition of Innovation in High-Technology Industries. Management Science 56, 2076–2093.

Rhéaume, L., Bhabra, H.S., 2008. Value creation in information-based industries through convergence: A study of U.S. mergers and acquisitions between 1993 and 2005. Information & Management 45, 304–311.

Rochet, J.-C., Tirole, J., 2003. Platform Competition in Two-Sided Markets. Journal of the European Economic Association 1, 990–1029.

Rochet, J.-C., Tirole, J., 2006. Two-sided markets: A progress report. The RAND Journal of Economics 37, 645–667.

Roll, R., 1986. The Hubris Hypothesis of Corporate Takeovers. The Journal of Business 59, 197–216.

Rumelt, R.P., 1974. Strategy, Structure and Economic Performance. Harvard University Press, Cambridge.

Ryan, C., 2019. The Diminishing Returns of Tech IPOs: Recent startup offerings tend to be less profitable, slower-growing and more aggressively priced than their predecessors. Wall Street Journal. August 20.

Schechner, S., Pop, V., 2019. Google Offers Choices For EU Android Users. Wall Street Journal. March 20.

Schief, M., Buxmann, P., Schiereck, D., 2013. Mergers and Acquisitions in the Software Industry. Business & Information Systems Engineering 5, 421–431.

Schlesinger, J.M., Kendall, B., McKinnon, J.D., 2019. Hunting For Giants: For decades, the Washington consensus was to let markets decide how big companies could get. No longer. 'Antitrust law now stands at its most fluid and negotiable moment in a generation.'. Wall Street Journal. June 8.

Schlingemann, F.P., 2004. Financing decisions and bidder gains. Journal of Corporate Finance 10, 683–701.

Schulze, C., Skiera, B., Wiesel, T., 2012. Linking Customer and Financial Metrics to Shareholder Value: The Leverage Effect in Customer-Based Valuation. Journal of Marketing 76, 17–32.

Seth, A., 1990. Sources of value creation in acquisitions: An empirical investigation. Strategic Management Journal 11, 431–446.

Shahrur, H., 2005. Industry structure and horizontal takeovers: Analysis of wealth effects on rivals, suppliers, and corporate customers. Journal of Financial Economics 76, 61–98.

Shapiro, C., 2019. Protecting Competition in the American Economy: Merger Control, Tech Titans, Labor Markets. Journal of Economic Perspectives 33, 69–93.

Shapiro, C., Varian, H.R., 1999. Information Rules: A Strategic Guide to the Network Economy. Harvard Business Review Press, Boston.

Shiller, R.J., 2015. Irrational Exuberance. Princeton University Press, Princeton.

Siegler, M.G., 2011. Exposed: Facebook's Secret iPhone Photo Sharing App (Which Looks Amazing). TechCrunch. https://techcrunch.com/2011/06/15/facebook-secret-photos-app. Accessed January 10, 2020.

Sirmon, D.G., Hitt, M.A., Ireland, R.D., 2007. Managing Firm Resources in Dynamic Environments to Create Value: Looking Inside the Black Box. Academy of Management Review 32, 273–292.

Smith, K.G., Ferrier, W.J., Ndofor, H., 2001. Competitive dynamics research: Critique and future directions, in: Hitt, M.A., Freeman, R.E., Harrison, J.S. (Eds.), The Blackwell Handbook of Strategic Management. Blackwell Publishers, London, pp. 315–359.

Smith, R.L., Kim, J.-H., 1994. The Combined Effects of Free Cash Flow and Financial Slack on Bidder and Target Stock Returns. The Journal of Business 67, 281–310.

Song, M.H., Walkling, R.A., 2000. Abnormal returns to rivals of acquisition targets: A test of the 'acquisition probability hypothesis'. Journal of Financial Economics 55, 143–171.

Spulber, D., Yoo, C., 2015. Antitrust, the Internet, and the Economics of Networks, in: Blair, R.D., Sokol, D.D. (Eds.), The Oxford Handbook of International Antitrust Economics, Volume 1. Oxford University Press, Oxford, 380–403.

Stahl, H.K., Matzler, K., Hinterhuber, H.H., 2003. Linking customer lifetime value with shareholder value. Industrial Marketing Management 32, 267–279.

Staykova, K.S., Damsgaard, J., 2017. Towards an Integrated View of Multi-sided Platforms Evolution, in: Proceedings of the 38th International Conference on Information Systems (ICIS), Seoul, South Korea.

Stillman, R., 1983. Examining antitrust policy towards horizontal mergers. Journal of Financial Economics 11, 225–240.

Trueman, B., Wong, M.H.F., Zhang, X.-J., 2000. The Eyeballs Have It: Searching for the Value in Internet Stocks. Journal of Accounting Research 38, 137–162.

Trueman, B., Wong, M.H.F., Zhang, X.-J., 2001. Back to Basics: Forecasting the Revenues of Internet Firms. Review of Accounting Studies 6, 305–329.

Uhlenbruck, K., Hitt, M.A., Semadeni, M., 2006. Market value effects of acquisitions involving internet firms: A resource-based analysis. Strategic Management Journal 27, 899–913.

van Gorp, N., Batura, O., 2015. Challenges for Competition Policy in a Digitalised Economy. Policy Department A: Economic and Scientific Policy, European Parliament, Brussels.

Wang, Q.-H., Hui, K.-L., 2017. Technology Mergers and Acquisitions in the Presence of an Installed Base: A Strategic Analysis. Information Systems Research 28, 46–63.

Wernerfelt, B., 1995. The resource-based view of the firm: Ten years after. Strategic Management Journal 16, 171–174.

Wilcox, D.H., Chang, K.-C., Grover, V., 2001. Valuation of mergers and acquisitions in the telecommunications industry: A study on diversification and firm size. Information & Management 38, 459–471.

Wunderlist, 2019. Join us on our new journey: We'll be with you every step of the way. Wunderlist. https://www.wunderlist.com/blog/join-us-on-our-new-journey. Accessed January 10, 2020.

Yang, S.H., Nam, C., Kim, S., 2018. The effects of M&As within the mobile ecosystem on the rival's shareholder value: The case of Google and Apple. Telecommunications Policy 42, 15–23.

Yoo, Y., Boland, R.J., Lyytinen, K., Majchrzak, A., 2012. Organizing for Innovation in the Digitized World. Organization Science 23, 1398–1408.

Yoo, Y., Henfridsson, O., Lyytinen, K., 2010. Research Commentary: The New Organizing Logic of Digital Innovation: An Agenda for Information Systems Research. Information Systems Research 21, 724–735.

Zhu, K., Xu, S., Dedrick, J., 2003. Assessing Drivers of E-Business Value: Results of a Cross-Country Study, in: Proceedings of the 24th International Conference on Information Systems (ICIS), Seattle, Washington.

Zweig, J., 2018. The Intelligent Investor: Big Tech Companies Test Limits of Growth. Wall Street Journal. April 7.

Appendix

Abstract: English Version

Digital technology companies dominate the list of the largest publicly traded companies worldwide. This group of digital technology giants (Alibaba, Alphabet, Amazon, Apple, Facebook, Microsoft and Tencent) has not only experienced high market valuations and strong economical and societal influence but also conducted a large number of mergers and acquisitions in the recent decade.

The dissertation analyzes mergers and acquisitions by digital technology giants from three perspectives – it examines the effect of the activity on the value of the acquiring firm and on the value of different groups of rivals, and compares it with the effect of other firms' acquisitions. For this purpose, the thesis defines the group of digital giants and gathers a unique sample of transactions that were conducted by this group between 2008 and 2017. It integrates research from different areas, including finance, information systems, strategy and economics, and investigates the value effects on different types of companies and compares the value effects of different groups of acquirers. In addition, the thesis identifies factors that drive value creation and discusses them in relation to the market environment, the digital giants' special role and potential managerial motives.

The results indicate that the market dynamics in the digital technology industry support the value creation in mergers and acquisitions but that it is counteracted by the distinct financial strength of the digital giants in terms of high liquidity. A field of tension can be seen between the positive influence of network effects, complementarities and decreasing competition on the one hand and the negative influence of managerial motives on the other. Additionally, the mergers and acquisitions activity of digital technology giants has signaling effects on competitors in the industry, thus further emphasizing the special role of the giants. Rivals experience a return reaction similar to that of the acquirer. Rivals' shareholders appear to expect their companies to utilize the transactions as guidance and imitate the competitive moves of the digital giants. However, the dominant position of market leaders in the digital technology industry can rapidly change and, with it, the effect of transactions on the industry and its players.

The results of this dissertation provide several implications for researchers and managers, owners and regulators of companies in the digital technology industry.

Abstract: German Version

Digitale Technologieunternehmen führen die Liste der weltweit größten börsennotierten Unternehmen an. Diese Gruppe von digitalen Technologiegiganten (Alibaba, Alphabet, Amazon, Apple, Facebook, Microsoft und Tencent) hat im letzten Jahrzehnt nicht nur hohe Marktbewertungen und starken ökonomischen und gesellschaftlichen Einfluss erfahren, sondern auch eine große Anzahl an Fusionen und Übernahmen getätigt.

Die Dissertation analysiert Fusionen und Übernahmen von digitalen Technologiegiganten aus drei Perspektiven – sie untersucht den Effekt der Aktivität auf den Wert des Käuferunternehmens sowie auf den Wert unterschiedlicher Gruppen von Wettbewerbern und vergleicht ihn mit dem Effekt von Übernahmen durch andere Unternehmen. Hierfür definiert die Thesis die Gruppe der digitalen Technologiegiganten und erstellt eine unikale Stichprobe an Transaktionen, die die Gruppe zwischen 2008 und 2017 getätigt hat. Sie integriert Forschung aus verschiedenen Bereichen einschließlich Finanzwirtschaft, Wirtschaftsinformatik, Strategie und Volkswirtschaftslehre, untersucht die Werteffekte auf verschiedene Arten von Unternehmen und vergleicht die Werteffekte von verschiedenen Gruppen an Käufern. Darüber hinaus identifiziert die Thesis werttreibende Faktoren und diskutiert diese in Verbindung mit dem Marktumfeld, der besonderen Rolle der digitalen Giganten und potenziellen managementgetriebenen Motiven.

Die Resultate indizieren, dass die Marktdynamiken in der digitalen Technologieindustrie die Wertschöpfung von Fusionen und Übernahmen unterstützen, aber die ausgeprägte finanzielle Stärke der digitalen Giganten in Form von hoher Liquidität dagegenwirkt. Ein Spannungsfeld zwischen dem positiven Einfluss von Netzwerkeffekten, Komplementaritäten und abnehmenden Wettbewerb auf der einen Seite und dem negativen Einfluss von managementgetriebenen Motiven auf der anderen kann beobachtet werden. Des Weiteren hat die Fusions- und Übernahmen-Aktivität der digitalen Technologiegiganten Signalwirkung für Wettbewerber in der Industrie, was die besondere Rolle der Giganten weiter unterstreicht. Die Rivalen vermerken eine ähnliche Renditereaktion wie der Käufer. Die Anteilseigener der Rivalen scheinen zu erwarten, dass ihre Unternehmen die Transaktionen als Orientierungshilfe nutzen und das wettbewerbliche Vorgehen der digitalen Giganten imitieren. Jedoch kann sich die dominierende Position von Marktführern in der digitalen Technologieindustrie schnell ändern und zugleich auch der Effekt von Transaktionen auf die Industrie und ihre Akteure.

Die Resultate dieser Dissertation beinhalten verschiedene Implikationen sowohl für Forscher als auch Führungskräfte, Inhaber und Aufsichtsbehörden von Unternehmen in der digitalen Technologieindustrie.